I0109495

Parties and Prejudice

Parties and Prejudice

The Normalization of Antiminority Rhetoric in US Politics

MANEESH ARORA

THE UNIVERSITY OF CHICAGO PRESS   CHICAGO AND LONDON

The University of Chicago Press, Chicago 60637
The University of Chicago Press, Ltd., London
© 2025 by The University of Chicago
All rights reserved. No part of this book may be used or reproduced in any manner
whatsoever without written permission, except in the case of brief quotations in critical
articles and reviews. For more information, contact the University of Chicago Press,
1427 E. 60th St., Chicago, IL 60637.
Published 2025
Printed in the United States of America

34 33 32 31 30 29 28 27 26 25   1 2 3 4 5

ISBN-13: 978-0-226-84238-7 (cloth)
ISBN-13: 978-0-226-84240-0 (paper)
ISBN-13: 978-0-226-84239-4 (ebook)
DOI: https://doi.org/10.7208/chicago/9780226842394.001.0001

Library of Congress Cataloging-in-Publication Data

Names: Arora, Maneesh, author.
Title: Parties and prejudice : the normalization of antiminority rhetoric in US politics /
    Maneesh Arora.
Other titles: Normalization of antiminority rhetoric in US politics
Description: Chicago : The University of Chicago Press, 2025. |
    Includes bibliographical references and index.
Identifiers: LCCN 2024056937 | ISBN 9780226842387 (cloth) | ISBN 9780226842400 (paper) |
    ISBN 9780226842394 (ebook)
Subjects: LCSH: Political oratory—United States—History—21st century. | Communication
    in politics—United States—History—21st century. | Political parties—United States—
    History—21st century. | Politicians—United States—Attitudes. | Minorities—United
    States—Public opinion. | Prejudices—Political aspects—United States. | Social norms—
    Political aspects—United States. | Islamophobia—United States. | Homophobia—
    United States. | Race discrimination—United States. | White supremacy (Social
    structure)—United States.
Classification: LCC E184.A1 A765 2025 | DDC 305.800973/0905—dc23/eng/20250122
LC record available at https://lccn.loc.gov/2024056937

♾ This paper meets the requirements of ANSI/NISO Z39.48-1992 (Permanence of Paper).

FOR ROBIN AND KAVI

Contents

Figures and Tables

TABLES

CHAPTER ONE

Introduction

Here's a thought that occurred to me. I didn't look at the population of Germany at the beginning of the Third Reich but it's probably in the area of seventy–eighty million is my guess. And out of that Hitler in a few years build something that cost the lives of roughly sixty million people. The radical Islamists have 1.3 or more billion Muslims to work with. Now they aren't all supporters. Daniel [inaudible] says 10%–15% of them, but that is a huge population to draw from. —Steve King (Kaczynski 2014)

White nationalist, white supremacist, Western civilization—how did that language become offensive? Why did I sit in classes teaching me about the merits of our history and our civilization? —Steve King (Gabriel 2019)

In 2014, Steve King, a Republican member of the US House of Representatives from Iowa, sounded the alarm on supposed Islamic State recruiters in the United States during an appearance on a radio show (Kaczynski 2014). King claimed that 10%–15% of Muslims were "radical Islamists" and were actively recruiting fighters from states like Minnesota and Virginia. He urged the federal government to surveil mosques, saying: "We ought to have people in those mosques watching to see what's going on." One year later, King continued pushing his stereotype of Muslims as anti-American by questioning the loyalty of Muslim Representative Keith Ellison during an interview with MSNBC: "When Congressman Ellison takes an oath to support and defend the Constitution of the United States . . . which is superior, the Constitution or Sharia law? Sharia law by their teachings is superior to everything else. It replaces everything else. It replaces the Constitution itself" (MSNBC 2015).

King faced no material political consequences for his overtly prejudicial comments about Muslims. He was not subject to any disciplinary action from Congress and was subsequently reelected to his seat in 2016 and again in 2018. In fact, King has a long history of making Islamophobic comments and pushing tropes that paint Muslims as threatening and anti-American without facing social censure. King's political career once flourished in spite of, or possibly because of, his frequent expression of antiminority prejudice.

However, in an interview with *The New York Times* in January 2019, King crossed his party's line with the following statement about white nationalism: "White nationalist, white supremacist, Western civilization — how did that language become offensive? Why did I sit in classes teaching me about the merits of our history and our civilization?" (Gabriel 2019). King's comments were condemned by the media, Democrats, and even by members of his own party as racist. The Republican steering committee removed him from all of his House committee assignments and the House voted 424–1 to approve a measure rebuking him.[1] His reelection chances took a severe hit as he had lost the support of most of the Republican Party leadership and was subsequently out-fundraised almost three to one by his GOP primary opponent (Sprunt 2020). After eighteen years in the House of Representatives, King lost his reelection bid to a primary challenge in 2020, about a year after his comments about white nationalism.

King's political career thrived when he was explicitly prejudicial toward Muslims and Islam, but it ended in large part over his praise of white nationalism and white supremacy — comments that were perceived as openly racist. This anecdote highlights some of this book's most important points about contemporary US politics. Because of a set of interconnected factors, prejudice directed at certain minority groups, like Muslims, is generally acceptable to the American public and has become normalized in political discourse. Some of the groups for whom egalitarian social norms are lacking are also perceived as highly threatening. This combination of inegalitarian norms and threat incentivizes politicians, in certain circumstances, to use messaging strategies that appeal to the antiminority sentiments of key constituents. Conversely, overt anti-Black prejudice is less acceptable to the American public. Anti-Black tropes, while still prevalent in our politics, tend to be communicated through racial code words or dog whistles instead of overtly to avoid violating a norm of racial equality. Consequently, King could be overtly Islamophobic for years without facing social censure, but his praise of white supremacy was quickly condemned by Democrats and the media and derided as an "embrace of racism" by a colleague in his own party (Barrón-López and Bresnahan 2019).

The target audience of the message is another important element in determining which antiminority political appeals will benefit a politician and which messages will not. Social norms do not always develop uniformly across a large population. Members of one social group may even adhere to a completely different set of norms than members of another social group. In this book, I show that social norms of acceptable political rhetoric have developed to be more inegalitarian within the Republican Party than within the Democratic Party. Thus, a Republican politician like King has different political incentives and faces different consequences for his speech than his Democratic counterparts.

Several key questions arise from King's story that will be answered in this book. Why is it socially acceptable to openly discriminate against some minority groups and not others? What is the role of social norms in understanding antiminority political rhetoric? Why are norms developing differently within the Republican Party than within the Democratic Party? Finally, in a political environment that appears to be defined by antiminority prejudice, are there effective strategies to counter prejudice? This book's answers clarify the link between social norms and expressions of prejudice and have important implications for political communication, party politics, and the current and future state of American democracy.

Central Argument

Social norms are key to understanding political prejudice. Social norms determine whether overt prejudice is accepted by the public and what, if any, the political consequence of prejudicial speech will be. Chapter 2 introduces and details the primary theoretical framework of the manuscript, the theory of differential norms, which posits that norms guiding political messaging vary based on the subject group of a message and the audience who receives it. To determine whether a particular message will benefit (by increasing public support for) or harm (by decreasing public support for) a political elite, both factors need to be considered.

Social norms develop through a mutually reinforcing interaction between signals from influential actors and mass attitudes. Importantly, there is no one uniform norm that guides rhetoric directed at all minority groups in society. Norms, the book shows, develop distinctly for each minority group. A line demarcates what is and what is not socially acceptable based on the way social norms have developed for each minority group based on a set of identifiable factors. For example, the civil rights movement helped develop a norm of racial equality in principle[2] for Black

Americans through pervasive signals supporting equality from a massive social movement, politicians, political institutions, and media elites. However, most of the factors that helped develop this norm of racial equality are missing for Muslims. Thus, King's comments about Muslims were generally accepted while his anti-Black comments led to censure.

Moreover, norms develop distinctly within segments of the broader population. More specifically, norms of acceptable political rhetoric have developed differently within the Republican Party than within the Democratic Party. Consistent and pervasive inegalitarian signals from conservative elites, in conjunction with right-wing activism in opposition to minority rights, have activated festering out-group animus from much of the Republican base. A combination of political circumstance and elite signaling have also situated some of these groups as threatening in the imaginations of GOP voters. These processes have destabilized egalitarian norms for some minority groups and propagated inegalitarian norms for others. Consequently, Republican elites are more likely to utilize antiminority messaging and Republican voters are more receptive to and mobilized by these messages. Meanwhile, Democrats trust their copartisan elected officials, progressive activists, and liberal media who are much less likely to signal opposition to minority rights; and in recent years are increasingly signaling a commitment to protecting and expanding minority rights. These distinct informational pathways and group constructions have led to social norms developing differently within the two political parties. This can also be measured at the individual level: Some people, because of the networks or social groups they are part of and the information they are receiving, adhere to egalitarian norms more strongly than others.

Thus, to understand how prejudice functions in politics, we have to know the status of social norms regarding the subject group of the prejudicial message and the characteristics of the audience that's intended to receive it. The differential construction of social norms, with variation based on the subject group and the target audience, makes it possible for political elites to openly signal negative sentiments toward certain groups deemed to be high threat. Indeed, rhetorically attacking groups of people who have become high-threat boogeymen in the imaginations of the target audience, and for whom a norm of equality has not been established, can be politically beneficial. However, politicians remain wary of explicitly derogating minority groups for whom a norm of equality has developed, as they are likely to face political costs if they do so.

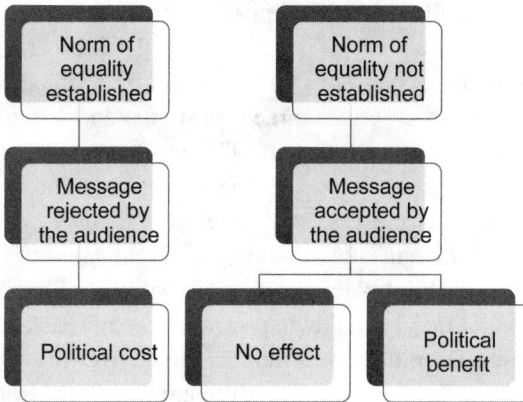

FIGURE I.I. Expected pathway of prejudicial political messaging.

Politicians gain and maintain power through public support, so political costs come in the form of decreases in public support, while benefits are measured through increases in support. Of course, like many other political messages, there are situations where antiminority messaging will have no impact on public evaluations of a politician. Figure I.I illustrates this pathway. The theory presented in this book sheds light on which groups are more likely to receive negative political attention, and why. It also illuminates who is most likely to accept antiminority messages and who is most likely to reject them.

Summary of Key Findings

The empirical findings begin in chapter 3 with the development of an original individual-level measure of social norm adherence, the social norms index (SNI). This measure tests my expectation that norm adherence varies throughout the population and that adherence to egalitarian/inegalitarian norms leads to rejection/acceptance of antiminority messaging. The chapter then presents several statistical analyses to show that the SNI has high scale validity, is moderately correlated with other attitudinal measures that influence reactions to prejudice and has predictable demographic profiles across its range. These tests demonstrate the appropriateness of using the SNI to test the hypotheses presented in the remainder of the book.

My theory of differential norms posits that overt prejudice of groups for whom a norm of equality *has not* developed will be accepted by the public. Overt prejudice of groups for whom a norm of equality *has* developed should be rejected. Across three case studies and using survey data, dozens of original survey experiments, TV news coverage, and real-world examples, I find consistent support for this expectation. Chapter 4 presents the first of three empirical case studies testing the theory of differential norms. The chapter begins by outlining the development of norms guiding political speech about Black people. The civil rights movement helped develop a norm of racial equality in principle that internalized within the public over time. Despite a concerted conservative effort to destabilize[3] the norm, the Black Lives Matter movement, political institutions, and prominent political elites have helped maintain it. Thus, my expectation is that political speech is guided by a norm of racial equality, but that norm is actively destabilizing within the Republican Party.

The findings in chapter 4 strongly support that hypothesis. Democrats and Independents consistently reject overt anti-Black political rhetoric and punish candidates who use such language in experimental and survey settings. Most Republicans reject such messaging as well, but there is a sizable segment within the GOP who accepts both overt anti-Black messaging and the candidates who use it. The SNI shows that respondents who adhere to inegalitarian norms are most likely to accept overt anti-Black prejudice, while those who adhere to egalitarian norms are most likely to reject it. I supplement these findings with analysis of TV news coverage that provides further evidence for the destabilization of egalitarian norms within the GOP.

Chapter 5, in contrast, argues political messaging about Muslims is guided more by a norm of inequality. Particularly since the September 11, 2001, terrorist attacks, a plethora of anti-Muslim signals from political institutions, social movement leaders, political elites, and the news media have interacted with widespread fear, threat, and resentment of Muslims among much of the public, to push norms in an inegalitarian direction. Moreover, factors that could help develop a norm of equality—like a strong social movement demonstrating deep and broad public support for Muslim rights or major legislation enshrining equal rights into law—are mostly nonexistent. Survey and experimental results demonstrate high levels of overt anti-Muslim sentiment, high levels of perceived threat from Muslims, and majority support for politicians who use overt anti-Muslim campaign appeals.

However, norms have still developed differently within the Democratic and Republican Parties. Signals from GOP leaders, conservative media, and right-wing activists have been consistent in spreading anti-Muslim ideas and endorsing discrimination. Meanwhile, a growing number of influential voices within the Democratic Party advocate for equal rights for Muslim Americans. Survey findings indicate that Republicans are much less supportive than Democrats of equal rights for Muslims and are much more threatened by Muslims than Democrats are. A series of survey experiments show that overt anti-Muslim messaging can garner significant support across the political spectrum but that Republicans are much more supportive than Democrats and Independents of candidates who use this messaging.

Chapters 4 and 5 present case studies that are relatively clear-cut. A norm of racial equality in principle generally guides messaging toward Black people, while a norm of inequality guides messaging toward Muslim people. Chapter 6 complicates that dichotomy by focusing on messaging about the LGBTQ+ community, a group for whom norms are stratified and in flux. Norms vary across multiple segments of the US population and do not uniformly apply to groups within the broader LGBTQ+ community. The chapter first outlines the recent historical development of LGBTQ+-related norms and lays out empirical expectations. Then, the chapter presents survey and experimental findings to show that acceptance of overt anti-LGBTQ+ messaging varies based on party identification, religious identity, and age. The chapter compares the effects of antigay and anti-transgender messaging on candidate support, showing that antitransgender messaging is only slightly more palatable to the general public, despite being the focal point of recent right-wing attacks on LGBTQ+ rights. That said, I argue that the normalization and legitimization of antitransgender political messaging is actively destabilizing the already tenuous norm of equality that was recently developed for gay and lesbian people. Table 1.1 summarizes the hypothesized social norm development and resulting empirical expectations of each case study subject group. The figure presents a simplified guiding framework — further complexity will be added to this framework in subsequent chapters.

The findings from these chapters support the theory of differential norms, showing that norms of acceptable rhetoric vary by the subject group of the message and by the partisan identity and individual social norm adherence of the target audience. The three case studies presented in these chapters demonstrate the spectrum of support for antiminority

TABLE 1.1 **Summary of case studies**

Subject group	Social norm development	Empirical expectations
Black Americans	Norm of equality in principle.	Overt anti-Blackness will be rejected by Democrats and Republicans.
Muslim Americans	Norm of inequality.	Overt Islamophobia will be accepted more readily than overt anti-Blackness.
LGBTQ+ Americans	Norm of equality for gay and lesbian people has destabilized among some segments of the population. Norm of inequality for transgender people.	Overt anti-LGBTQ+ messaging will be accepted by Republicans, evangelicals, and older Americans but rejected by their counterparts. Overt antitransgender messaging will be accepted at higher rates than overt homophobia.

messaging, with overt anti-Muslim messaging being most consistently accepted by the public and overt anti-Black messaging being most consistently rejected. Overall support for anti-LGBTQ+ messaging is in between and highly stratified across social groups. Republicans consistently support antiminority messaging of all kinds more than Democrats do. The results also show that general adherence to inegalitarian norms is a powerful predictor of acceptance of antiminority political messages. Using an original measure of social norms, the SNI, regression analysis in each empirical chapter demonstrates that those who adhere to inegalitarian norms are substantially more likely to support candidates who overtly appeal to prejudice. Respondents who adhere to egalitarian norms are more likely to reject these candidates in favor of their opponents.

The upshot is that elections will increasingly pit candidates against each other who take very different positions on issues of race and ethnicity; with Republican candidates often incentivized to overtly appeal to the antiminority prejudices of key constituents. This has a myriad of downstream effects on society, including deepening dislike for the opposition party (e.g., Valentino and Zhirkov 2018), harming the mental and physical well-being of members of minority communities (e.g., Chavez et al. 2019), and enflaming antiminority violence (e.g., Feinberg et al. 2022). Chapter 7 turns to the normative question of how to counteract prejudicial political messaging. In this chapter, I develop and test four strategies to neutralize the effects of overt prejudice on candidate and policy evaluations. The findings indicate that countering prejudice is difficult but not impossible. Because Republicans are driving the acceptability of overt prejudice, meaningful strategies to counter prejudice will likely have to come from Republican elites. It is less likely that Republicans will be convinced that a message or act is a violation of social norms if the condemnation comes from someone outside of their trusted reference group. I also find evidence that when Democrats forcefully denounce antiminority messaging as violations of social norms, or when information is provided about the dangerous real-world effects of prejudicial rhetoric, it can weaken support for candidates who use such messaging in low-information elections, even among Republicans.

Implications

On March 8, 2023, amid a wave of antitransgender legislation and overt hatred coming from politicians, conservative media, and right-wing activists, a well-known transgender rights activist tweeted: "Michael Knowles' speech about eradicating transgenderism and Matt Walsh's rants about Dylan Mulvaney are gifts to the movement for trans equality. Normal people watch these angry maniacs with revulsion" (Drennen 2023a). The activist seemed to be arguing that overt and extreme hostility directed at the transgender community would aid the movement for equality by stoking backlash to antitransgender attacks among the public. To an extent, this is happening. There have been protests and demonstrations across the country opposing legislation that seeks to curtail the rights of transgender people. Some states, like Minnesota, are taking proactive measures to defend the rights of transgender people by protecting access to gender-affirming health care. Hostility toward the LGBTQ+ community during the 2022 midterm elections may also have backfired on Republicans. A record number of candidates who identified with the LGBTQ+ community ran for, and were elected to, public office in 2022 (Branigin 2022). Almost all of these candidates were Democrats, and several said they were motivated to run by the extreme attacks on their community's rights (Moreau 2022).

Yet most Republican controlled states are continuing to enact legislation that restricts the rights of the LGBTQ+ community, and popular party leaders like Ron DeSantis have made opposition to LGBTQ+ rights central to their campaigns. Protests of drag shows and other similar events have become important rallying points for the conservative movement. We also saw Trump get elected president twice using a messaging strategy rife with overt attacks on Muslims, immigrants, women, and many other minority groups. Republican politicians like Representative Lauren Boebert and Representative Marjorie Taylor Greene have risen to prominence largely because of their antiminority hostility. Public demonstrations opposing the rights of many different minority groups have become increasingly common across the country. Conservative media from Fox News to Newsmax and Breitbart have doubled down on openly antiminority narratives. Indeed, conservatives are increasingly, and overtly, engaging in a dangerous brand of grievance politics that blames minorities for actual or perceived societal problems.

This book helps us understand this moment and the likely future of US politics. First, it clarifies the relationship between social norms and political messaging by specifying the central power of norms in conditioning evaluations of prejudice. It demonstrates that norms of acceptable rhetoric vary based on the message's subject group and target audience. We can thus better understand why certain groups face the brunt of negative political attention and who among the public is mobilized by this brand of politics. We can also better predict when politicians will face social censure. For example, this book sheds light on why King was punished for his comments about white nationalism but not for his anti-Muslim rhetoric and why Trump's explicit Islamophobia, beyond not costing him his election bid, actually contributed to his victory. It also sheds light on why transgender people have become the latest target of right-wing hostility and how that hostility is destabilizing egalitarian norms for the rest of the LGBTQ+ community.

Second, this book illuminates the role of party politics. The case studies show that Republicans readily accept overt anti-Muslim, antitransgender, and antigay campaign appeals. Even overt anti-Black messaging was accepted by a substantial portion of Republicans. The particular brand of grievance politics that the GOP is using shows no signs of abating. Indeed, antiminority messaging is likely to only increase, especially given demographic changes, growing income inequality, and the high levels of status threat among white Americans. Moreover, social conservatives have incentives to espouse antiminority ideas beyond short-term election wins. Political, media, and societal elites exert a great deal of influence on their followers. By repeatedly endorsing antiminority ideas, they can shift social norms in an inegalitarian direction in the long term even while taking short-term electoral losses or losses in popularity. For example, Republicans have opposition to the transgender community as a central part of their platform and messaging strategy despite evidence that these stances are unpopular among the public and may have hurt the party in the 2022 midterm election. Yet, if the GOP successfully positions the transgender community as a high-threat boogeyman in the eyes of the public, it may help the party build and maintain political power in the future. By positioning the transgender community as a threat to society and shifting norms in an inegalitarian direction, GOP candidates and elected officials can more successfully use fear of and opposition to the community to mobilize the social conservatives and evangelicals who comprise a large portion of their base. GOP candidates can also launder antigay and antilesbian messages through antitransgender frames to appeal to religious conservatives who continue to oppose equal rights to the broader LGBTQ+ community without facing censure for violating egalitarian norms. Indeed, this strategy may have paid off just two years later in the 2024 election. A postelection survey of more than three thousand swing voters found that one of the most common reasons given for not voting for Kamala Harris was that she "focused more on cultural issues like transgender issues rather than helping the middle class" (Blueprint 2024).

Meanwhile, Democrats have little to gain from most forms of overt antiminority messaging (though see Stephens-Dougan 2020). In fact, Democratic politicians may benefit politically from calling out Republicans for their antiminority hostility. Democrats would also be well served to combat the long-term strategy of the Republican Party and their allies. The GOP often relies on grievance politics that blame out-groups for social and economic ills, thus stoking outrage from their base. If they sit by while the GOP creates boogeymen of the Muslim and LGBTQ+ communities, Democrats allow Republicans to play into a proven strategy. Indeed, the old strategy of staying silent on issues of race and ethnicity to appease white moderates and conservatives (see Kinder and Sanders 1996) plays right into the hands of the GOP.

To that end, this book helps diagnose an issue that I hope will lead to innovative social change. As Bicchieri (2016, 1) stated, "Understanding the nature of collective behaviors and why people engage in them is critical for the design of appropriate interventions aimed at social change." In other words, by understanding what sustains the use of antiminority political messaging, we can develop methods to counteract political prejudice. The findings from chapter 7 provide multiple short-term ways to counteract expressions of prejudice and neutralize their electoral effects. More importantly, the theoretical framework and findings from the case studies can be helpful for developing long-term strategies to combat prejudice and shift social norms in an egalitarian direction.

CHAPTER TWO

Theory of Differential Norms

Well, lookey there, it's the jihad squad. — Lauren Boebert (Kaczynski 2021)

Many in the party see that they no longer need to pretend and they can go back to voicing what they really believe. —Stuart Stevens[1] (Leonhardt and Philbrick 2022)

In November 2021, a video surfaced of Representative Lauren Boebert (R-CO) calling Representative Ilhan Omar (D-MN) "blackhearted" and "evil" as a crowd of donors cheered. Boebert repeatedly referred to Omar as the "jihad squad" and likened her to a suicide bomber, saying she only felt safe in an elevator with her because Omar was not wearing a backpack (Kaczynski 2021). Soon after, forty-one Democratic members of Congress wrote a letter calling for Boebert to be stripped of her committee assignments because of her comments (Alfaro et al. 2021). Republicans, however, largely remained silent on the matter. When Republican House Minority Leader Kevin McCarthy was asked to condemn Boebert's remarks, he instead said, "This party is for anyone and everyone who craves freedom and supports religious liberty" (Alemany and Sotomayor 2021). Boebert has yet to face any public censure from her party or any material political consequences for her overt anti-Muslim remarks. Though her victory was narrow, Boebert was reelected to her seat a year after the video surfaced.

Although a norm of equality has not been established for Muslims, it appears that political messaging is still somewhat guided by a norm of racial equality. As discussed in the opening to chapter 1, Republican Representative Steve King faced major political repercussions for his praise of white nationalism and white supremacy because the comments were perceived as racist. He was quickly stripped of his committee assignments and soon after, all but one of his colleagues in the House, including every single one of his Republican colleagues, voted yes on a measure to rebuke him.[2] Many Republicans even called for his resignation. The following year, King failed to make it out of the GOP primary. While Boebert's political career survived, King's political career came to an end after eighteen years in office.[3]

There is clearly a difference in the way the public reacts to anti-Black and anti-Muslim messaging. Overt prejudice against some minority groups is met with tacit acceptance by politicians and the public at large. Some of these messages are even met with enthusiasm from key constituents and can contribute to the electoral success of candidates. However, overt prejudice against other minority groups is condemned for violating egalitarian social norms and can have disastrous political consequences for the purveyor of the message. In other words, social norms about what is acceptable vary based on the subject group of the message. For certain groups, collective pro-equality initiatives have cultivated egalitarian norms that shape the way messaging about those groups is framed. In these cases, the public will typically reject explicit prejudice because it violates established social norms. As a result, politicians either have to avoid denigrating these groups or they have to disguise the prejudicial intent of their rhetoric by shrouding it in coded language. For other groups, like Muslims, a norm of equality has not developed. Messaging for those groups is sometimes guided by a norm of inequality instead. Thus, when politicians like Boebert or Donald Trump want to appeal to the anti-Muslim sentiments of their voters, they can do so explicitly without worrying about facing social censure.

The anti-Muslim comments described above are just the latest salvo of such rhetoric, mostly from Republican politicians and right-wing leaders. Trump's rise to political power exemplifies the inegalitarian norm environment. In 2011, Trump popularized the "birther myth" by insinuating that President Barack Obama had been born outside of the United States. He called on Obama to release his birth certificate and claimed he had hired a team of investigators to find Obama's birth records (Graham et al. 2019). While announcing his presidential bid in 2015, Trump said, "When Mexico sends its people, they're not sending their best. They're not sending you. They're not sending you. They're sending people that have lots of problems, and they're bringing those problems with us [sic]. They're bringing drugs. They're bringing crime. They're rapists. And some, I assume, are good people." (Phillips 2017) This statement is emblematic of a campaign that was characterized by explicit attacks on racial, ethnic, religious, and gender minority groups. Trump's primary policy proposals during his first presidential campaign were building a wall on the Mexican border and a "total and complete shutdown" of Muslims entering the US "until our country's representatives can figure out what is going on" (J. Johnson 2015b). Not only did Trump escape social censure or negative political consequences for his rhetoric, he won the nomination over a crowded Republican field. He went on to capture the presidency.

Data from surveys and exit polls in 2016, 2018, and 2020 show that antiminority attitudes like racism, Islamophobia, and xenophobia were powerful predictors of support for Trump and the Republican Party. For example, low favorability ratings of African Americans, immigrants, and Muslims and the belief that racial inequality is due to lack of effort from African Americans were all associated with strong support for Trump during the 2016 Republican presidential primary and general election (Sides et al. 2018). These attitudes have remained strongly predictive of support for Trump and the GOP in the years since (e.g., Sides et al. 2018; Lajevardi and Abrajano 2019; Sides et al. 2022).

In other words, Trump's explicit and frequent attacks on minority groups contributed to his political success by activating negative attitudes toward minorities among much of the Republican voter base. Trump also influenced the norm environment by normalizing and legitimizing antiminority rhetoric in the eyes of his supporters. Indeed, Trump's presidential campaign and political success exacerbated the force of prejudice by bringing explicit antiminority rhetoric to the forefront of American politics. He demonstrated to fellow Republicans like Boebert that explicit prejudice can be a winning electoral strategy.

In the years since Trump's presidential campaign, overt antiminority political messaging has become even more widespread. A report commissioned by the organization Muslim Advocates (2018) found that more than eighty political candidates across thirty-three states in the 2018 midterm election utilized Islamophobic rhetoric in their election campaigns. According to a database of campaign ads compiled by America's Voice (2021), anti-immigrant rhetoric dominated the 2018 midterm elections and Islamophobic ads were featured in state and congressional races in Alabama, Georgia, Kansas, Maryland, Minnesota, Missouri, New York, and Virginia in 2020. Leading up to the 2022 midterm election, America's Voice identified hundreds of political ads and messages from GOP politicians that focused on racist conspiracy theories, such as "white replacement" and a "migrant invasion" (Mueller 2022). Even after Trump's defeat in the 2020 presidential race, antiminority messaging continued to dominate US politics, particularly among the right wing.

This represents a dramatic shift from the era when Republican President George W. Bush repeatedly called on Americans to oppose terrorism while supporting Islam and Muslims in general (White House 2002). Despite many policies passed during his administration that curtailed the rights of Muslim Americans, Bush and his copartisans were careful not to overtly signal their opposition to the rights of minority groups. When politicians were more explicit with their antiminority stances, they tended to face social censure. For example, in 2002, Republican Senator Trent Lott praised Strom Thurmond, a former presidential candidate and strong proponent of racial segregation (Edsall and Faler 2002). Lott's comments proved so controversial that he resigned his post as Senate minority leader two weeks later.

Today's Republican Party is very different. For decades, the GOP relied on racially coded language or dog whistles to activate antiminority attitudes from key constituents while avoiding overtly signaling antiminority sentiment. Now, prominent members of the party openly appeal to antiminority sentiments by denigrating groups such as immigrants, Muslims, and the LGBTQ+ community. I argue that norms of acceptable political rhetoric vary not just based on the subject group of the message, but based on the target audience as well. More specifically, I argue that norms have developed in a more inegalitarian way within the Republican Party than within the Democratic Party. Thus, antiminority messaging is more acceptable to Republicans, and GOP elites are more likely to use such messaging to appeal to their supporters.

Clearly, things have changed in US politics. Many elected officials and candidates now openly signal their antiminority sentiments and, in many circumstances, benefit politically by doing so. The rise in and implications of explicit prejudicial messaging has not been fully explained by current scholarship. How did we get to this place in American politics? What has happened since the early 2000s, when praising a former segregationist held major political consequences? The answers to these questions are meant to shed light on the rise of Trump but also go beyond Trump. How did we get to a place where right-wing elites are able to endorse the great replacement theory (Mansfield and Woodall 2022) and refer to a Muslim member of the House of Representatives as a suicide bomber (Arora 2021) without ruining their political careers? How did we get to a place where 58% of Republicans believe that demographic changes "pose a threat to white Americans and their culture and values" (Miller 2022), and where 37% of the American public is worried that Sharia law could be applied in America (Smietana 2015)? What are the broader implications of the rise in overt prejudice in politics? Finally, can anything be done to temper the effects of explicit prejudicial political messaging?

This chapter sheds light on this situation by explaining the integral role that party politics and social norms play in understanding the use of and response to political rhetoric. In this chapter, I present the theory of differential norms, which explains why political elites can openly denigrate certain minority groups without incurring significant political repercussions and, in certain situations, even bolster their own political fortunes.

When Party Politics Clash with Social Norms

For decades following the civil rights era, Republicans and Democrats found themselves locked in an equilibrium that Kinder and Sanders (1996) adroitly termed "the electoral temptations of race." Republicans generally relied on racial code words or dog whistles so they could appeal to the anti-Black attitudes of key constituents while maintaining plausible deniability about racism. Meanwhile, Democrats tended to be silent on racial issues so they could maintain their non-white voting base without alienating racially conservative white voters. The tendencies of the two major political parties were based on incentives stemming from the clash between party politics and social norms. Democrats were better off avoiding the topic of race because of competing interests within their coalition. Republicans had incentives to appeal to the engrained antiminority attitudes of key members of their base, but they had to do so without violating a developed norm of racial equality in principle (see Mendelberg 2001; Valentino et al. 2002; White 2007).

Indeed, coded language was more effective than explicit anti-Black appeals because it could "bypass the self-censorship mechanisms of whites" and "activate negative racial predispositions" (Mendelberg 2001, 20). In other words, because a norm of racial equality in principle existed and because white individuals did not want to be viewed as racist, explicit anti-Black political messaging was likely to be rejected. However, implicit appeals that disguised the racial subject matter could more effectively activate the negative racial attitudes that existed among much of the public. This theory held up to several empirical tests over multiple decades (Mendelberg 1997; Mendelberg 2001; Valentino et al. 2002; White 2007; Winter 2008; Tokeshi and Mendelberg 2015; though see Huber and Lapinski 2006). Thus, race was a focal topic in political messaging due to incentives to activate particular racial attitudes from voters. But the manner in which political and societal elites talked about race was guided by social norms. Essentially, a party structure based on anti-Black cleavages came into conflict with a norm of racial equality in principle which shifted messaging strategies accordingly. Therefore, to understand why contemporary elites now more overtly signal certain antiminority sentiments, it is essential to understand the social norms at play.

Among the various definitions of social norms, there is consensus that they have to be "social" and must "inform action-oriented decision-making" (Legros and Cislaghi 2020, 66). Norms are social because they arise from an individual's perceptions of other people, which shape what actions and behaviors that individual believes are typical and appropriate. Norms then inform decision-making because people tend to want their behavior to fit with their perception of what is typical and appropriate. Essentially, a norm is a grammar of social interactions, helping to specify what is and is not acceptable in any given situation (Bicchieri 2006; Legros and Cislaghi 2020).

Almost a century of scholarship in social psychology has demonstrated that social norms can have a large influence on individual opinions, attitudes, and beliefs (for a review, see Morris et al. 2015). Social norms influence individual opinions and decision-making through two mechanisms. First, when individuals are aware of the norm, the criteria they use to process information and make decisions shift in favor of a response that is congruent with the norm (Germar and Mojzisch 2019). As Mendelberg (2001, 17) put it, the purpose of following a norm is "to avoid social censure or the pangs of conscience." People who follow a norm of racial equality in principle may not have internalized the norm. Put another way, someone who adheres to this norm may not necessarily believe racism to be morally bad. However, they understand that it is socially unacceptable to be racist and they want to demonstrate that they accept the norm.

Similarly, individuals are incentivized to try and control the impressions other people receive of them. People put on a performance—an activity, verbal or otherwise—in front of others that has an effect on outside observers (Goffman 1956, 13). Individuals work to create a positive image, which is delineated by social attributes that have been approved by society (Goffman 1967). Thus, people's words and actions in front of others are a performance put on to adhere to accepted norms and attributes. For example, if there is a norm against using a particular derogatory term, an individual may not use the term as a way of indicating to others that they accept the norm, regardless of how they actually feel about it.

The second mechanism through which social norms influence opinions and decision-making is by "evoking a persistent perceptual bias leading to lasting norm adherence" (Germar and Mojzisch 2019, 11). Social norms have a strong cognitive effect on the acquisition and processing of information, which then influences individual opinions and attitudes. As norms change, the opinions and decision-making processes of the public should change in a corresponding fashion, helping to internalize the new norm. A social norm becomes most powerful when it is internalized and becomes personal (Cialdini and Trost 1998). Someone who initially follows a norm simply because they want to avoid social censure may over time internalize that norm and follow it because they have internalized the value of the behavior.

Therefore, social norms perform two important functions in society. First, norms help us understand "that particular behavioral responses are warranted in situations that are sufficiently similar to each other" (Bicchieri 2016, 30). Second, norms "express social approval or disapproval of such behaviors—they tell us how we ought to act" (30). Indeed, norms have been found to guide individual behaviors in a host of important areas, including energy conservation, voting, and alcohol consumption (Tankard and Paluck 2016). Not only do social norms guide individual behavior and decision-making, but they also "structure people's *awareness* and *consideration* of the behavioral options available to them" in any given situation (Kalkstein et al. 2022, 3).

For our purposes, then, social norms help voters understand how they ought to react to antiminority appeals based on their perception of what behavior is appropriate. If an individual adheres to a norm of equality, then they are likely to perceive an openly racist or prejudicial message as inappropriate, which will lead them to reject the message along with the messenger. Conversely, if an individual adheres to a norm of inequality, then they will perceive those same messages as appropriate and will accept the political message along with the messenger.

Indeed, more than two decades of racial priming scholarship has demonstrated the powerful influence of social norms on how political elites discuss race and how the public reacts to these messages. Mendelberg's (2001, 67) seminal work demonstrated that the transformation of racial or anti-Black political messaging from explicit to implicit was predicated on inegalitarian norms being "displaced by an ideology of racial equality." As norms transitioned from inegalitarian to egalitarian in the mid-1900s, she argued, there was a corresponding shift from explicit to implicit appeals to anti-Black sentiments. Similarly, we should be able to explain the recent rise in overt antiminority prejudice in politics by investigating the role of social norms and their interaction with party politics.

How Norms Develop

Social norms develop through consistent signals of commitment to a norm from influential actors who interact with mass attitudes in a mutually reinforcing way. This process can be driven by political or media elites, or major political institutions, who hold significant influence over the public. Signals from elites can shift or activate mass attitudes and, over time, destabilize an old norm and develop a new one in its place. Social norm transformation can also be driven by social movements or other forms of organized social action. In this case, activists directly influence mass attitudes and simultaneously leverage elites who further sway the masses. While elites strongly influence public attitudes and behavior, mass attitudes, especially when organized, can also shift national dialogue and guide elite rhetoric and behavior. The process of developing social norms is not a simple top-down or bottom-up process. Rather, elites and the masses interact in particular ways to establish norms. Exogenous shocks to the system like the September 11, 2001, terrorist attacks or the COVID-19 pandemic can also greatly impact mass attitudes and provide leverage for elites to dictate social norm transformation. Below, I detail the forces at play in social norm development and provide illustrative examples to underscore the process.

Elites can play a crucial role in norm development when they actively and deliberately communicate their commitment to a particular norm (see Mendelberg 2001). Signals from influential leaders are very important because we adjust our behavior to fit the expectations of political, societal, and media elites, who have enormous influence over our opinions, behaviors, and decision-making (e.g., Zaller 1992; Berinsky 2009; Levendusky 2009; Tesler 2015). In situations involving interdependent collective behaviors, where the choices of individuals are influenced by the actions of others, the decisions made by people an individual trusts will significantly impact that individual's own choices (see Bicchieri 2016). People tend to trust political elites and political institutions and, especially in the political realm, be influenced by them. If trusted elites communicate their support for equal rights while rejecting messages that discriminate against minorities, then the public will see such messages as violations of a norm of equality. But if elites signal their opposition to equal rights and accept discriminatory messages, then a norm of equality is unlikely to develop.

Political institutions play an important role in the development of norms through signaling lack of commitment to an old norm or commitment to a new norm. For example, *Loving v. Virginia*, the 1967 Supreme Court decision that prohibited bans on interracial marriage, contributed to a dramatic shift in support for interracial marriage from under 25% to well over 80% (Marshall 1987). Similarly, Tankard and Paluck (2017) found that a 2015 Supreme Court ruling in favor of same-sex marriage increased individual perceptions of a norm that favors gay marriage. Through two landmark rulings, the Supreme Court helped develop norms of equality for Black Americans and gay and lesbian Americans by signaling to the public a commitment to protecting and expanding their rights.

Tankard and Paluck (2017) theorized two primary reasons why institutions shape social norms. First, if an institution is perceived by the public as democratic, then a decision it makes could be viewed as a signal of where the public stands on a topic. This can lead people to update their own perceptions of public opinion. Second, decisions from "legitimate" institutions such as the Supreme Court and US Congress may be viewed as expert takes on the future direction of public support for a group or issue. So, if an institution enacts a policy that curtails the rights of a minority group, it legitimates discrimination against that group in the eyes of the public. Through both mechanisms, a decision from an institution can influence perceptions of status quo support for a group or issue, thereby helping shape social norms.

Another important set of actors with major influence on the public is members of the media. The media can have a powerful effect on politics through shaping the political agenda (Iyengar and Kinder 1987); influencing the political preferences of the public (Brummett 1994); and shaping people's views on issues such as race, crime, and welfare (Gilens 1999; Gilliam and Iyengar 2000; Dixon 2017). Conservative media in particular has played a crucial role in molding the attitudes and preferences of its audience and has turned this audience into reliable voters for the Republican Party (see Hemmer 2016). Indeed, extant scholarship shows that

Fox News has had a major effect on voting behavior (e.g., DellaVigna and Kaplan 2007; Martin and Yurukoglu 2017), COVID-19 pandemic-related behavior (e.g., Simonov et al. 2022), and attitudes toward salient policy issues such as immigration and climate change (e.g., Hoewe et al. 2020). If Fox News endorses overt prejudice and signals strong opposition to minority rights, it will contribute to the development of a norm of inequality.

As just one example, in April 2021, Tucker Carlson appeared to endorse the great replacement theory, a white nationalist idea that the white European population in the West is being demographically and culturally replaced by immigrants, Muslims, and people of color. He said, "I know that the left and all the little gatekeepers on Twitter become literally hysterical if you use the term 'replacement,' if you suggest that the Democratic Party is trying to replace the current electorate—the voters now casting ballots—with new people, more obedient voters from the third world. But they become hysterical because that's what's happening, actually. Let's just say it. That's true" (Petrizzo 2021).

Carlson's comments garnered praise throughout the white nationalist community. The white nationalist website VDARE called his comments "one of the best things Fox News has ever aired" (Place 2021). Nicholas Fuentes, a prominent white nationalist and founder of the Groyper Army, said Carlson had just "red-pilled four million people, and there is nothing liberals can do about it" (Anti-Defamation League 2021). Indeed, a large national poll conducted later that year by AP-NORC found that more than 30% of US adults, including almost 50% of Republicans, agreed with the following statement: "There is a group of people in this country who are trying to replace native-born Americans with immigrants who agree with their political views" (Bump 2022c). This example illustrates the way that elites and organized social groups can interact with one another to shape norms. White nationalist organizations and their allies had been pushing the great replacement theory for years. Their efforts gave the theory momentum and made it a prominent part of far-right discourse. But the white nationalist movement, acting through sites like Stormfront and other similar forums, did not have the reach or legitimacy to make the idea palatable to a broad audience. Carlson then used his position as a popular member of the mainstream media to legitimize the theory among the large audience who regularly watch and trust Fox News. He captured the imaginations of millions of Americans with the great replacement theory, or "red-pilled" them, in a way that the movement on its own, without the aid of mainstream media, likely would not have been able to do. The process snowballed further in 2022 as many Republican political candidates endorsed the theory and used it in their electoral campaigns to activate the xenophobic sentiments of key constituents (Mueller 2022). In sum, the mutually reinforcing efforts of white supremacists and mainstream right-wing elites helped normalize and legitimize a racist, xenophobic idea.

Social movements are an effective, mass-driven way to mobilize and activate public support for a new norm. Mendelberg (2001, 68) showed that an important contributing factor to the creation of the norm of racial equality was collective efforts by African Americans to "shift the norm of public discourse." The efforts of the civil rights movement led elites such as the mass media and politicians from both major political parties, and the public to increasingly reject the ideology of white supremacy (Lee 2002; Schuman et al. 1997). Lee (2002) succinctly described the mutually reinforcing process of mass-based activism and elite rhetoric: "In this case, the mobilization of Black resistance and insurgency begins the sequence, which then provokes a reaction of southern whites and both local and national parties, which in turn activates mass audiences throughout the land" (6). As racial norms changed, beliefs about supposed biological inferiority were relegated to the fringes of society and both major political parties strived to align themselves against this ideology. In the years following the civil rights era, there was growing recognition that it was no longer acceptable for citizens or elites to appear racist (Schuman et al. 1997; Van Dijk 2015). Of course, these efforts did not eliminate racial conflict and racial appeals were not altogether abandoned; rather, there was a transition to using racial code words to activate anti-Black attitudes without appearing to violate the newly constructed norm of racial equality in principle (Kinder and Sanders 1996; Mendelberg 2001).

A prominent example of an exogenous shock precipitating social norm development can be found in the shaping of the norm environment for Muslims in the first decade of the twenty-first century. Following the 9/11 terrorist attacks, a major exogenous shock to the political system, much of the US public held negative views of Muslims and of Islam. Yet, for several years following the attacks, anti-Muslim attitudes remained mostly disconnected from partisan politics and did not meaningfully influence voting behavior or other political decisions. Tesler and Sears (2010, 127) found that public views of Muslims "did not have significant independent effects on presidential vote choice, evaluations of the president, or even opinions about going to war with the predominantly Islamic nation of Iraq." Moreover, a study by Kalkan et al. (2009) showed that partisan identity and ideology only weakly influenced attitudes about Muslims during Bush's time in office.

Then, during Barack Obama's 2008 presidential run, prominent conservatives saw an opportunity to activate existing anti-Muslim hostility in a way that would benefit the Republican Party. The subsequent barrage of anti-Muslim rhetoric from conservatives tied these attitudes to partisan politics (see Tesler and Sears 2010; Tesler 2016; Lajevardi and Abrajano 2019). Negative views of Muslims and Islam became an important component of identifying with the Republican Party and voting for conservative politicians. Conservatives successfully leveraged public fear, anger, and resentment stemming from the terrorist attacks to pass laws that restricted Muslim rights, which further stoked negative public sentiment. The success of this strategy incentivized some Republicans to increase the frequency and intensity of Islamophobic campaign appeals, exemplifying the mutually reinforcing interaction between an exogenous shock, mass attitudes, and elite signals. Though Obama won in 2008 (and was reelected in 2012), the Republican strategy pushed norms of acceptable rhetoric for Muslims in an inegalitarian direction and helped pave the way for Trump's victory in 2016.

In sum, social norm transformation can take place in a mass-driven or elite-driven way and can involve any subset of the influential actors discussed above. Changes to social norms can also be precipitated by exogenous shocks. For norm development to be most effective, signals of commitment to the norm must be communicated actively and deliberately by influential actors like political and media elites, political institutions, and social movement leaders and must interact with mass attitudes in a mutually reinforcing fashion. In the next section, I will discuss the nuanced ways that social norms influence politics. I argue that norms can shift in an egalitarian way for some subject groups while shifting in an inegalitarian direction for other subject groups. Similarly, norms within some audience groups might shift in an egalitarian direction at the same time that norms of equality are destabilizing within other audience groups. Thus, the subject group of a political message and the target audience of the message condition the use and effect of antiminority political messaging.

Theory of Differential Norms

Why the Subject Group Matters

Throughout different time periods, certain groups have been more subject to overt negative political attention than others. For almost a century, at

least from the rise of the national party system in the 1860s through the Jim
Crow era, Black Americans were the primary target of overt antiminority
political messaging. Democrats during this time made their opposition to
Black citizenship clear. Explicit attacks on the supposed biological and
cultural deficiencies of Black Americans were a central part of the party's
messaging strategy (see Mendelberg 2001). Other groups—like Chinese
Americans in the late nineteenth and early twentieth century (Daniels
2004; Ngai 2004), Japanese Americans around World War II (Daniels
et al. 1991), and Muslim Americans after September 11, 2001 (Abdo 2005;
Rivera 2014)—have also become primary targets of antiminority sentiment for periods of time. The political, economic, and social forces at any
given time can influence which groups face the brunt of antiminority political rhetoric and behavior. Indeed, I argue that there is no one norm
that universally applies to all minority groups. For each group, there is a
line that demarcates what is and is not socially acceptable. For example, a
line separates covert white supremacy, which is often socially acceptable,
from more overt white supremacy, which is generally not socially acceptable. This demarcation line is different for political messaging and behavior regarding Black Americans, Muslim Americans, LGBTQ+ Americans,
and other minority groups.

Many different minority groups have faced negative political attention in recent years. During Trump's 2016 presidential campaign, he took
aim at Muslims, immigrants, Latinos, women, and people with disabilities.
Trump called for the "total and complete shutdown" of Muslims entering
the United States; referred to Mexican immigrants as drug abusers, criminals, and rapists; and mocked reporter Serge Kovaleski for his arthrogry-
posis (Gass 2015). These are just a few examples of Trump's many hostile
and overtly prejudicial messages targeting minorities. Many politicians
and media elites, mostly on the right wing, have followed Trump's lead.
As I will discuss in chapter 5, there has been a notable rise in anti-Muslim
and xenophobic political messaging and political advertisements following Trump's rise to power.

During the last few years, the LGBTQ+ community has become one
of the GOP's most frequent targets. States across the country have introduced hundreds of bills aimed at curtailing the community's rights since
2020. According to data from the American Civil Liberties Union (2023),
the number of anti-LGBTQ+ legislative bills introduced and passed at
the state level has increased significantly each year from 2020 to 2022.
Republican candidates across the country took aim at the LGBTQ+ com-

munity in speeches and political ads to such an extent that David Stacey, the government affairs director for the Human Rights Campaign (HRC) said that anti-LGBTQ+ political messaging is "on another level from prior years" (Rummler 2022). Republicans doubled down on this strategy in 2024, spending more than $200 million just on antitransgender TV ads (AdImpact 2024).

There are several reasons to expect norms of acceptable political rhetoric to vary based on the subject group. First, the factors that contribute to the development of a norm of equality are not equally present for all minority groups. Few groups have had a strong social movement advocating for equal rights akin to the civil rights movement or Black Lives Matter movement. Landmark legislation and judicial decisions like the Civil Rights Act, Voting Rights Act, and *Brown v. Board of Education* were focused on equal rights for Black Americans. Other groups like Muslim Americans have not had a similar social movement advocating for their rights or similar institutional signals of equality. For some minority groups, the dominant signals from influential leaders are instead in opposition to equal rights, which can lead to political rhetoric about them being guided by inegalitarian norms.

Second, in various time periods and due to social and political phenomena, certain minority groups are more likely than others to be cast as urgent threats in the public imagination, which can push norms in an inegalitarian direction. This outcome is evident when examining, again, the treatment of Muslim Americans, Arab Americans, and South Asian Americans following the September 11, 2001, terrorist attacks. Hate crimes against these communities skyrocketed after 9/11. These incidents included physical assault, arson, vandalism of places of worship, and even murder. A survey of Muslim Americans conducted in July 2002 by the Council on American–Islamic Relations (2002) found that 57% of respondents had experienced discrimination since 9/11. Many media and political elites fanned the flames of anti-Muslim fear and resentment during this period by disseminating anti-Muslim tropes (see Dabashi 2017; Lajevardi 2020). The 9/11 attacks, an exogenous shock to the political system, also ushered in what Alsultany (2022, 546) referred to as a "perpetual state of exception" in which the government felt justified to expand its power to combat the supposed Muslim threat. Discriminatory measures like the passage of the PATRIOT Act, the implementation of a special registration program to collect information on visitors from the Middle East, and the opening of the Guantanamo Bay prison were justified as part of the global war on terror. Echoes of the legitimization of anti-Muslim rhetoric and behavior can be seen in Boebert's comments discussed at the beginning of this chapter, Trump's electoral success on the back of an openly Islamophobic campaign strategy, and the recent efforts of state legislatures to combat the perceived threat of Sharia law.

This example corresponds with extant scholarship, which systematically demonstrates the relationship between perceptions of threat and prejudice. Feeling threatened, particularly through perceptions that the power of the dominant group is being challenged in some way, has long been found to activate prejudice (Blumer 1958; Bobo and Hutchings 1996; Kinder and Kam 2010). More recent studies have used survey, lab, and field experiments to show that when white Americans feel threatened, they are more likely to express prejudice and accept overt prejudice toward minority groups. Craig et al. (2018) found that when white Americans were informed that their neighborhood would become more racially diverse, they felt their status as the dominant group was being threatened; this led to expressions of in-group favoritism and expressions of bias toward racial minority groups (see also Craig and Richeson 2014). Similarly, Christiani (2021) used survey experiments to show that white respondents were more accepting of overt anti-Black political messages when they felt threatened.

These findings are particularly important given the current political landscape. Changing racial and ethnic demographics have increased perceptions of threat, largely because many white people view any status gains by non-white groups as a detriment to their own racial group (Wilkins and Kaiser 2014). Trump supporters in particular are prone to the belief that white people are losing out to racial and ethnic minorities (De Jonge 2016). Obama's 2008 election caused anxiety among white individuals that they were losing political power (Parker and Barreto 2013) and activated prejudicial attitudes like old-fashioned racism (Tesler 2013) and Islamophobia (Sides et al. 2018). A major economic recession, growing wealth disparity, and a slow economic recovery period have also contributed to threat perceptions and a tendency to blame minority groups (Vargas et al. 2018). All these factors have contributed to Jardina's (2019) finding that white people perceive a greater threat to their dominant status from minority groups today than they did in the past.

Social and political conditions that heighten threat levels associated with a group can also lead to more pervasive signals of inequality from leaders and political institutions. Crisis situations such as the 9/11 terrorist attacks or public health emergencies like the AIDS epidemic and the COVID-19 pandemic were used by political actors to justify curtailing minority rights. Actors can capitalize on raw emotions like fear and anger in reaction to crises to justify enacting discriminatory or prejudicial laws in the name of public safety. Actions that may have violated social norms prior to the crisis may become acceptable because of the exceptional circumstances. This can snowball: It is easier to justify each subsequent infringement on a group's rights after the first one. Over time, this can erode a norm of equality and replace it with a norm of inequality.

Influential actors often not only capitalize on heightened threat levels but contribute to the phenomenon. During the COVID-19 pandemic, Trump used his position of power to place blame for the pandemic on a minority group. This led people to blame Chinese Americans and other Asian Americans for their supposed role in creating the pandemic and heightened the level of threat associated with the group, which increased anti-Asian sentiments among the public (Reny and Barreto 2022) and even influenced behaviors such as rating Chinese restaurants more poorly than in the past (Kim and Kam 2023). This example highlights the mutually constitutive relationship between perceived threat levels and elite signals, one of the main ingredients of social norm development.

In sum, institutional signals of commitment to equal rights (or to inequality) vary by group, which leads to different constructions of social norms of acceptable rhetoric and behavior. Further, the urgency of the threat felt toward a group increases the likelihood that overt prejudice will be directed at the group. Together, these factors help us understand why certain groups face negative political attention, but not others, and why overt prejudice leveled at certain groups is accepted by the public while similar prejudice leveled at other groups is rejected. Essentially, if a group has developed a norm of equality, then overt political messaging targeting the group is likely to be rejected. If a norm of inequality has developed, then overt political messaging targeting the group is likely to be accepted.

It is important to note that the norm environment is not always so clearly constructed. Sometimes, the factors that influence norm development are in competition. For example, a social movement advocating for the protection of minority rights might arise at least partially in response to institutional curtailment of minority rights (or vice versa). This can lead to periods of transition between norms. When one norm is destabilized, a new norm does not automatically arise and take its place. During transition periods, individuals who internalized the old norm will have a difficult time letting go of it. The new norm will more quickly influence those who never internalized the old one. During these periods of transition, the state of social norms is in flux, so we should find predictable variation in the acceptance and rejection of antiminority messages across segments of the population. For example, chapter 6 shows that support for same-sex marriage increased more quickly among younger people who were socialized during the marriage equality movement than among older generations who were socialized during periods of pervasive inegalitarian norms. As discussed in the next subsection, this relationship between norms and political messaging is complicated by striations within large population units.

Why the Audience Matters

The first crucial piece of information that determines how the public will respond to an antiminority political message is the specific norm for the subject group of the message. The second crucial piece of information is how norms have developed within the target audience of the message. Even when a norm of equality has been established for a group, an overt political message targeting that group will not necessarily be universally rejected. Similarly, an antiminority political message targeting a group for whom a norm of inequality has been established will not necessarily be universally accepted. The impact of an antiminority message also depends on how norms have developed within segments of a larger population. Practices like political messaging, which are guided by social norms, are interdependent. Individuals make choices based on their perception of what other people think or do. But the individual's perception of what all other people think or do does not matter as much as their perception of what people they trust think or do. Thus, the networks, or social groups, within which an individual is embedded will greatly influence which norms they adhere to.

Indeed, scholarship has found that major societal cleavages like racial identity, education, and gender can help predict acceptance or rejection of antiminority messaging among a broader population group. Huber and Lapinski (2006) found that education level and racially resentful attitudes conditioned the effects of anti-Black messages on individual policy preferences. Hutchings et al. (2010) found differences across gender: Women were more likely than men to reject explicit anti-Black messages. While these past studies have focused on demographic characteristics or the effects of education, I argue that the nature of group dynamics can explain much of the variation in social norm development. I developed this argument by building from Cialdini and Trost's (1998) summary of how norms develop within groups. They contend that this process is based on three connected factors: (1) opportunities for communication within groups; (2) the cohesiveness of the group and the extent to which uniformity is valued; and (3) how important a particular norm is for the group. Below, I apply this framework to the US political party system to show that norms of acceptable political rhetoric have developed in distinct ways within the Republican and Democratic Parties.

The first factor in the process is the development of partisan communication channels. Spatial segregation of Republicans and Democrats, in conjunction with a highly polarized media environment, present communication opportunities and shape norm-influencing information that party members receive. Extant scholarship shows that the groups or social networks an individual is embedded in influence the information that individual receives, which then influences norm development (Goode et al. 2014; Bicchieri 2016; Tankard and Paluck 2016). For example, Anoll (2022) demonstrated that racial segregation has influenced the strength, enforcement, and even the content of political participation norms across racial groups. Groups that are spatially segregated, like Democrats and Republicans, are thus more likely to develop distinct norms than groups that are more integrated. As far back as the eighteenth century, urban areas became hubs for liberal political supporters (Rodden 2019). Over the ensuing century and a half, forces such as racial and class segregation exacerbated partisan segregation (Massey and Denton 1993; Trounstine 2018). Recent scholarship has found that Republicans and Democrats are highly geographically segregated and spatially isolated from one another (Brown and Enos 2021) and that segregation rates are actively increasing (Brown et al. 2022). This makes it less likely for people to interact with out-partisans. Indeed, Brown and Enos (2021, 1002) found that among Republicans and Democrats, "only about three in ten of their interactions in their residential environment will, on average, be with a member of the other party." Most Republicans and Democrats are relatively siloed in their partisan geographic and social networks, which influences the political information they receive, making it more likely for norms to develop in distinct ways across partisan groups.

In conjunction with geographic segregation, the media environment and the way that people tend to consume media exacerbate the distance between the two major political parties. In the 1970s and 1980s, three television networks—ABC, CBS, and NBC—dominated the media market (Lotz 2007). Programming coming from these networks was largely similar and was rarely partisan. The media environment is now much more ideological and partisan. Consumers can self-select information that fits their worldview, which can result in partisan echo chambers (Sunstein 2001). One recent study found that roughly one in seven Americans consume more than eight hours of partisan media per month (Broockman and Kalla 2023). The study further showed that partisans were very likely to consume their side's media and unlikely to supplement it with national broadcast news or the other side's media output. In many cases, liberal media elites are speaking directly to Democrats and conservative media elites are speaking directly to Republicans. Consuming news this way can intensify dislike of members of the other party and reduced support for bipartisanship (Levendusky 2013). Further, the influence of partisan media on public opinion extends beyond the direct audience. Partisan media consumers spread its influence by discussing content with nonviewers (Druckman et al. 2018).

This is particularly important for the development of egalitarian/inegalitarian social norms because of the normalization of far-right actors and extremist right-wing ideas in conservative media. Studies of Fox News, one of the main players in conservative media, show it has major influence on its viewers' attitudes and behaviors (e.g., Broockman and Kalla 2022). Fox News holds a unique position in partisan politics: More than 40% of Republicans and Republican-leaning Independents cite it as their main source of political and government news (Bump 2022b). It also platforms white nationalists and frequently espouses racist and antiminority tropes (Confessore 2022). Digital media has also emerged as a prominent platform for right-wing extremism and antiminority messaging. YouTube, the most used social network in the US, has seen an explosion of white nationalist and alt-right content in recent years (Forestal 2019; Munger and Phillips 2022). Much of conservative media content is overtly prejudicial and signals opposition to equal rights for minority groups. Americans' tendency to self-select partisan media that does not challenge their worldviews and to exist within digital echo chambers means Republicans are much more likely to receive prejudicial and antiminority messaging than Democrats, and to communicate those messages to copartisans. In sum, the media environment and partisan segregation reinforce partisan communication channels and lead to disparate information networks among Democrats and Republicans, which has led to social norms of acceptable political rhetoric developing in distinct ways among the two groups.

The second factor is group cohesion and uniformity. Democrats and Republicans are increasingly cohesive, and value uniform behavior of party members. A partisan realignment stemming from national and subnational differences in support for civil rights initiatives led to racial conservatives identifying with the GOP and racial liberals with the Democratic Party (Carmines and Stimson 1989; Edsall and Edsall 1992; Schickler 2016). By the early 2000s, the partisan realignment had sorted most racially resentful white individuals into the GOP (Valentino and Sears 2005). This realignment further intensified after Obama's election in 2008. Racial attitudes became an even stronger predictor of partisanship among white Americans after Obama's election, with racial conservatism strongly predicting Republican Party identity (Tesler 2016). This contributed to a "white flight" of racially resentful white individuals without college degrees away from the Democratic Party and into the GOP (Tesler 2016). As just one example, the Republican advantage among white people who attribute racial inequality to a supposed lack of effort by Black people increased from 15 percentage points in 2004 to 39 points in 2012 (see Sides et al. 2018).

Trump's presidency further exacerbated party differences. Trump activated hostility and prejudice toward racial, ethnic, and religious minority groups. Meanwhile, Democrats shifted decidedly in favor of racially liberal policies and took more favorable views of these same minority groups in response to Trump's rise to power. Data from the American National Election Study and Pew Research Center polls show that evaluations of African Americans, immigrants, Islam, and Muslims among Democrats and Republicans have sharply widened in recent years, particularly after the 2016 presidential election (see Sides et al. 2018; Sides et al. 2024).

Partisanship, which was already viewed as among the most stable political attitudes (e.g., Campbell 1960; Converse 1964; Green et al. 2002), has also become one of the most salient identities for many Americans. The effects of partisanship have seeped into many areas of personal life. Republicans and Democrats alike would rather spend time with, be friends with, and live near members of their own party than people from the opposing party (Mason 2018). Dislike for the opposing party and preference for one's own party are not isolated to elected officials or party leaders. It now influences how people relate to one another. Indeed, partisan identities have grown so strong that they are powerful influencers of our "human judgment, emotion, and behavior" (Mason 2018, 140). Americans are more likely than ever to silo themselves within their political bubbles and be influenced by leaders within their own political parties while rejecting messages coming from members of the opposing party.

The saliency of partisan identity is important to the uniformity of behavior. In developing their racialized social constraint model, White and Laird (2020) argued that the interconnectedness of the Black community, and indeed their identification as a cohesive community, led to behavioral constraint. The authors argued that when making political decisions, Black Americans weighed the social costs and benefits of conforming to a group norm or defecting from it. This theory can apply to highly cohesive partisan groups. Political parties, like most groups, are most powerful when their members are a cohesive bloc that consistently support party candidates, issues, and platforms. As much as possible, parties want to minimize defectors and will sanction deviations in behavior from party elites and members. Party leadership will sanction copartisans when they act against party interests. And, given the cohesion of partisan groups, the saliency of partisan identity, and the high levels of spatial and media segregation, party members are more acutely aware of the benefits of adhering to partisan norms and the costs of defecting.

The third factor for group norm development is making a particular norm important to group members. Norms surrounding political rhetoric are important to both major political parties. This is particularly clear for the Republican Party. It benefits the GOP's electoral chances for their members to adhere to inegalitarian norms. Decades of scholarship has demonstrated that Republican candidates are most successful when they appeal to the prejudicial sentiments of white voters (e.g., Carmines and Stimson 1989; Edsall and Edsall 1992; Kinder and Sanders 1996; Mendelberg 2001). When inegalitarian norms are pervasive, Republican candidates and party leaders can more directly and more successfully activate prejudicial sentiments without worrying about violating egalitarian norms.

In recent election cycles, Republican candidates have increasingly embraced a strategy of openly conveying antiminority messages. Muslim Advocates (2022) compiled a report of anti-Muslim campaign messaging during the 2018 US election and found that almost all of the eighty anti-Muslim candidates were Republican. Similarly, a report from America's Voice (2021) found that anti-immigrant messaging in the 2020 election came almost exclusively from candidates in GOP primaries and Republican candidates in the generals. Anti-LGBTQ+ rhetoric and campaign messaging during the 2022 election had a similar partisan split. This messaging came almost exclusively from Republican candidates (Rummler 2022) and conservative news outlets like Fox News (Paterson 2022). Anti-LGBTQ+ advertisements were funded by conservative organizations associated with right-wing stalwarts like Stephen Miller (HRC 2022a). This is not to say that antiminority messaging is coming exclusively from the conservative Right, or that not a single Democrat uses or benefits from such messaging (see Stephens-Dougan 2020), but the vast majority of antiminority messaging is being produced by the GOP and its allies.

The Democratic Party faces a different set of electoral incentives. For decades, Democrats were incentivized to remain silent on issues of race so they could maintain their base of Black voters while not alienating racially conservative white voters (Kinder and Sanders 1996). Yet, there is evidence that the incentive structure for Democrats has changed. Stout (2020) argues that a set of interrelated factors, including widespread efforts for racial equality like the Black Lives Matter movement, ideological sorting by partisanship, and changing demographics have created a political environment in which Democratic politicians are more incentivized to advance a racially progressive agenda. My own research shows that fictional candidates who make pro-Black and pro-Latino appeals garner significant support from Democratic voters[4], which corresponds with other recent empirical findings (Tesler and Sears 2010; Stout 2015). If egalitarian norms are widespread, Democrats can more successfully activate pro-minority sentiments to mobilize voters; and more successfully combat the GOP's antiminority messaging strategy. Thus, norms of acceptable political rhetoric are important to both parties and can greatly influence the messaging and mobilization strategies of party elites.

In sum, the Democratic and Republican Parties clearly fit the framework developed by Cialdini and Trost (1998) for group-based norm development. Both major political parties have significant opportunities for communication due to high levels of partisan segregation and the highly polarized media environment. Both parties are cohesive and relatively uniform, particularly in the current hyperpolarized political environment. Both parties also gain advantages in the ability to mobilize constituents from developed norms of political rhetoric—Republicans from inegalitarian norms and Democrats from egalitarian norms. Therefore, in examining social norm adherence and the acceptance and rejection of antiminority messaging, I argue that the different ways norms have been constructed across party lines must be considered. Norms of acceptable rhetoric depend on the subject group of the message and also vary by the party purveying the message and the partisan identity of the individual receiving it. Given the factors discussed above, we should expect Republicans to be much more accepting of, and even enthusiastic about, overt antiminority political messaging compared to Democrats.

Conclusion

The acceptance of overt prejudice has both short- and long-term consequences. In the short term, as evidenced by changes in US politics over the past decade, it leads to more intensely racialized elections, greater political polarization, and increased public hatred and violence directed at minority groups. Drawing from the second function of social norms—that internalization of norms leads to lasting norms adherence—the long-term consequences of normalizing overt prejudice may be even more disastrous. The development of inegalitarian norms engrains the acceptance of prejudice in public opinions and attitudes; and incentivizes political parties and candidates to mobilize constituents by appealing to antiminority sentiments. The development of inegalitarian norms not only paves the way for overt prejudicial political rhetoric but can have long-term consequences for the treatment of minority groups and can stymie the development of true multiracial democracy. Understanding the ways that inegalitarian norms are developed and the ways that norms guide the acceptance of overt prejudice is essential to analyzing this threat and to developing solutions.

Consequently, this book focuses on when and why antiminority political messages are accepted or rejected by the public. The first prong of the answer is that social norms guide the public's reaction to antiminority messaging. If a norm of equality has been developed through the process described in this chapter, then an overt antiminority message is likely to be rejected along with its messenger. But if a norm of inequality is in place, then that same message and messenger are likely to be accepted. The second prong of the answer is that no all-pervading norm guides reactions to all antiminority messaging. We need specific information about the message's subject group and target audience to predict whether it will be accepted or rejected.

Throughout the remainder of the book, this theory of differential norms will be applied to better understand the relationship between norm adherence and reactions to antiminority political messaging. Chapter 3 will use this theory to develop an original empirical measure of individual social norm adherence. This measure will allow me to test the theory at the individual level. In chapters 4, 5, and 6, the theory will be applied to analyze the effects of overt anti-Black, anti-Muslim, and anti-LGBTQ+ political messages on the public. If the theory is correct, we should see overt prejudicial messages against a group with a developed norm of equality (Black Americans) be rejected; overt prejudicial messages against a group with a developed norm of inequality (Muslims) be accepted; and overt prejudicial messages against a group for whom norms are currently in flux (the LGBTQ+ community) have large variation across predictable cleavages. We should also see Republicans consistently accept antiminority messages directed at each of the case study groups at higher rates than Democrats or Independents.

CHAPTER THREE

The Social Norms Index

The messages that [Gillespie] was driving home, apparently to try to energize a base vote, really very clearly backfired. —Henry Fernandez[1] (Schneider 2017)

Ed Gillespie, the Republican candidate for Governor in Virginia in 2017, used a campaign messaging strategy that featured numerous overt anti-Latino and anti-immigrant appeals. Based on the available data, these appeals clearly backfired. According to public opinion polls conducted by Latino Decisions and the African American Research Collaborative, Gillespie's anti-immigrant advertisements produced a net drop of 23 percentage points in enthusiasm for the candidate among white voters in Virginia (Latino Decisions 2017). Among every racial/ethnic group that reported seeing anti-immigrant ads or discussions of Gillespie as the anti-immigrant candidate, there was overwhelming support for his Democratic opponent, Ralph Northam: 89% of African Americans, 82% of Latinos, 73% of Asian Americans and Pacific Islanders (AAPI), and 57% of white individuals voted for Northam. Among people who did not report seeing Gillespie's anti-immigrant ads, support for Northam was lower: 88% among African Americans, 57% among Latinos, 66% among AAPI, and 29% among white people. Moreover, Northam used Gillespie's anti-minority messaging to his advantage. Northam ran numerous ads attacking Gillespie and Donald Trump for the openly hostile rhetoric they were using. Turnout in Virginia, particularly among minority communities, was large, and Northam won the race in a landslide.

Gillespie was banking on activating anti-immigrant animus among a large enough portion of potential voters for his messaging strategy to be effective. There is some evidence that Gillespie's strategy should have worked. According to my analysis of the 2016 Cooperative Congressional

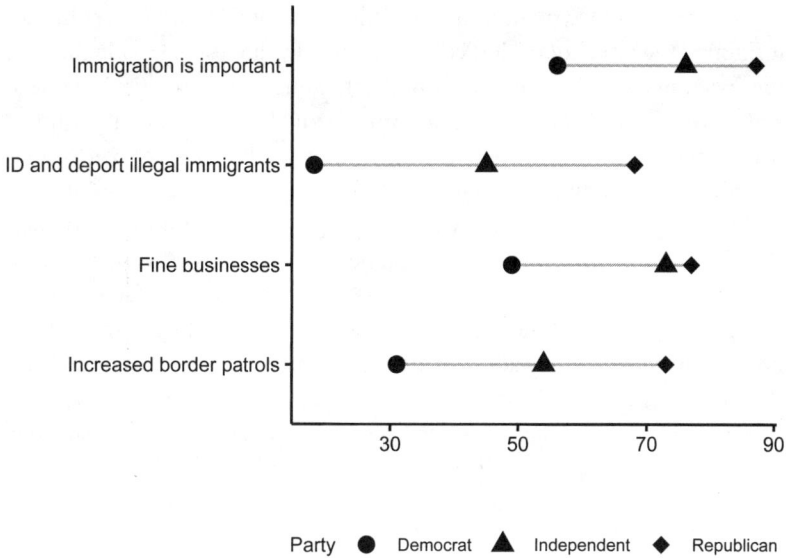

FIGURE 3.1. Anti-immigrant attitudes among Republicans, Independents, and Democrats in Virginia. Data from the 2016 Cooperative Congressional Election Study.

Election Study, which includes 2,008 respondents from Virginia, antiminority attitudes were high among Republicans and Independents. Figure 3.1 shows that 73% of Republicans and 54% of Independents in Virginia agreed that the number of patrols at the US–Mexico border should be increased and 77% of Republicans and 73% of Independents said the government should fine US businesses that hire "illegal" immigrants. Moreover, 68% of Republicans and 45% of Independents supported efforts by the government to identify and deport all "illegal" immigrants. In short, a large majority of Republicans and a majority of Independents supported curtailing the rights of immigrants. Immigration was also a very important issue for both groups. Large majorities—87% of Republicans and 76% of Independents—rated immigration as a very or somewhat important problem. Just looking at these results, it would be reasonable to conclude that Gillespie's messaging strategy should have worked. Among the constituencies that Gillespie most needed to mobilize, anti-immigrant animus was high and immigration was a mobilizing issue. Even many Democrats agreed on these issues as demonstrated by the almost 50% who supported the government levying fines on businesses who hire "illegal" immigrants.

Yet, the existence of antiminority animus is not all that matters for determining the effect of prejudicial messaging. In chapter 2, I made the case for social norms as the basis for understanding how a political message will be received by the public. If a norm of equality exists, overt prejudice will be rejected. Thus, a politician or candidate who uses an overt prejudicial campaign appeal will face negative political consequences, even if antiminority animus is strongly held among most of the target audience. But if there is an inegalitarian norm, people will accept overt prejudice and a politician who uses an overt prejudicial appeal will not face negative consequences. Candidates may even benefit from appealing to the antiminority sentiments of certain constituents. Social norms will also influence the effectiveness of advertisements condemning prejudice like the ones Northam ran. Thus, measuring the social norm adherence of prospective voters, particularly among Republicans and Independents, would have been necessary to understand why Gillespie's overt anti-immigrant messaging strategy backfired in Virginia in 2017.

Social norms also show why some messaging strategies are overtly prejudicial and other strategies more subtly appeal to antiminority animus. For example, politicians often rely on coded language like "states' rights," "welfare queen," and "inner-city crime" to appeal to the anti-Black attitudes of key constituents (see Kinder and Sanders 1996; Mendelberg 2001; Hurwitz and Peffley 2005; Haney López 2014). Politicians do this because anti-Black attitudes are widely held throughout society. But, because there is a shared understanding or social norm that it is generally unacceptable to openly express these sentiments, the messages are not overt. Though it might be easier to be explicit, politicians use coded language or dog whistles to avoid social censure for violating the norm of racial equality in principle (Mendelberg 2001).

Scholars have long recognized the important role that social norms play in a host of political and social phenomena. In examining reactions to expressed prejudice, Crandall et al. (2002) found that people's reaction to a prejudicial joke was based on whether they believed the joke violated social norms. Other scholars have found that being told one's voting record will be made public to their neighbors increased their likelihood of voting in the subsequent election (Gerber et al. 2008; Davenport et al. 2010). Social norms influence behaviors as far ranging as smoking (Bell and Cox 2015), energy consumption (Tankard and Paluck 2016), and female genital cutting (Vaitla et al. 2017).

Although large bodies of scholarship are devoted to the effects of social norms on individual behaviors and attitudes, there is no consensus measure of individual adherence to norms. This is particularly true of norms regarding prejudicial political messaging. Studies have theorized the role that social norms play in guiding reactions to prejudice but have not directly tested its effect. A measure of social norm adherence would allow better empirical tests of not just the hypotheses put forth in this manuscript but of any others that posit a relationship between social norms and reactions to prejudice.

In this chapter, I first reviewed existing measures of social norm adherence. The purpose of this discussion was to point out the limitations of these measures and make the case that a new measure is needed. I then presented an original measure of social norm adherence that I call the social norms index (SNI) that builds upon existing measures. I argue that the SNI is a subtle measure of egalitarian/inegalitarian norm adherence that is specifically applicable to expressions of prejudice. Finally, I detailed the construction of the SNI and presented evidence of its validity for the analyses conducted in subsequent chapters.

Measures of Social Norm Adherence

The cornerstone of much of the research on racial priming is the idea that social norms guide the use of and response to anti-Black political messages. Racial priming theory suggests that subtle appeals using coded language or images can effectively activate racial attitudes, but more explicit appeals are less effective because they clash with societal norms of racial equality in principle (Mendelberg 2001; also see Valentino et al. 2002; White 2007; Winter 2008). The notion that explicit anti-Black appeals should be rejected assumes that individuals adhere to a pervasive norm of equality. But more recent research found no difference between implicit and explicit anti-Black appeals among white individuals (Valentino et al. 2018a; see also Banks and Hicks 2019; Reny et al. 2020), a finding attributed to the growing acceptability of explicit anti-Black messaging. Yet these studies did not empirically test the role of individual social norm adherence. A primary challenge to testing this mechanism is that there is no broadly accepted measure for gauging adherence to the egalitarian norms that underlie racial priming theory.

There are, however, several useful measures to build upon. Blinder et al. (2013) used two questions to measure adherence to egalitarian norms: "I aim to be nonprejudiced toward immigrants due to my own convictions" and "I feel guilty when I have a negative thought about immigrants."[2] The authors argued there is a dual process at play. Many people have negative or prejudicial opinions about immigrants and other minority groups. Those same people often also recognize that there is a social norm against discrimination and prejudice. They found that the internalization of antiprejudice norms led majority-group Europeans to reject antiminority messaging and discriminatory policies. This is a valuable measurement, but it has several limitations for testing the hypotheses in this book. First, words like "nonprejudiced" and "negative" are obtrusive and have normative connotations that can influence how respondents answer. Including these words may introduce social desirability bias into the measure of norm adherence. Second, the questions only get at the internalization of norms. Asking whether people are acting a certain way due to their own convictions and whether they feel guilty is valuable for understanding whether a norm has internalized but less helpful for gauging the extent to which people act a certain way due to their perception of what is more broadly acceptable or unacceptable. Put another way, this measurement of norm adherence does not capture respondents' normative expectations of the societal appropriateness of anti-immigrant prejudice and the external motivation that comes from recognizing these expectations. Thus, this measure is less applicable for broadly examining the influence of social norm adherence on reactions to prejudice.

Crandall et al. (2002) asked respondents about the social acceptability of prejudice directed toward various groups. They then asked a second set of respondents to rate their personal attitudes toward the same set of groups. They compared these two ratings and found a high level of correlation between the perceived acceptability of prejudice and actual attitudes across almost all 105 groups the study asked about. They argued "expressed prejudice is a direct function of its social acceptability" (363). This is an interesting finding because it demonstrates that personal prejudice is strongly connected to norms regarding prejudice. While this is a helpful empirical exercise for understanding the function of social norms, it cannot be used as a standard measure for gauging adherence to egalitarian/inegalitarian norms. First, the measure requires two sets of respondents, which makes it difficult to determine the influence of individual norm adherence on that same individual's reaction to prejudice. Second, there is not a perfect correlation between prejudicial attitudes and the social acceptability of prejudice. Indeed, many studies have used lab experiments to show that manipulating norms influence both the public expression and private acceptance of prejudice (e.g., Blanchard et al. 1994; Stangor et al. 2001). Thus, examining the relationship between norms and reactions to prejudice requires a measure that is better able to determine an individual's adherence to socially acceptable ideas about prejudice.

Another potentially applicable measure is the self-monitoring scale (SM), which is a battery of twenty-five questions (Snyder 1974). The idea behind this scale is that individuals use self-awareness and self-control to guide their behavior in social situations. High self-monitors are highly sensitive to social norms and more aware of situations in which they need to act according to accepted social decorum. Low self-monitors are less sensitive to social norms and instead act on their own personal judgment. If applied to the research questions presented in this book, the argument would be that respondents who are high self-monitors would reject expressions of prejudice that violate social norms. There are multiple limitations of this scale with respect to measuring adherence to egalitarian/inegalitarian norms. First, it relies on respondents' awareness of the social norm. Those who are highly sensitive to a norm will only act on it if they know it exists and if it is activated in a given scenario. Second and more importantly, the SM consists of questions about oneself and does not ask any questions that are specific to prejudice. For example, one of the questions in the scale is: "True or false: When I am uncertain how to act in social situations I look to the behavior of others." While this scale does a better job of capturing external motivation to act a certain way based on normative expectations than Crandall et al. (2002), these types of questions are less useful to norms about prejudice specifically.

In sum, while these existing measures are valuable in their own right, they are less useful for assessing the relationship between egalitarian/inegalitarian social norm adherence and responses to overt antiminority political rhetoric. The scale used by Blinder et al. (2013) is topical, but not subtle, making the measure susceptible to social desirability bias. The measure also does not capture normative expectations, which are crucial for measuring norm adherence. Similarly, the scale used by Crandall et al. (2002) also captures personal prejudice instead of normative expectations. The self-monitoring scale overcomes some of these limitations but is not specific to egalitarian/inegalitarian norms about expressed prejudice, making it less useful for testing the specific hypotheses proposed in this book.

Constructing the Social Norms Index

As discussed in chapter 2, social norms perform two important functions in society. First, norms help people understand what behavioral responses are warranted in a given situation. Second, norms provide people with an understanding of which behaviors are acceptable or unacceptable in a given situation. In the case of expressions of antiminority prejudice, social norms help people determine which reactions are acceptable and which are unacceptable. With these ideas in mind, I created a new measure of social norm adherence that takes seriously the need to measure perceptions of normative expectations but is also innocuous and appropriate for measuring the particular norms that guide antiminority prejudice.

In developing this new measure, I was guided by existing literature. First, I constructed the SNI to measure respondents' normative beliefs about what others think they should do. Mackie et al. (2015) suggested this as an appropriate method for measuring social norms and cautioned that it is the "social should" rather than the "prudential or moral should" that is important. As such, the SNI asks respondents what is socially acceptable or unacceptable (social should) rather than what is best for society (prudential should) or morally correct (moral should). Second, by asking what is socially acceptable or unacceptable, the SNI identifies the reference group. This is important because it asks respondents to consider the beliefs of society (see Mackie et al. 2015). However, the question wording also allows for variation because what a respondent believes is acceptable or unacceptable within society is likely to vary based on the social networks they are embedded in or the social groups they identify with.

To construct an effective measure of social norm adherence, I developed a battery of four vignettes.[3] Each vignette presents respondents with a scenario in which an individual's behavior may be prejudicial. The first vignette was taken from Newman et al. (2021); I developed the other three. Respondents were asked to judge the individual's behavior on a five-point Likert scale ranging from "completely socially unacceptable" (1) to "completely socially acceptable" (5). I then recoded the measure into a 0 to 1 scale. Lower scores indicate recognition of an egalitarian norm and higher scores indicate recognition of an inegalitarian norm. In each vignette, the individual's behavior references a stereotype and matches it with the salient group. For example, the vignette regarding African Americans invokes the stereotype of laziness while the vignette regarding Muslims invokes the stereotype of terrorism. Respondents' answers to the four questions were then combined into an additive scale to create a unique measure of social norm adherence. Table 3.1 presents full wording of the four vignettes that comprise the SNI.

TABLE 3.1 **The social norms index**

Vignette	Description
1	Darren Smith is a middle manager at an accounting firm and has been working at the firm for nearly eight years. One part of Darren's job is to supervise the new interns for the accounting firm. While Darren usually likes the interns, he does not like a new intern named Miguel. Darren regularly throws away Miguel's leftover food in the break room fridge, claiming that "Miguel's food is greasy and smells up the fridge."
2	One day you overhear Brian and Mark having a discussion. Brian says, "Antoine told me that at the grocery store yesterday a security guard kept following him because he's Black." Mark grimaced and replied, "Antoine is always playing the race card."
3	As you are walking through your neighborhood one day, you see two high school students, one white and one Black. The two are talking in raised voices as if having an argument. The white student says, "It's not your fault; laziness is just a trait among you people."
4	You are talking to two of your friends one day. Your friend says that he is nervous about the Muslim family that moved in up the street. "Something needs to be done about the terrorism problem in America," he says. "I shouldn't need to be afraid of my kids playing outside in my own neighborhood."

This is a useful measure for testing the influence of social norm adherence on the likelihood of individuals accepting or rejecting antiminority political messages for several reasons. First, the vignettes that comprise the SNI include high-salience minority groups, which creates a more generalized measure of individual recognition of egalitarian/inegalitarian social norms. In subsequent sections, I show that respondents' answers are similar across the four vignettes despite different minority groups being featured in the vignette questions. This generalized measure of norm adherence should allow researchers to analyze the effects of prejudicial rhetoric regardless of the minority group being discussed, even if the group is not included in any of the vignettes that comprise the measure. Second, each vignette pairs the minority group with a congruent stereotype. This is important because it makes the vignettes more realistic and provides a more accurate measure of respondents' reactions, because they are more likely to recognize the prejudicial nature of the behavior when matched with a congruent stereotype (see Reny et al. 2020). Consequently, when individuals are provided with external information such as endorsement of a stereotype or racial trope, the information often activates the racial animus of the individual. If that individual adheres to egalitarianism, then the racial animus can be suppressed through a process called controlled processing (see Terkildsen 1993).

A third benefit of the SNI is that it was designed to determine respondents' normative expectations of what is or is not appropriate. This is key because people's normative expectations of what is socially acceptable is a powerful indicator of how they will behave (see Bicchieri 2016). The concept of a norm of equality is based on the idea that people will find antiminority behavior socially unacceptable, which leads them to reject such behavior. If an individual believes an action is socially unacceptable, they are unlikely to engage in that norm-violating behavior because of the social costs that could follow. However, if an individual believes an action is socially acceptable, then they likely do not believe they will face any social costs for engaging in that behavior. Thus, landing on the egalitarian end of the SNI can be a proxy for adhering to egalitarian norms, and landing on the inegalitarian end of the SNI can be a proxy for adhering to inegalitarian norms.

A fourth benefit of the SNI is that it is structured to avoid social desirability bias, which is when a respondent answers a question based on what they believe will be viewed favorably by others rather than providing their true opinion. The SNI is a subtle measure that asks respondents to evaluate the behavior of others in terms of social acceptability rather than asking about a respondents' own views on the subject. The questions used in the scale also avoid using words like "prejudice" (as in Crandall et al. 2002), which can lead to social desirability effects and bias the measure.

Validating the Social Norms Index

Before I examined the effect of the SNI on reactions to candidates who use prejudicial campaign appeals, it was important to validate the measure. In this section, I first present the results of empirical tests that show high scale reliability. These test results demonstrate that the vignettes used to construct the SNI fit together well and are measuring a single phenomenon. Second, I show that the SNI is moderately, but not too strongly correlated, with other attitudinal measures that influence reactions to prejudice. These correlation tests provide clarity about the nature of the SNI as an instrument for explaining reactions to prejudicial political messaging. Third, I show distribution of the SNI across respondents' demographic profiles, finding that Republicans, men, Latinos, people fifty and older, and those without college degrees score closer to the inegalitarian end of the scale than their counterparts. These discussions lay the groundwork for the analyses in subsequent chapters that demonstrate the explanatory power of the SNI on reactions to prejudicial political speech.

These results come from six national samples of US adults I collected between 2018 and 2023. In all six surveys, respondents were asked the full set of questions that comprise the SNI. Five of these surveys were collected through the survey firm, Lucid. These samples were collected from October to November 2018 ($N = 1{,}010$), January to February 2019 ($N = 1{,}039$), May 2019 ($N = 1{,}488$), March 2023 ($N = 2{,}994$), and June 2023 ($N = 4{,}074$).[4] Lucid constructs a national sample by matching census demographics for age, gender, ethnicity, Hispanic identification, political party identification, and region. Recent tests of the Lucid platform have found that its demographic and experimental results are similar to those from nationally representative probability samples (Coppock and McClellan 2019). Appendix table A.1 shows that each sample was similar to the US population on several key demographics. A sixth survey was conducted in October 2020 through YouGov. It included a nationally representative sample of 800 non-Hispanic white Americans. YouGov creates high-quality survey samples by drawing from a stratified sample and using sample matching to approximate the demographics of the US population. Appendix table A.2 shows that this sample was similar to the US population of non-Hispanic white people.

At the beginning of each survey, respondents were assured that their responses would remain anonymous. Given the sensitivity of many of the survey questions and the potential for social desirability effects, it was important to include this language. Respondents were then provided with the following instructions before being shown the vignettes:

> One component of this study is to explore the way people think about daily events and the way people communicate and interact with one another. We would now like to ask you to read over some short stories describing day-to-day social situations and interactions. We will present you with a series of short stories and ask for your opinion about each story.

Table 3.2 displays descriptive statistics for the SNI and the four questions that comprise it. For ease of presentation and because of the relatively short time span during which the samples were drawn, the top row presents results from the pooled samples collected through Lucid from 2018 to 2019. The other rows present results from the 2020 YouGov survey, the March 2023 Lucid survey, and the June 2023 Lucid survey. The

TABLE 3.2 **Descriptive statistics of the social norms index**

Measure	N	Mean	SD	Min	Max
Pooled Lucid 2018–2019					
SNI	3,538	.287	.258	0	1
SNI Q1	3,538	.248	.312	0	1
SNI Q2	3,538	.356	.290	0	1
SNI Q3	3,538	.212	.292	0	1
SNI Q4	3,538	.334	.322	0	1
YouGov 2020					
SNI	800	.204	.193	0	1
SNI Q1	800	.171	.234	0	1
SNI Q2	800	.291	.245	0	1
SNI Q3	800	.122	.209	0	1
SNI Q4	800	.231	.275	0	1
Lucid March 2023					
SNI	2,994	.321	.284	0	1
SNI Q1	2,994	.305	.343	0	1
SNI Q2	2,994	.382	.307	0	1
SNI Q3	2,994	.262	.321	0	1
SNI Q4	2,994	.335	.326	0	1
Lucid June 2023					
SNI	4,074	.283	.266	0	1
SNI Q1	4,074	.263	.325	0	1
SNI Q2	4,074	.353	.294	0	1
SNI Q3	4,074	.221	.298	0	1
SNI Q4	4,074	.296	.313	0	1

means for the SNI across each sample (.287, .204, .321, and .283 out of
1) indicate that, on average, respondents tended to adhere to egalitarian
norms. However, the standard deviations indicate wide variation. Indeed,
in the pooled Lucid sample and both of the 2023 Lucid samples, more
than 20% of respondents were on the inegalitarian end of the scale (i.e.,
scored more than a .5 on the SNI), and about 4% of the sample scored a 1
out of 1. While most respondents tended to score on the egalitarian side of
the scale, many were on the inegalitarian end. There was some variation in
means across the question items, but no more than roughly .15 on a 0 to 1
scale. This variation was consistent across samples. For example, the mean
for question 2 was consistently the highest and the mean for question 3
was consistently the lowest.

Component Fit

The descriptive data about the SNI and its individual components provide information about the general placement of respondents on the scale. However, it remains unclear how well the four individual components of the scale fit together. Even though different groups were asked about in the vignettes, a series of statistical tests indicate high scale reliability. This suggests that the index measures an underlying construct of adherence to norms of acceptable behavior and rhetoric targeting underrepresented minority groups. Factor analysis using promax oblique rotation show that responses to each of the four vignettes load heavily into a single factor. The eigenvalues of each individual component of the SNI, presented in table 3.3, show that the components fit strongly together.

Moreover, the three Lucid surveys conducted between 2018 and 2019 on national samples of more than 1,000 respondents returned Cronbach's alpha scores of .86, .86, and .88, respectively, demonstrating high internal consistency.[5] The fourth study of 800 white Americans returned an alpha score of .81. Finally, the March 2023 Lucid sample of 2,994 respondents returned an alpha score of .90 and the June 2023 Lucid sample of 4,074 respondents returned an alpha score of .89. These results indicate that, across six different studies spanning more than five years and including more than 10,000 total respondents, the scale scores consistently contained more than 80% of the common variance. The number of samples allows for replication of the SNI results over time and among different respondent groups; and the consistent results across these various samples indicates stability over time. Between October 2018, the date of the first sample, and June 2023, the date of the final sample, we have had presidents from both major political parties, a "racial reckoning" in the

TABLE 3.3 **Confirmatory factor analyses of responses to the social norms index**

Variable	Factor 1
PFA results	2.6627
Vignette 1: Miguel, "greasy food"	0.8165
Vignette 2: Antoine, "playing the race card"	0.7820
Vignette 3: Black student, "laziness"	0.8561
Vignette 4: Muslim family, "terrorism"	0.8073

Source: Data come from the pooled 2018–2019 Lucid samples.
Notes: See appendix table A.3 for confirmatory factor analysis results for the additional samples. CFA results are similar across all samples.

summer of 2020, an attempted insurrection in 2021, and other potentially norm-shifting events like the anti-CRT (critical race theory), anti-DEI (diversity, equity, and inclusion), and antitransgender movements. Yet, the mean, standard deviation, and various measures of the internal consistency of the SNI have remained fairly consistent. Thus, the large number of samples and total respondents improves the internal validity of the measure and provides confidence that the SNI is a valid measure to use in the hypothesis tests found in the case study chapters.

Theoretical Correlates of the SNI

Another potential concern is that the SNI may be too similar to standard measures of racial attitudes, such as the racial resentment or old-fashioned racism scales, or to other political attitude measures like ideology. This concern is twofold. One, the SNI may simply be duplicating an existing measure rather than measuring something unique: namely, adherence to egalitarian/inegalitarian social norms. Second, the measure may not be correlated with existing measures of attitudes toward minority groups, which would mean that even though it is tapping into something unique, it is probably not a useful mechanism for assessing reactions to expressions of antiminority prejudice. As such, table 3.4 presents pairwise correlations between the SNI and standard measures of racial attitudes including racial resentment, old-fashioned racism, and racial sympathy (see Chudy 2021). Correlations between the SNI and party identification, ideology, favorability of Donald Trump, a self-monitoring scale, and a measure of the respondent's belief in the importance of being politically correct are also presented.[6]

The results indicate that the SNI is correlated with standard racial attitude measures but, in most cases, only moderately. The correlation coefficient between the SNI and racial resentment is .26 in the pooled Lucid surveys. The coefficient for the old-fashioned racism scale is a little bit higher at .37, and the coefficient for racial sympathy is quite strong at −.60.[7] One might expect that those who are most likely to subscribe to inegalitarian social norms would also be most likely to hold personally prejudicial beliefs. However, social norms are different from personal beliefs on issues such as race. A moderate level of correlation with these racial attitude measures provides confidence that adherence to inegalitarianism measured through the SNI is not wholly disconnected from racial animus. Given the relatively modest correlation scores, the SNI proves to be dis-

TABLE 3.4 **Pairwise correlation coefficients with the social norms index**

Variable	Sample	Pairwise correlation coefficient
Racial resentment	Pooled Lucid samples 2018–2019	.26***
Old-fashioned racism	Pooled Lucid samples 2018–2019	.37***
Party ID [Republican]	Pooled Lucid samples 2018–2019	.18***
Ideology [conservative]	Pooled Lucid samples 2018–2019	.06**
Trump favorability	Pooled Lucid samples 2018–2019	.38***
Self-monitoring scale	Lucid May 2019	−.25***
Political correctness	Lucid March 2023	−.21***
Racial sympathy	YouGov 2020	−.60***

Notes: * $p < 0.05$; ** $p < 0.01$; *** $p < 0.001$.

tinct from standard measures of racial prejudice and a useful measure for understanding reactions to antiminority messaging.

The SNI is weakly correlated with political attitudes like conservative ideology (.06) and Republican Party identification (.18). The SNI is also moderately correlated (.38) with reported favorability of Donald Trump. These findings were expected given the theoretical expectation from chapter 2 that Democrats would be more likely to recognize and adhere to egalitarian norms than Republicans.

Respondents in the May 2019 survey were asked an abridged version of the self-monitoring scale that included eight of the twenty-five questions. This abridged version has been used in other empirical studies (see Terkildsen 1993). The correlation coefficient of −.25 suggests a moderate level of correlation. The negative sign indicates that adherence to inegalitarian norms (i.e., scoring high on the SNI) is negatively correlated with high levels of self-monitoring (i.e., scoring high on the SM). This was expected, as people who are sensitive to social norms should be less likely to adhere to potentially problematic inegalitarian norms. Another question included in the March 2023 survey asked respondents how strongly they agree or disagree that it is important for people to be politically correct. Again, there was a moderate negative correlation (−.21) between the SNI and the political correctness measure.

Respondent Profiles

Another helpful way to validate the SNI is to compare profiles of respondents who adhere to norms on the inegalitarian end of the scale to those on the egalitarian end of the scale. Table 3.5 presents mean SNI scores

TABLE 3.5 **Mean distribution of the SNI across demographic characteristics**

Characteristic	Mean	SE
Democrat	.25	.007
Republican	.37	.007
Independent	.26	.007
Women	.24	.005
Men	.34	.007
White	.29	.005
Black	.30	.014
Latino	.34	.015
College degree	.28	.005
No college degree	.30	.007
Aged over fifty	.32	.006
Aged less than fifty	.25	.005

Source: Data come from the pooled 2018–2019 Lucid samples.

for respondents in a variety of demographic groups for which we would expect variation in norm adherence. For example, chapter 2 laid out the theoretical expectation that Republicans would adhere to more inegalitarian norms than Democrats. Indeed, table 3.4 showed that the SNI is moderately correlated with Republican identification, conservative ideology, and support for Trump. Distribution of the scale provides further evidence that norms vary by political party. Table 3.5 shows that a substantially higher percentage of Republican respondents adhere to inegalitarian norms than Democrats. The mean score for Republican respondents (.37 out of 1) is 12 percentage points closer to the inegalitarian end of the scale than Democratic respondents (.25) and 11 points closer than Independents (.26). Results from the 2020 YouGov survey, which included only white respondents, show an even starker partisan split. The mean SNI score for Republican respondents is .32 out of 1. For Democrats, the mean is .13, and for Independents, the mean is .19. To put these differences in context, the partisan fissure in SNI scores is larger than the gender, race, education, or age splits. Partisanship is among the most important factors in determining an individual's adherence to egalitarian/inegalitarian norms.

Though not as large as partisanship, there are also significant differences across gender and age. Men (.34) are about 10 percentage points closer to the inegalitarian end of the scale than women (.24) and respondents fifty or older (.32) are about 7 points more inegalitarian on average than respondents younger than fifty (.25). There are also small dif-

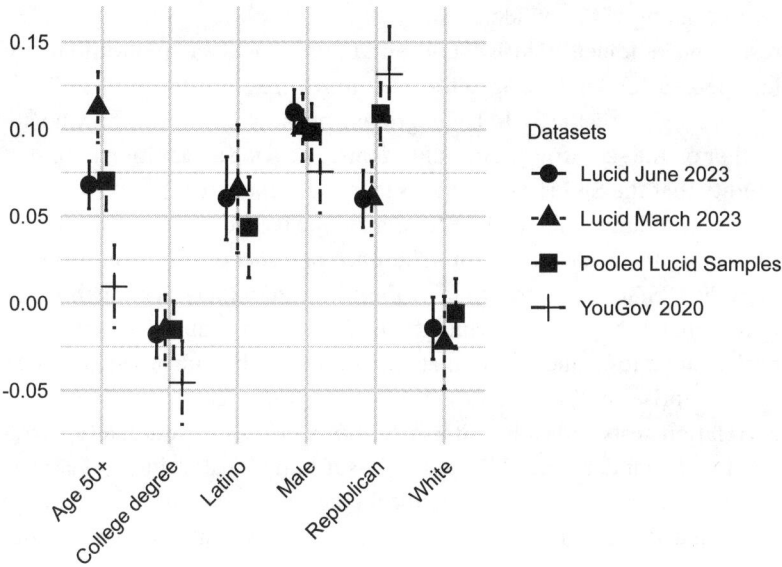

FIGURE 3.2. Predictors of social norms index (SNI) scores. Data come from the pooled Lucid samples, the 2020 YouGov sample, the March 2023 Lucid sample, and the June 2023 Lucid sample.

ferences across education and race. Respondents who have less than a college degree (.30) are about 2 points closer to the inegalitarian end of the scale than respondents who have a college degree (.28) and Latino respondents are further on the scale toward inegalitarianism than other racial groups. These results fit with scholarly expectations of variation in adherence to egalitarianism. For example, studies show that anti-Black messaging is more influential on people with lower levels of education than those with higher levels (Huber and Lapinski 2006) and that men are less likely than women to reject overt anti-Black messaging (Hutchings et al. 2010). Moreover, younger people were quicker to adhere to racial egalitarianism following major events in the civil rights movement than older people (Schuman et al. 1997). These findings demonstrate variation in social norm adherence across predictable demographic categories, providing further confidence in the internal validity of the measure.

Figure 3.2 displays results from multivariate ordinary least squares (OLS) regression models that predict scores on the SNI in the pooled Lucid samples, the 2020 YouGov sample, the March 2023 Lucid sample, and the June 2023 Lucid sample. Coefficients for each variable from each sample, along with confidence intervals, are displayed in the figure. The results make it clear that Republicans, Latinos, men, people without college degrees, and people aged fifty and above are consistently more likely to score higher on the SNI.[8] Demographic profiles of respondents who are further on the scale toward inegalitarianism provide an additional form of validity that the SNI is capturing social norm adherence.

These findings validate the SNI as a unique measure that is appropriate for testing the effects of norm adherence on reactions to expressions of prejudice. First, the distribution of the SNI shows there is enough variation to make the scale a meaningful explanatory variable. Second, Cronbach's alpha tests and factor analyses show that the individual questions that comprise the SNI reliably fit together into a scaled variable. Third, correlation tests indicate that the SNI is weakly or moderately correlated with standard racial attitude measures, political attitude measures, a self-monitoring scale, and a political correctness measure. The findings show that the SNI is correlated with expected measures but is not duplicating them. It makes sense that people who adhere to inegalitarian norms also have higher levels of racial animus. It also makes sense, given the discussion in chapter 2, that adherence to inegalitarian norms would be connected to Republican Party identity and support for Trump. These findings also help validate the scale by showing that, while the SNI is correlated with these measures, it is also clearly distinct from all of them. Finally, constructing profiles of respondents who adhere to inegalitarian norms showed that norm adherence breaks down across expected demographic characteristics. Republicans, men, people aged fifty and older, and people without college degrees are further on the scale toward inegalitarianism than their counterparts. In sum, the findings from this chapter indicate that the SNI is a sound, internally valid measure that is tapping into a unique phenomenon adjacent to, but distinct from, racial animus and conservative ideology. Accordingly, the SNI may be a valuable tool for examining why people react the way they do to expressions of prejudice.

The Social Norms Index and Antiminority Political Messaging

In subsequent chapters, the SNI will be used to test the effect of social norm adherence on the evaluation of candidates who issue antiminority political messages. This dependent variable—candidate evaluation—is a better test than direct evaluation of a message because it examines the actual political effect of reactions to political messaging. An individual may not like a particular message but may vote for the candidate anyway. That speaks to the acceptability of prejudice. On the other hand, if a message leads that individual to not vote for a candidate they were otherwise planning to support, then the message has had an important political effect. In chapters 4, 5, and 6, I find that the SNI strongly predicts support for candidates who use explicit antiminority appeals and that the measure is useful for explaining differing levels of support for candidates based on their use of explicit anti-Black, anti-Muslim, or anti-LGBTQ+, messaging. Respondents who score high on the SNI are consistently more supportive of candidates who use prejudicial campaign appeals than those who score low on it.

Though the case studies feature different minority groups, there are reasons to expect the SNI to be a useful predictor of reactions to antiminority messaging targeting each group. First, a long line of scholarship points to a generalized prejudice toward out-groups. Social identity theory posits an ethnocentric or in-group bias in the way people approach their own identities. The construction of this in-group identity is buttressed against out-groups who are viewed as inferior (Tajfel and Turner 1979). Thus, prejudice against one out-group is connected to a tendency toward prejudice against out-groups in general (Allport 1954; Sniderman and Hagendoorn 2007). Tajfel (1982, 21) summarizes this idea: "One of the principal features, discussed earlier, of intergroup behavior and attitudes was the tendency shown by members of an in-group to consider members of out-groups in a relatively uniform manner, as 'undifferentiated items in a unified social category.'" So, while social norms differ across subject group, there is also an internalized general prejudice that may influence some individuals to reject a constructed norm of equality and adhere to inegalitarian norms.

Relatedly, the broader political environment likely influences expressions of prejudice and reactions to prejudice across subject group. For example, Trump's prejudicial rhetoric has influenced attitudes and behaviors toward many minority groups, even those that he has not directly targeted with his vitriol. A political environment that normalizes antiminority prejudice directed at one group may give rise to a belief that prejudice of other out-groups is also acceptable. Third, the internal consistency of the measure demonstrated by numerous statistical tests and distribution across predictable demographic characteristics indicates a general adherence to egalitarian/inegalitarian norms. This should lead to some amount of consistency in response to antiminority prejudice despite the differential construction across subject group.

The findings from chapter 7 show that the SNI is also useful for determining who is influenced by efforts to counteract overt prejudice. The specific models and hypotheses stemming from the SNI will be discussed in more detail in subsequent chapters. These results clarify the ways that social norms vary across subject groups and target audiences and have the potential to push political messaging strategies in new directions.

CHAPTER FOUR

Anti-Black Messaging
and Political Evaluations

When someone has so recently endorsed Nazism, it is inconceivable that someone can reason-
ably aspire to a leadership role in a free society. —George H. W. Bush (Suro 1991)

The 1991 Louisiana gubernatorial election resulted in Democrat Ed-
win Edwards defeating Republican David Duke. Though Duke was
a member of his own party, President George Bush was strongly critical
of the former grand wizard of the Ku Klux Klan (KKK). Bush said Duke
was unfit for public office because of his long record of racist comments
and open endorsement of Nazism (Suro 1991). Bush made it clear that he
opposed Duke's campaign and that there was no room in the GOP for
people like him. Almost everyone within the Republican Party leadership joined Bush in rejecting Duke's candidacy. Ultimately, Duke received
only 38% of the vote in the election runoff and lost soundly to his Democratic opponent.

Bush's strong rejection of Duke may be surprising to some because
Bush's presidential campaign just a few years earlier benefited from the
infamous Willie Horton ad. Horton was a Black prisoner in Massachusetts
who had raped a white woman and stabbed her boyfriend while released
on a furlough program. Bush's presidential campaign used the incident to
paint his opponent, Michael Dukakis, as soft on crime. Horton's mug shot
was featured for months on television broadcasts and in newspapers, leav-
ing an indelible mark on the presidential race. The Horton ad has come to
be synonymous with *dog whistles*, implicit racial appeals that covertly appeal to the anti-Black sentiments of the audience (see Mendelberg 2001;
McIlwain and Caliendo 2011). If Bush's own campaign prominently featured a race-based attack ad, why was he against Duke so strongly that

his condemnation of a member of his own party likely helped a Democrat become governor of Louisiana? The answer to this question lies at the intersection of social norms and party politics.

Politicians routinely used (and continue to use) coded language to activate anti-Black animus from certain constituents (e.g., McIlwain and Caliendo 2011; Stephens-Dougan 2020). Yet, Duke, because of the overt nature of his racism, was criticized by members of both major political parties and deemed unfit to hold public office. The reaction to Duke's overt racism is indicative of a period in which US politics was characterized by a stable racial equilibrium: Republicans relied on racial code words or dog whistles to activate anti-Black sentiment while Democrats largely remained silent on issues of race (Kinder and Sanders 1996). Politicians, particularly Republicans, were frequently incentivized to appeal to the anti-Black sentiments of key constituents because it boosted their electoral chances. But they were careful to disguise any racial intent by using code words and images rather than being explicit about their anti-Black stances to avoid charges of racism. Politicians believed they and their party would face negative political consequences if they were openly racist.

We got to this point because the civil rights movement—which featured large, public demonstrations in support of civil rights; major institutional commitments to protecting Black rights such as the Civil Rights Act and Voting Rights Act; and clear signals from influential leaders that Black rights are important and must be protected—helped push social norms toward racial equality (Lee 2002; Gillion 2013; Mazumder 2018). However, anti-Black attitudes continued to be held by large portions of the American public. Further, the US political party system was divided by racial attitudes, with racial liberals concentrated in the Democratic Party and racial conservatives in the GOP (Valentino and Sears 2005). Thus, it was still electorally beneficial for politicians in certain contexts to appeal to anti-Black sentiments. But they had to do so in ways that allowed them to pretend the political message was not about race to avoid violating the developed norm of racial equality in principle.

The idea behind this framing is formalized in the implicit–explicit (IE) model of racial priming (Mendelberg 2001). The IE model suggests that when race is subtly cued, the effect of racial attitudes on evaluations of political elites and policies is heightened, but explicit racial appeals are ineffective because they violate the norm of racial equality in principle. The contradictory elements of this norm and a party system based on racial attitudes meant that politicians who wanted to activate the anti-

Black attitudes of voters needed to avoid overtly signaling their intention. Thus, dog whistles became an important and pervasive messaging strategy.

There is recent evidence that the norm of racial equality may be destabilizing, which would lead to overt anti-Black messaging being more acceptable than before. Recent experimental tests of the IE model have found no major differences in the effect of implicit and explicit anti-Black messages (Reny et al. 2020; Valentino et al. 2018a). Moreover, an analysis of racial rhetoric from 1984 to 2016 found that campaign stories in 2016 contained significantly more negative comments about racial and ethnic minority groups than prior election cycles (Valentino et al. 2018b). The share of all group-based stories that included direct negative comments about at least one racial group increased from 30% in 1984 to more than 45% in 2012, and then spiked to 70% in 2016. Not coincidentally, racial attitudes were more strongly connected to vote choice in 2016 than in any previous election on record (Sides et al. 2018).

For several years, anecdotal evidence has suggested that social norms about the acceptability of overt anti-Black rhetoric are changing. After the election of Barack Obama in 2008, explicitly racist posters began regularly appearing at Tea Party rallies (Parker and Barreto 2013). The use of white supremacist online platforms like Stormfront and Parler skyrocketed in the last fifteen years, particularly after Donald Trump's election in 2016. Indeed, racism on social media and in other virtual spaces has become rampant to the extent that, in 2020, half of Black teenagers in the US said they experienced online racial discrimination (Del Toro and Wang 2023). This leads to three important questions: Is anti-Black political messaging still guided by a norm of equality, or has that norm destabilized? Can we pinpoint the role of social norms in determining how individuals will respond to overt anti-Black messaging? Finally, are the two major political parties so ensconced in their own information environments that social norms have fractured along party lines?

In this chapter, I apply the theory of differential norms, detailed in chapter 2, to answer these questions. I first focus on the specific way that norms of acceptable political rhetoric have developed for the subject group—in this case, Black Americans. I argue that a set of interrelated factors have helped maintain the norm of racial equality in principle. One, the norm of racial equality has existed for so long that it has been internalized by much of the public. Norms are especially difficult to change when they have been internalized over long periods of time. Two, a major social movement, Black Lives Matter (BLM), has demonstrated broad and deep public support for protecting and expanding Black rights. Three, the American public continues to receive signals from influential leaders, political institutions, and the media that racial equality is important and explicit racism is unacceptable. Results from a set of survey experiments provide ample empirical evidence for the assertion that political messaging targeting Black Americans continues to be, at least to an extent, guided by a norm of racial equality in principle.

I then examine variation in adherence to egalitarian racial norms among the American public and find that the norm is being fractured along party lines. I argue that the concentration of racial conservatives within the GOP, reactions to Barack Obama's election, and the prevalence of anti-Black narratives from conservative media and right-wing activists have at least partially eroded the norm of racial equality within the Republican Party. Meanwhile, the concentration of racial liberals within the Democratic Party, growing recognition of racial inequality, and the increased prevalence of overt pro-Black messaging from some Democratic politicians have helped maintain the norm of racial equality in that party. Consequently, survey and experimental results show that Republicans are much more supportive than Democrats of politicians who use overt anti-Black campaign appeals.

The theoretical framework in this manuscript is predicated on the notion that social norms guide the use of and responses to antiminority political messaging. As such, I constructed the social norms index (SNI) to directly test the effect of individual social norm adherence on reactions to candidates who espouse antiminority sentiments and on support for antiminority policies. In this chapter, I find that the SNI does an effective job of predicting support for these candidates and policies. Survey respondents who adhere to inegalitarian norms according to the SNI tend to support candidates who use overt anti-Black campaign appeals and policies that are explicitly anti-Black. Meanwhile, survey respondents who adhere to egalitarian norms tend to reject these same candidates and policies.

Hypothesis Development

Norms of Racial Equality

As discussed in chapter 2, the efforts of the civil rights movement pushed racial norms in an egalitarian direction. Basic principles of equal treatment became broadly accepted by the American public. For example, in

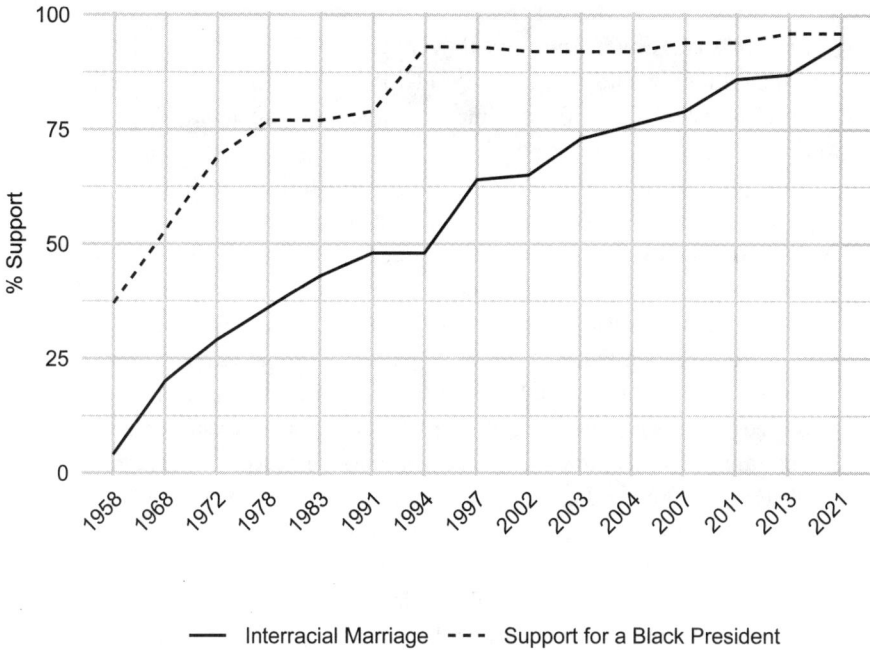

FIGURE 4.1. Percentages of respondents who approve of interracial marriage and would vote for a well-qualified Black presidential candidate. Data from Gallup.

1942, only 32% of white people thought Black and white students should attend the same schools. This number had doubled by the 1960s (65%). By the mid-1990s a full 96% of white people thought Black and white students should attend school together.[1] Similarly, support for integration in transportation and public accommodations like parks, restaurants, and hotels also reached almost full support by the 1970s (Schuman et al. 1997).

Another racial attitude that changed dramatically was support for interracial marriage. Gallup asked samples of national adults how much they approve or disapprove of marriage between Black and white people many times between 1958 and 2021.[2] Figure 4.1 shows the percentage of respondents who approved over time. In 1958, only 4% of respondents said they approved and 94% said they disapproved. By 2021, these numbers had flipped: 94% approved and only 4% disapproved.[3]

Figure 4.1 also shows the percentage of respondents in a series of Gallup polls who said they would vote for a generally well-qualified Black presidential candidate.[4] We see a similarly dramatic rise in abstract support for a hypothetical Black presidential candidate from 1958 to 2021. In 1958, 37% of respondents said they would vote for the candidate and 53% said they would not. By the mid-1990s, more than 90% of respondents consistently said they would vote for a well-qualified Black presidential candidate.

Support for basic principles of racial equality have risen dramatically in the last seventy years (see also Engelhardt 2023). Indeed, basic principles of racial equality like interracial marriage; racial integration of schools, transportation, and public accommodations; and abstract principles like acceptance of a Black president have enjoyed majority support from the public for decades. During that same period, there has been growing recognition that it is unacceptable for citizens or elites to appear racist (Van Dijk 2015). This is crucial because social norms that consistently guide or constrain people's opinions and decision-making processes become internalized over time and can lead to lasting norm adherence (Germar and Mojzisch 2019). Because this norm of racial equality has existed for most people's entire lifetimes, it has likely internalized in most people, making the norm more resistant to destabilization efforts.

A second important reason why the norm of racial equality in principle still exists is the efforts of the Black Lives Matter movement and allied groups working to achieve racial justice. The BLM movement formally began in 2013 with the posting #BlackLivesMatter in protest of George Zimmerman's acquittal in the killing of Trayvon Martin. It morphed from a hashtag into a prominent contemporary global civil rights movement. In summer 2020, the protests following the deaths of George Floyd, Ahmaud Arbery, and Breonna Taylor were labeled the largest and broadest protests in the history of the United States (Putnam et al. 2020). The Crowd Counting Consortium estimated between fifteen million and twenty-six million people participated in more than four thousand demonstrations across the US (Buchanan et al. 2020). BLM provided a resounding signal of broad and deep support for Black rights.

In response, public awareness of racial inequality increased, as did support for government programs to address racial inequality. For example, a June 2020 poll found that a large majority of Americans (71%) believed racism is at least somewhat of a problem (Monmouth University Polling Institute 2020). A poll conducted in July 2020 found that 46% of people agreed that "people of color experience racial discrimination because it is built into our society, including into our policies and institutions" (*NBC News* and *Wall Street Journal* 2020). Recognition of structural racism has translated into support for addressing the problem. A survey conducted by YouGov (2020) found that 60% of respondents believed systemic racism should be addressed by the 2020 presidential candidates. Several questions asked in Gallup polls also show increased support for addressing racial inequality. Support for affirmative action programs for racial minorities among the national adult population increased from 47% in 2001 to 62% in 2021.[5] Among white respondents, support increased from 44% to 57%. Another question asked by Gallup is whether respondents think new civil rights laws are needed to reduce discrimination against Black people. In 2011, only 21% of respondents and only 15% of white respondents thought such programs were needed. By 2020 this number had tripled, with 61% of respondents, including 53% of white individuals, saying such programs are needed. Even support for reparations in the form of cash payments to Black Americans who are descendants of slaves has sharply increased. In 2019, 29% of respondents said the government should make such payments, including 16% of white respondents. In 2002, only 14% of respondents and only 6% of white respondents had supported these payments. In sum, the American public has, on average, become much more cognizant of racial inequality and much more supportive of structural measures to address the issue in recent years.

This is an especially important development because of the principle-implementation gap (see Sears and Kinder 1971; Schuman et al. 1985). As shown in figure 4.1, Americans consistently accept racial equality as an ideal and demonstrate it through support for general principles like support for interracial marriage and abstract support for a qualified Black presidential candidate. Despite broad support for the principle of racial equality, Americans tend to reject government interventions that are designed to actually achieve racial equality. The rejection of these interventions is largely due to newer forms of cultural and symbolic racism that have replaced older forms of racism like the belief in Black biological inferiority. The efforts of the Black Lives Matter movement are not only solidifying support for general principles of racial equality, but they are also helping bridge the principle-implementation gap by buoying support for affirmative action programs, new civil rights law, and other structural actions to combat racial inequality.

Crucially, BLM, and the broader Movement for Black Lives, has developed and articulated a set of "ideas, policy proposals, and political infrastructure" to seize back the "grounds of politics" (Woodly 2021, 162). As one example of BLM's influence on public discourse, a recent study used

Google's digital book archive, Google searches, and news media tran-
scripts to show a dramatic rise in terminology associated with the movement's goals. The authors found that terms such as white supremacy, systemic racism, and mass incarceration were used more often in published
books, were searched for on Google much more frequently, and received
substantially more news coverage post-2013 (Dunivin et al. 2022). BLM
has caused a cultural shift: Americans, particularly liberals, have become
more aware of racial injustice and more interested in antiracism efforts,
which can be seen through their choice of movies and books, internet
searches, and day-to-day conversations.

Democratic elites followed suit by using these terms more frequently
in their own rhetoric and becoming more overtly supportive, at least rhetorically, of combating racial injustice. For example, during the 2016 presidential election, Hillary Clinton spoke more explicitly about race and racial issues than previous Democratic presidential nominees. In campaign
speeches, she invoked concepts such as white privilege, implicit bias, and
systemic racism (see Sides et al. 2018). Clinton's mention of systemic racism and its effects on African Americans in her speech at the Democratic
National Convention marked a clear departure from the Democratic
Party's earlier racial reticence. During a speech in Harlem, Clinton again
discussed systemic racism, this time calling on white Americans to do their
part to end racial inequality. In 2020, every single Democratic presidential candidate acknowledged racial inequality and stressed the importance
of racial justice (*New York Times* 2020). Indeed, the "Achieving Racial
Justice and Equity" section of the Democratic Party's 2020 platform was
much stronger and more explicit in its support for racial justice than in
previous years: "We will take a comprehensive approach to embed racial justice in every element of our governing agenda, including in jobs
and job creation, workforce and economic development, small business
and entrepreneurship, eliminating poverty and closing the racial wealth
gap, promoting asset building and homeownership, education, health care,
criminal justice reform, environmental justice, and voting rights."[6]

Consequently, government institutions have been influenced by BLM
and allied groups to pass legislation that signals institutional support for
equal rights. The number of policing-related bills introduced in state legislatures increased from fifty-six in 2013 to 406 in 2015 following the for-
mal creation of the BLM movement (Arora et al. 2019). State action on
police reform further surged after the massive 2020 protests. More than
three thousand policing-related bills were introduced in state legislatures

following George Floyd's death in May 2020, according to data from the National Conference of State Legislatures (2022). Several city councils took action by reducing their city's police budgets (Axios 2020), removing police officers from school premises (Axios 2020), and approving tactical rule changes to police departments to reduce the likelihood of police brutality (Weil and Nirappil 2020). Though much of the enacted legislation will have little to no impact on police brutality rates or racial inequality more broadly; these measures still serve as signals to the public that political institutions are committed to improving racial equality, whether or not that commitment actually exists.

Although overt pro-Black messaging from the GOP is rare, Republican politicians have faced censure from their own party over blatant racist comments in support of white supremacy. As discussed in the opening chapters of this book, Republican Steve King was rebuked by Democrats and Republicans alike for his racist comments about white supremacy and then lost in the subsequent Republican primary election (Killough et al. 2019). More recently, Republican Representatives Marjorie Taylor Greene and Paul Gosar were criticized by GOP leaders in both the House and Senate for speaking at the annual white nationalist event, the America First Political Action Conference. Senate Minority Leader Mitch McConnell was clear in denouncing their actions: "There's no place in the Republican Party for white supremacists or anti-Semitism" (Wong 2022). These rebukes from leaders within the GOP help reinforce racial norms of equality.

In sum, important signals of commitment to equal rights for Black Americans continue to come from social movements, institutions, and political and media elites. These signals help maintain a norm of racial equality in principle that has likely internalized over time in many Americans. Despite some evidence of destabilization, I argue that the norm of racial equality in principle continues to be widely held. I expect overtly racist political messaging, along with its messengers, to be broadly rejected by the American public.

Hypothesis 4.1. Candidates who use explicit anti-Black campaign appeals will be rejected by the public.

Partisan Polarization

In August 2017, hundreds of white supremacists and their allies descended on Charlottesville, Virginia, over the planned removal of a statue of Confederate

General Robert E. Lee. On the evening of August 11, neo-Nazis, Ku Klux Klansmen, and their allies marched through the University of Virginia campus with torches chanting "The South will rise again" and "You will not replace us" (Neiwert 2017). The next day, as they organized around the statue of Lee, things turned violent. Clashes between white supremacists and counterprotesters left people bloodied and bruised. An alt-right protester drove a vehicle through a crowd of counterprotesters, killing one person and injuring more than a dozen others.

The Unite the Right rally was one of the largest public gatherings of white supremacists in decades. It was also far from an isolated incident. White supremacists and other far-right extremists have held rallies in states across the country that are larger and more frequent than in past years. Moreover, data from the Center for Strategic and International Studies shows that 63% of the 405 domestic terror attacks that occurred between 2015 and 2020 were carried out by far-right extremists (Glaun 2021). The rally was just one prominent example of white supremacy moving further into mainstream politics.

Democratic leaders were quick to condemn the actions of those who participated in the Unite the Right rally. Notable Democrats like Obama, Clinton, Nancy Pelosi, Joe Biden, Kamala Harris, and Bernie Sanders used words like "white supremacy," "racism," "bigotry," and "hatred" in their condemnations (Hansler 2017). Trump, however, refused to call evil by its name. He instead condemned "hatred, bigotry, and violence on many sides, on many sides." He doubled down on these comments during an interview in the coming days. In response to a question about the events in Charlottesville, he said, "Excuse me, they didn't put themselves down as neo-Nazis, and you had some very bad people in that group. But you also had people that were very fine people on both sides. You had people in that group—excuse me, excuse me. I saw the same pictures as you did. You had people in that group that were there to protest the taking down, of to them, a very, very important statue and the renaming of a park from Robert E. Lee to another name" (*Politico* 2017). Indeed, the organizers of the Unite the Right rally seemed to be emboldened by Donald Trump. David Duke, who was the leader of the KKK at the time, said, "This represents a turning point for the people of this country. We're going to fulfill the promise of Donald Trump because he said he's going to take our country back."

The different reactions to the Unite the Right rally exemplify how far apart segments of the population are on issues of race. Though the distance has grown in recent years, the fact that Republicans and Democrats have vastly different views on race and racial issues is nothing new. Scholarship has long shown that racial attitudes are one of the primary dividing lines between the two major political parties (see Carmines and Stimson 1989; Edsall and Edsall 1992; Schickler 2016). Starting almost one hundred years ago, a partisan realignment shifted most racial conservatives into the GOP. Reactions from many white people to the election of the first Black president in the US in 2008 deepened partisan rifts and racialized the political environment in an even more intense way (Tesler and Sears 2010; Tesler 2016; Yadon and Piston 2019). Obama's election also more closely tied anti-Black attitudes to Republican Party support.

In the decades prior to Obama's presidency, overt endorsements of segregation and white supremacy had all but disappeared from mainstream political debate (Kinder and Sanders 1996; Mendelberg 2001). Debates over racial policy shifted away from emphasis on segregation and white racial dominance to an equality of outcomes framework, evoking anti-Black ideas about lack of work ethic and cultural inferiority (Virtanen and Huddy 1998). Consequently, old-fashioned racism (opposition to interracial relations and belief in Black intellectual inferiority) became uncorrelated with partisan preferences and most political evaluations. From 1987 to 2007, there was essentially no relationship between old-fashioned racism and partisanship (Tesler 2013). This changed following Obama's election. Racist attitudes that had lain dormant in many people's reservoirs of attitudes rose back to the surface. Obama's rise to political power, and the resulting strong cognitive association that was created between Democrats and the Black community, caused old-fashioned racism to again play a role in politics. Not only did old-fashioned racism have major influence in opposition to Obama in 2008 and 2012, but it has also become a strong predictor of white partisanship in the years since (Tesler 2013). Similarly, another study found that dehumanizing attitudes—the view that Black people are less than fully human—are held by sizable numbers of white people and are directly associated with support for Trump (Jardina and Piston 2022).

The news media have played a prominent role, particularly during and after the Obama era, in normalizing anti-Blackness within the GOP. One study found that negative media articles about Black Americans were more prevalent in 2016 than other recent election years (Valentino et al. 2018b). Fox News in particular has played an outsized role in amplifying anti-Black messaging and ideas. A *New York Times* report analyzed 1,150 episodes of *Tucker Carlson Tonight* and interviewed dozens of current or

former Fox News employees. The report concluded that Carlson "had constructed what may be the most racist show in the history of cable news—
and also, by some measures, the most successful" (Confessore 2022). The
analysis showed that Carlson frequently used racist tropes and endorsed
racist conspiracy theories that tended to be found in white nationalist outlets like *The Daily Stormer* and VDARE. Indeed, a former Fox employee
admitted that the research used for the show at times originated from
white supremacist platforms like Stormfront.

This matters because, at the time, *Tucker Carlson Tonight* was the most
watched cable news show (Joyella 2023). It also matters because Carlson
was at the forefront of a transformation within Fox News. The network,
which already leaned to the right, had sidelined or ousted contributors
who were left leaning or who criticized Donald Trump. They leaned so
far into stories about Black violence and undocumented immigration that
employees referred to the network's coverage as "brown menace" (Confessore 2022). Fox News is also the main source of news about politics for
more than 40% of Republicans (Bump 2022b). Thus, when Tucker Carlson and other Fox News anchors spread racist tropes and conspiracy theories, a large portion of Republicans are listening.

Meanwhile, Democrats have moved in the opposite direction. As discussed above, Democratic presidential candidates have more overtly signaled support for Black rights in recent elections. But the transformation
in racialized rhetoric within the Democratic Party is not only at the top of
the ticket. Alexandria Ocasio-Cortez, Ayanna Pressley, Ilhan Omar and
other Democratic elected officials have emphasized such issues as criminal justice reform and structural racism in their successful primary and
general election campaigns and during their time in office. Progressive
Democratic candidates appear more comfortable explicitly signaling their
stances on racial issues after 2016 than in past elections, buoyed as they are
by growing racial liberalism among Democratic voters (see Stout 2020)
and successful efforts from racial justice groups such as Launch Progress
and Run for Something that are recruiting and supporting young, progressive, diverse candidates (McElwee 2018).

After a period of "racial stasis" in the 1990s and 2000s in which ag-
gregate attitudes about systemic racism and Black Americans did not
change much (see DeSante and Smith 2019), there have been notable attitude shifts in recent years. Across several different measures of racial
attitudes, society has become more progressive (Engelhardt 2023). Moreover, Democrats evaluate the Black community more positively than Republicans do and are far more supportive of Black rights. One measure of

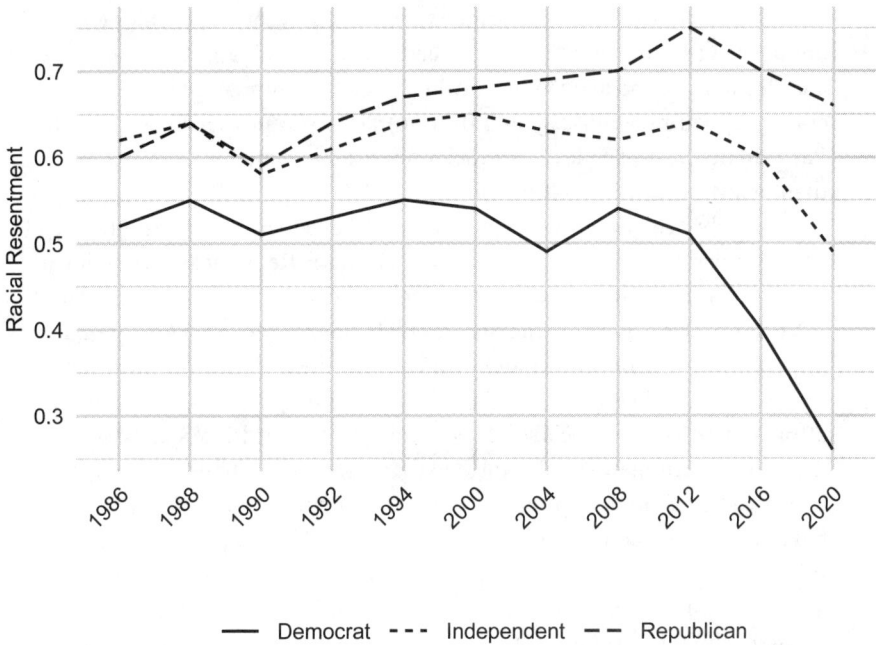

FIGURE 4.2. Racial resentment levels by party identification over time. Data from American National Election Studies.

this is the racial resentment scale, which captures individuals' beliefs in the cultural inferiority of Black Americans. Respondents are asked how strongly they agree or disagree with the following statements: "Over the past few years, Blacks have gotten less than they deserve;" "Irish, Italian, Jewish, and many other minorities overcame prejudice and worked their way up. Blacks should do the same without any special favors;" "It's really a matter of some people not trying hard enough; if Blacks would only try harder, they could be just as well of as whites;" "Generations of slavery and discrimination have created conditions that make it difficult for Blacks to work their way out of the lower class." Those who blame work ethic rather than structural factors get coded as racially resentful.

The American National Election Study (ANES), a large-scale survey conducted every presidential election year, consistently asks respondents these four questions. I coded the questions on a 0 to 1 scale, with higher numbers corresponding to respondents with higher levels of racial resentment. Figure 4.2 shows mean racial resentment among Democrats, Republicans, and Independents over time from 1986, when the questions were first included in the survey, to 2020. Racial resentment among Republicans has remained relatively steady, peaking at .74 out of 1 in 2012 and declining to .66 in 2020. Meanwhile, racial resentment among Democrats dropped precipitously in 2016 (.40) and even further in 2020 (.26). Partisan differences in levels of racial resentment were far higher in 2020 than in any other year that the survey has data for.

Not only are there major partisan differences in racial resentment, but Democrats are also much more likely than Republicans to believe that the government should take action to combat racial inequality. The ANES includes a question that gauges respondents' views on government intervention into the social and economic position of Black Americans: "Some people feel that the government in Washington should make every effort to improve the social and economic position of Blacks. Others feel that the government should not make any special effort to help Blacks because they should help themselves. And, of course, some other people have opinions somewhere in between. Where would you place yourself on this scale, or haven't you thought much about it?" I coded this variable on a 0 to 7 scale, with higher numbers corresponding to belief that the government should help. Figure 4.3 shows mean scores of this measure among Democrats, Republicans, and Independents from 1986 to 2020.

The results mirror the findings from the racial resentment scale. Republican respondents are consistently on the lower end of the spectrum, believing Black people should help themselves rather than receive help from the government. In fact, Republicans' score on this measure has decreased since 1986. Meanwhile, Democrats were more likely to agree that Black Americans should receive help from the government in 2020 than in any previous year. Similar to figure 4.2, partisan differences in 2020 were higher than any previous year on record. Democrats scored a 5.4 out of 7 while Republicans scored a 2.9. Independents were also more likely to agree that Black people should get help from the government (4.1) in 2020 than in any other year on record.

Other studies have found similar results. For example, a 2024 report published by the Democracy Fund's Voter Study Group, showed that Democrats became more racially liberal after 2016, at least partly in backlash to Trump (Sides et al. 2024). Republicans have mostly maintained high levels of racial resentment and other measures of anti-Black attitudes. Similar to my findings, the report shows Democrats have become less racially resentful and Republicans have remained fairly consistent. The report also finds that Democrats have become more likely to support

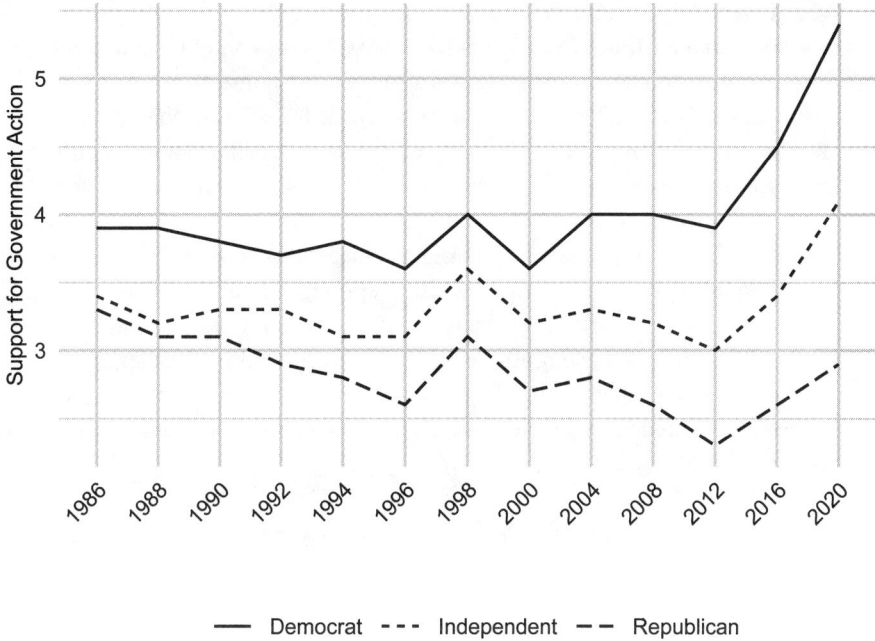

FIGURE 4.3. Support for government action to improve the social and economic position of Black Americans by party identification over time. Data from American National Election Studies.

affirmative action policies, with more than 70% support in 2020 (see also Jardina and Ollerenshaw 2022). Meanwhile, Republicans remain unsupportive, with less than 20% of the group in favor of such policies. Other recent survey data even shows that Republicans find the *n*-word less offensive than they did in prior years (Tesler 2018).

Although there are many reasons to believe a norm of racial equality in principle still exists within US society, some social groups likely adhere to the norm more strongly than others. The GOP in particular meets the criteria detailed in chapter 2 for the development of group norms. First, the polarized media and information environment has created numerous partisan communication avenues. Through these avenues, Republicans are receiving signals of opposition to Black rights and endorsement of racist tropes from their preferred media outlets like Fox News, from right-wing activists, and from some political elites within their party. Second, a partisan realignment has created a party that is relatively homogeneous across racial attitudes. Extant scholarship shows that people sort their partisanship on racial attitudes (e.g., Schickler 2016; Carmines and Stimson 1989) and people also change their racial attitudes in response to signals from party elites (e.g., Tesler 2016; Sides et al. 2018; Engelhardt 2021), which further homogenizes the parties. Consequently, survey data show Republicans have more negative evaluations of Black Americans and are less likely than Democrats or Independents to believe that structural efforts should be taken to promote equal rights. Third, destabilizing the norm of racial equality is important to the GOP. Republican politicians have long used anti-Black rhetoric to appeal to the racial animus of key voting blocs and will be able to do so more openly if egalitarian norms further erode within the party's base. Thus, Republicans should be more accepting of overt anti-Black messages, along with the messengers, than Democrats or Independents.

Hypothesis 4.2. Candidates who use explicit anti-Black appeals will receive more support from Republicans than from Democrats or Independents.

Social Norms

A set of factors during the civil rights movement developed a norm of racial equality in principle. This norm has been internalized by the public over time and has been maintained through the work of the Black Lives Matter movement and signals from prominent political and media elites and community leaders who support racial equality. Yet, not every member of society will adhere to the norm. Indeed, there is ample evidence that the norm is fracturing down political lines. Members of the Republican Party are unlikely to adhere to the norm as strongly as members of the Democratic Party.

Several studies have interrogated the effects of anti-Black political messages on opinion formation and found heterogeneous effects. For example, one study found that when respondents were made aware of the confederate flag's ties to the KKK, white women became substantially less supportive of that flag (Hutchings et al. 2010). Support for the confederate flag among white men did not change. The authors concluded that the norm of racial equality was internalized more strongly within white women than white men. Other studies have found that anti-Black messaging is an effective strategy for mobilizing racially moderate and conservative white people (see Stephens-Dougan 2020). Banks and Hicks (2019) found that support for politicians like Donald Trump and Ed Gillespie who used overt anti-Black messaging remained high among racially conservative white respondents even after credible accusations of racism; but decreased among some racially liberal white respondents.

The SNI, constructed in chapter 3, measures the extent to which an individual adheres to egalitarian or inegalitarian norms. This measure can help determine how much norm adherence conditions reactions to anti-Black messaging. Specifically, support for candidates who use overt prejudicial appeals should be highest among individuals who adhere to inegalitarian norms. In other words, norms condition the approval or disapproval of a given political message and candidates who use that message.

Hypothesis 4.3. Respondents who score high on the SNI (i.e., adhere to inegalitarian norms) will be most likely to support candidates who use explicit anti-Black appeals, and those who score low on the SNI (i.e., adhere to egalitarian norms) will be least likely to support such candidates.

Hypothesis Testing

Public Responses to Explicit Anti-Black Messaging

If norms guiding anti-Black political rhetoric are closer on the spectrum to egalitarianism, then we would expect overt anti-Black messaging to be rejected by the public. I found this to be true across a range of surveys. The first result comes from a survey conducted in August 2017 on a sample of 1,220 adult US residents collected through Amazon's Mechanical Turk (MTurk).[7] MTurk has been criticized because of its opt-in nature, but it provided several advantages to this study. Recent research has demonstrated that treatment effects from MTurk studies are comparable to those found in nationally representative surveys (e.g., Buhrmester et al. 2011; Mullinix et al. 2015). Studies of MTurk respondents also indicate that they are more representative of the population than other convenience samples (Buhrmester et al. 2011; Huff and Tingley 2015). Moreover, recent work by Clifford et al. (2015) showed that liberals and conservatives in MTurk samples closely mirror those in the mass public. The results of their study indicate MTurk is a valid tool for recruiting survey participants for questions regarding political ideology.

Embedded in the survey was an experiment in which one-third of respondents were randomly assigned to a treatment condition where they

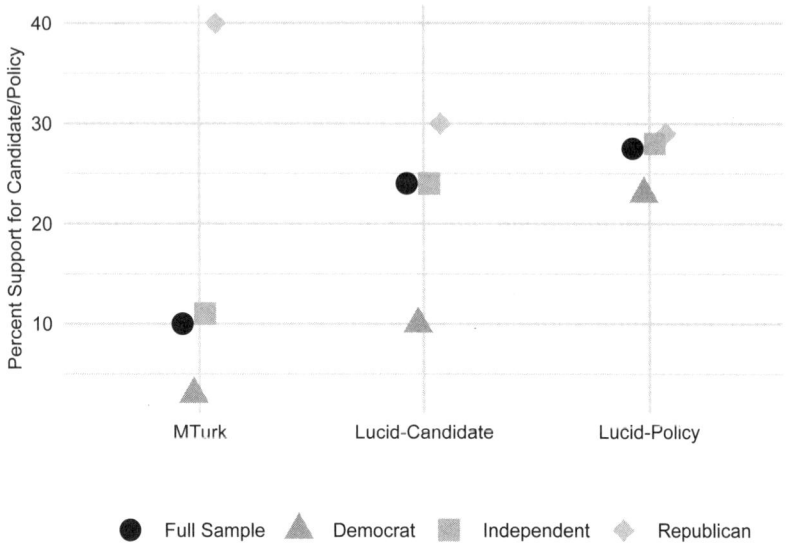

FIGURE 4.4. Public responses to explicit anti-Black messaging across three experiments. Data from the 2017 MTurk survey and the March 2023 Lucid survey.

were exposed to a fictional candidate for the US House of Representatives who used an explicit anti-Black campaign appeal, saying they would empower law enforcement to crack down on "violent Black criminals." Respondents were then asked how likely they would be to vote for the candidate. As shown in figure 4.4 in the MTurk column, only 10% of respondents in the treatment group said they would be somewhat or very likely to vote for the candidate. In other words, support for a candidate who made openly anti-Black comments was extremely low.[8]

The next set of experimental tests came from a survey conducted in March 2023 on a sample of 2,994 US residents collected through Lucid.[9] Half of the respondents in this survey were exposed to a fictional Senate candidate who said, "It is true that Blacks are more violent and choose to get involved with crime. Blacks have to stop being criminals. Stiffer penalties will act as a deterrent to crime." Respondents were then asked how likely they would be to vote for the candidate. There again was not much support among the general public for a political candidate who overtly denigrated Black Americans. As displayed in figure 4.4 in the Lucid-Candidate column, only 24% of respondents in the treatment group said they would be somewhat or very likely to vote for the candidate.[10]

In two surveys conducted almost six years apart, support for a candidate who used an overt anti-Black campaign appeal was very low. A candidate who receives 10% or 24% of the vote is unlikely to win an election in any scenario.

In the same March 2023 survey, half of the respondents were asked whether they would support a proposed policy that would create a special registration program to collect information on Black Americans. The text of the vignette question included the following line: "Proponents of the bill say that the group is a threat to the American way of life and need to be put under surveillance." This was a test of the public's support for an overt anti-Black policy. The Lucid-Policy column of figure 4.4 shows that 27.5% of respondents in the treatment group said they would strongly or somewhat support the proposed policy.[11] Across three tests conducted on two different samples six years apart, I found that the public is unlikely to broadly support explicit anti-Black messages from politicians or support a policy that is openly anti-Black. These results support hypothesis 4.1, which posits that the public will generally reject overt anti-Black political messaging.

The Role of Partisan Identification

Another aspect of the theory of differential norms is that the specific norm development among groups within the audience impacts the acceptance or rejection of antiminority messaging. There are clear differences in support for candidates who use overt anti-Black messaging between Republicans and Democrats. For example, figure 4.4 shows that in the MTurk sample, fielded in August of 2017, only 3% of Democrats and 11% of Independents said they would vote for the candidate who used the overt anti-Black campaign appeal. Meanwhile, almost 40% of Republicans said they would vote for the candidate. These differences are statistically significant at the $p < .001$ level according to two-sample t-tests. There were also partisan differences in support for the fictional Senate candidate who used an explicit anti-Black campaign appeal in the Lucid sample in March 2023. Roughly 30% of Republicans said they would vote for the candidate, while only 24% of Independents and 10% of Democrats said they would vote for him. The difference in support among Republicans and Democrats is significant at the $p < .01$ level.

There are two potential explanations for this partisan gap in support. One, Republicans are motivated to vote for the candidates by the anti-Black campaign appeals that they used. We could infer from this that a large number of Republicans find anti-Black messages acceptable enough that they would choose to vote for the candidates. Democrats, on the other hand, are generally not mobilized by anti-Black messages. A second explanation could be that respondents inferred the partisan identity of the fictional candidates (that information was not provided in either of the survey experiments). Because Republican candidates are much more likely to appeal to the anti-Black sentiments of their constituents, respondents may have assumed the candidates in the survey were Republicans. Thus, Republicans supported the candidates in both surveys while Democrats did not because of their partisan identities. Even if the latter explanation is the main reason for the partisan split, that still assumes the public strongly associates the GOP with anti-Blackness, which Republican voters find acceptable enough to continue identifying as Republican and to continue supporting Republican candidates.

Results from another survey conducted in October 2020 through YouGov on a nationally representative sample of 800 white Americans provides further evidence of partisan differences in support for overt anti-Black political messaging. Respondents in this survey were asked whether it is acceptable or unacceptable to discriminate against a set of groups. Among Republicans, almost 18% said it is "always acceptable" or "acceptable in some situations" to discriminate against Black Americans. Only 7% of Democrats and 8% of Independents agreed. Respondents were also asked how often they feel threatened by a set of groups. There was again a large partisan split. Among Republicans, 24% reported feeling threatened by Black Americans often or sometimes. Among Democrats and Independents, the percentages were 7% and 14%, respectively. These percentage point differences are all statistically significant to at least the $p < .05$ level according to two-sample t-tests.

In sum, Republicans are more likely than Democrats and Independents to support political candidates who use overt anti-Black messaging and are more supportive of a policy that is framed as anti-Black. Republicans are also more likely than Democrats or Independents to believe it is acceptable to discriminate against Black Americans and more often feel threatened by Black Americans. All these results provide support for hypothesis 4.2, which states Republicans will be most accepting of anti-Black messaging. It is important to caution that despite large partisan differences; the majority of Republicans still reject candidates and policies that are overtly anti-Black. The next set of tests further interrogates this idea by examining the reactions of Republican respondents to copartisan candidates who use overt anti-Black campaign appeals.

Election Tests

PRIMARY ELECTIONS. Another way to test the first two hypotheses is by examining reactions to overt antiminority messaging in election contexts—first in primaries and then in general elections. Explicit antiminority campaign appeals are more likely to be used in primary elections because candidates are speaking directly to their party base. They do not have to worry as much about persuading swing voters or making cross-party appeals. Therefore, I included two scenarios featuring fictional primary election candidates in surveys conducted in July 2018 and October 2018. Both surveys were conducted through Lucid on samples of 1,010 adult US residents.[12] Scholarship has demonstrated that social norms tend to influence behavior especially when individuals are choosing between options they do not have strong preferences about (e.g., Anderson and Dunning 2014; Bell and Cox 2015; Cialdini and Trost 1998). A primary election in which the voters have never heard of either candidate and the candidates have similar issue positions is an example of this type of situation. A primary election also holds party identification constant, which removes it as a factor in people's decision-making and helps isolate the effect of the political message. It also helps put the earlier results, which showed that Republicans were much more supportive than Democrats of a candidate who used anti-Black campaign appeals, in perspective. More specifically, findings from the primary election scenarios will clarify how many Republicans are mobilized by anti-Black campaign appeals when there is a viable alternative available to them.

Half of all respondents in each survey who self-identified as Republican were shown a matchup between two Republican candidates for the US House of Representatives.[13] In the scenario, the fictional candidates had the same stances across a range of typical Republican policies. The only difference between candidates Kyle Anderson and Peter Miller is that Anderson used an explicit anti-Black appeal while Miller did not. This is the text presented to respondents:

> The following is an excerpt of a media article written about a Republican primary election to fill a seat in the US House of Representatives from your state. After reading the excerpt, you will be asked to evaluate the candidates in the election.

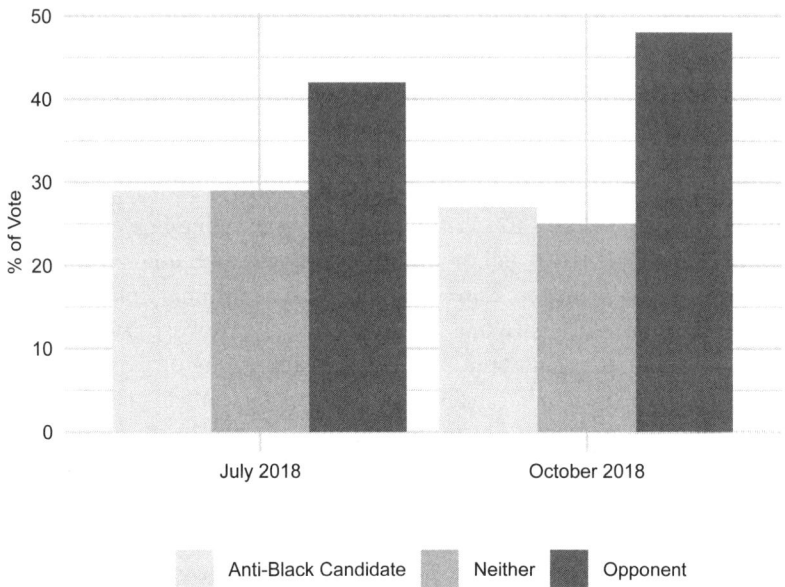

FIGURE 4.5. Republican primary election results featuring an anti-Black candidate versus an opponent. Data from Lucid surveys conducted in July 2018 and October 2018.

Kyle Anderson and Peter Miller, the two candidates in the Republican primary election, have similar views on most important policy issues. Both have promised to repeal Obamacare, simplify the tax code, and decrease entitlement spending. The two candidates differ slightly in their policies and rhetoric on law enforcement. While both candidates want to increase spending for law enforcement, Anderson has taken a hard-line stance, saying the United States is being destroyed by "Black gang members."

Respondents were then asked who they would vote for: Kyle Anderson, the candidate who used a racist campaign appeal; Peter Miller, the candidate who did not use a racist campaign appeal; or neither. Given that the two candidates had the same stance on a range of policy positions, with the only difference the use of a prejudicial appeal by one candidate, if the anti-Black message had no effect, then the two candidates would receive roughly the same number of votes. The results are shown in figure 4.5.

Respondents were much less supportive of the overtly anti-Black candidate (Kyle Anderson) relative to the opponent who did not use an overt anti-Black appeal (Peter Miller). Indeed, Anderson received only 29%

of the vote in the July 2018 sample and 27% in the October 2018 sample. A plurality of voters chose Anderson's opponent while a large proportion of respondents—29% in July 2018 and 25% in October 2018—said they would vote for neither candidate. In a real election, the anti-Black candidate would have been soundly defeated in both cases. Results from two-sample t-tests indicate that mean differences between vote intention for the anti-Black candidate and his opponent were statistically significant in both election scenarios to at least the $p < .05$ level.

Results from the nonpartisan election experiments showed that Republicans are more supportive of candidates who use overt anti-Black campaign appeals than Democrats and Independents. However, results from these primary election scenarios show that Republicans will reject the anti-Black candidate in favor of a similar candidate who does not overtly communicate an anti-Black message. This indicates that while egalitarian norms are less internalized within Republicans than Democrats and Independents; the norm of racial equality in principle has not destabilized to the point that Republicans have embraced openly racist candidates and public policies—at least, not when there are viable alternatives available.

GENERAL ELECTION. In two separate national samples, Republican respondents rejected a primary election candidate who used an overt anti-Black message in favor of a similar candidate who did not. What if a candidate used an anti-Black campaign appeal in a general election? Would Republicans back the candidate over a Democratic opponent? Will they abstain from voting? Given that the two parties are moving in opposite directions on racial issues and rhetoric, general elections are increasingly likely to pit candidates against each other who are sharply polarized on racial issues. Thus, voters will often be faced with the decision to vote for a Republican candidate who has overtly endorsed antiminority ideas and a Democratic candidate who has not.

To test these questions, the October 2018 Lucid survey included a series of fictional general election matchups. Respondents were randomly assigned to one of four general election scenarios, which are displayed in detail in table 4.1. In all four, the Republican candidate used an overt anti-Black campaign appeal. The scenarios vary by whether the Democratic opponent's message was pro-Black, pro-Latino, or pro-Muslim, or advocated a reduction in crime rates without naming a specific minority group. Respondents were asked which candidate they would vote for:

TABLE 4.1 **Hypothetical general election scenarios**

	Republican candidate's message	Democratic candidate's message
Anti-Black vs. Pro-Black	"The United States is being destroyed by Black gang members."	"End systemic racism."
Anti-Black vs. Pro-Latino	"The United States is being destroyed by Black gang members."	"Protect vulnerable Latino communities."
Anti-Black vs. Pro-Muslim	"The United States is being destroyed by Black gang members."	"Protect Muslim communities from hate crimes."
Anti-Black vs. no racial appeal	"The United States is being destroyed by Black gang members."	"Reduce crime rates."

the Republican, the Democrat, or neither. This test helped illuminate two aspects of the use of anti-Black messaging. First, it addressed whether anti-Black messaging from Republican candidates is viable in a general election context. Second, it shed light on which general election contests increase or decrease the viability of anti-Black messaging. For example, Republicans may be turned off by their candidate's anti-Black message unless their other option is a Democrat who advocates for equal rights for a group they view negatively. Figure 4.6 displays the results of all four general election matchups and breaks down candidate support by full sample, Democrats, Independents, and Republicans.

The results indicate that the Democratic candidate would win all four elections, though the difference in support varies greatly. The Republican candidate fared best when pitted against a Democratic candidate who used an overt pro-Muslim or pro-Latino campaign appeal. In these two scenarios, the Democrat won by less than 10 percentage points. When the Democrat issued a pro-Black appeal or did not openly appeal to pro-minority sentiments, the Republican candidate lost by more than 20 points.

Breaking down support by partisan identity helps illuminate the variation in outcomes for the four fictional election scenarios. Most Republican respondents were willing to support their copartisan candidate, but the level of support depended on who the opponent was. When pitted against a pro-Muslim or pro-Latino Democrat, 62% and 63% of Republicans supported their copartisan candidate, respectively. But when facing a Democrat who did not overtly appeal to pro-minority sentiments, only

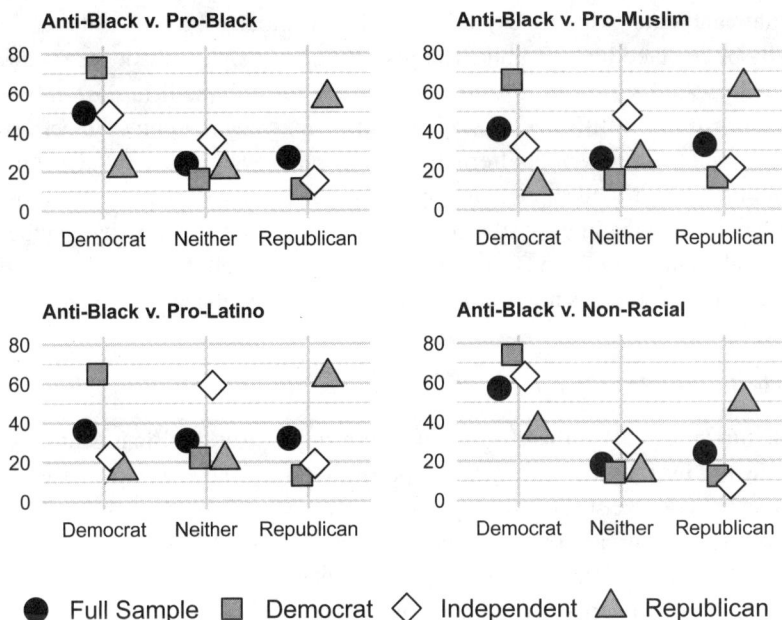

FIGURE 4.6. Percent support for anti-Black Republican candidates and their Democratic opponents in four different fictional general election scenarios. Data from the October 2018 Lucid survey.

50% of Republicans supported the Republican candidate. Though 50% or more of Republicans in each election scenario said they would vote for a copartisan candidate who was explicitly anti-Black, more than one-third of Republicans in each case chose to abstain or vote for the Democratic opponent. Democrats were also most supportive of their copartisan candidate when he made a pro-Black appeal or avoided race relative to scenarios where he was pro-Latino or pro-Muslim. The largest amount of variation came from Independents. When the choice was between an overtly anti-Black Republican and an overtly pro-Muslim Democrat, 21% of Independents chose the Republican. But when that same Republican was matched up against a Democrat who avoided race, only 8% of Independents said they would vote for the Republican candidate.

In sum, anti-Black campaign appeals do not improve Republican's electoral chances. These messages do not appeal to Independents or Democrats and do not mobilize Republican voters enough to overcome the lack of persuasive ability. The results buttress the evidence for hypothesis 4.1, that candidates who use explicit anti-Black campaign appeals will generally be rejected by the public. The results also qualify the evidence found for hypothesis 4.2 earlier in the chapter. Though Republicans are more supportive of anti-Black messaging and its messengers than Democrats, they will look to viable alternatives in primary elections and seem unlikely to give broad support to copartisan candidates who use overt anti-Black messaging in general elections. The norm of racial equality may be destabilizing within the GOP, but it has held up enough that openly signaling anti-Blackness is not a winning strategy for Republican candidates.

The Role of Social Norms

So far, the results in this chapter have shown that overt racism is generally rejected by the public. In two nonpartisan experiments, candidates who made openly racist campaign appeals received very little support. A policy that was framed around curtailing Black rights was also resoundingly rejected. Although Republicans were more inclined than Democrats or Independents to support candidates who espoused anti-Black sentiments, they rejected these candidates in primary election contexts in favor of similar candidates who did not make overt anti-Black appeals. Candidates who used overt anti-Black campaign appeals also fared poorly in general election scenarios. Given how deeply held anti-Black attitudes are in the US, why does explicit anti-Black messaging not garner more support? My theoretical framework indicates that the answer stems from social norms. The empirical evidence presented in this section powerfully demonstrates that social norms guide reactions to anti-Black messaging. In support of hypothesis 4.3, I show that the SNI predicts how people will react to overtly anti-Black candidates. Respondents who adhere to egalitarian norms tend to reject candidates who use overt anti-Black messaging. Respondents who adhere to inegalitarian norms tend to support these same candidates.

Table 4.2 presents the results from regression models that measure the effect of the SNI on several of the anti-Black political candidates presented above.[14] Each model includes control variables for party identification, gender, education, age, and racial resentment. For ease of presentation, only results for the primary independent variable of interest (the SNI) is displayed in the table. The full models can be found in the appendix. Model 1 presents results from an ordinary least squares (OLS) regression in which the dependent variable is respondent intention to vote for the anti-Black candidate presented in the March 2023 Lucid survey. The

TABLE 4.2 **OLS regression analysis of the social norms index (SNI) on support for anti-Black candidates**

	Model 1: Anti-Black candidate, Mar. 2023 Lucid	Model 2: Primary election, Oct. 2018 Lucid	Model 3: General election, Oct. 2018 Lucid
SNI	.78*** (.04)	.35** (.11)	.16** (.05)
Intercept	.11*	.06	.01
R^2	.51	.09	.20
N	744	236	869

Notes: * $p < .05$; ** $p < .01$; *** $p < .001$. Model 1 data from March 2023 Lucid survey. Model 2 and 3 data from October 2018 Lucid survey. The dependent variable in each model is stated intention to vote for an anti-Black political candidate in a US Senate race (model 1), US House Republican primary (model 2), and a US House general election (model 3). Response options for the dependent variable in each model range from 0 to 1. All three models control for party identification, gender, education, age, and racial resentment. For ease of presentation, only the primary independent variable of interest (SNI) is displayed. See appendix for full models.

dependent variable ranges from "very unlikely" (0) to "very likely" (1) to vote for the candidate who issued the anti-Black campaign appeal. The results indicate the SNI has a powerful effect on vote intention. Respondents who were closest on the SNI to inegalitarianism were 78 percentage points more likely to support the candidate than those who were closest to egalitarianism, holding all other variables at their means.

Model 2 presents results from an OLS regression that analyzed the effects of the SNI on support for the Republican primary candidate who used an overt anti-Black campaign appeal.[15] The dependent variable in the model is a dummy variable in which 1 represents choosing to vote for the anti-Black candidate and 0 represents choosing not to vote for that candidate (either choosing the opponent or neither).[16] Similar to model 1, adhering to inegalitarian norms predicts support for the anti-Black candidate. Those who most adhere to inegalitarian norms are 35 percentage points more likely to say they would vote for the anti-Black candidate than those who most adhere to egalitarian norms, controlling for all other factors.

I again find similar results when examining the effect of the SNI on support for the anti-Black candidate in the general election scenarios. Model 3 presents results from an OLS regression that analyzed the effect of the SNI on support for the anti-Black candidate pooled across all four general election matchups. As in model 2, the dependent variable in the model is a dummy variable in which 1 represents choosing to vote for the anti-Black candidate and 0 represents choosing not to vote for that candidate. Just like the first two models, I find that adherence to inegalitarian norms predicts support for the anti-Black candidate. Those who most adhere to inegalitarian norms were 16 points more likely to say they would vote for the anti-Black candidate than those who most adhere to egalitarian norms, controlling for all other factors.

In support of hypothesis 4.3, these results indicate that adherence to inegalitarian social norms is a strong predictor of support for candidates who use overt anti-Black campaign messages even after accounting for party identification, racial resentment, and standard demographic variables in a variety of experimental and election contexts. Adherence to egalitarian social norms predicts rejection of these same candidates. Although anti-Black attitudes are widespread in US society, overt anti-Black political messaging continues to be rejected for violating a norm of racial equality in principle.

Implicit Appeals

Congruent with existing scholarship, my findings show that people tend to find overt anti-Black racism unacceptable. However, this certainly does not mean that anti-Blackness is not central to political messaging strategies. Politicians in many situations are incentivized to appeal to the anti-Black sentiments of key constituents. Contradictory factors—a party system based on race and racial attitudes and a norm of racial equality in principle—mean that anti-Black messaging is pervasive but coded. Elites disguise their appeals to anti-Black attitudes in coded language to maintain plausible deniability about racism.

One prominent example of coded language being used to push an anti-Black agenda is the effort to undercut the work of the Black Lives Matter movement. In 2020, following the murders of George Floyd, Ahmaud Arbery, and Breonna Taylor, massive public demonstrations in support of BLM and racial justice took place across the country. During and after the summer of protests, it looked like the movement was changing hearts and minds and had potential to win major legislative victories. State, county, and city legislative bodies enacted dozens of reforms to police procedures. At the federal level, the US House of Representatives passed an ambitious bill to decrease the likelihood of future instances of police brutality. The events of that summer also precipitated a shift in public opinion. A set of attitudes—including support for the BLM movement, recognition of widespread racial discrimination, and unfavorable views of the police— all increased according to multiple tracking polls by the Democracy Fund, UCLA Nationscape, and Civiqs. Importantly, support for BLM increased among Democrats and Republicans alike and across racial groups. This moment was thought to be a racial reckoning that would lead to meaningful progress for racial justice. Then the backlash began in earnest.

One aspect of the backlash was conservative politicians and media focusing negative attention on protesters rather than on the violent actions of police officers. Just three days after Floyd's murder, Trump tweeted, "When the looting starts, the shooting starts" (Hatewatch 2020). Conservatives seized onto the slogan "defund the police" to paint BLM activists and Democrats as radical and soft on crime. Republicans ran ads in races across the country that accused Democrats of supporting efforts to defund the police (Dale 2022). The GOP made it an important part of their 2022 messaging strategy to win back the House and Senate. In June 2022, House Minority Leader Kevin McCarthy tweeted, "The 'Defund the Police' campaign—endorsed by Democrats—has decimated our law enforcement. . . . When Republicans are in the majority, we will *fund* the police" (Hackett 2021).

Around the time of the summer 2020 protests, right-wing attacks on diversity, equity, and inclusion (DEI) initiatives, critical race theory (CRT), and wokeness also increased in frequency and intensity. These ideas became code words for anti-Blackness. Florida Governor Ron DeSantis became one of the most prominent champions of antiwokeness. He signed into law the Stop WOKE Act, which prohibits any educational instruction that would cause someone to "feel guilt, anguish, or any form of psychological distress" due to their race. DeSantis proudly proclaimed, "Florida is where woke goes to die" (Harriot 2022). Donald Trump made opposition to DEI a central part of his 2024 campaign and presidential agenda. Indeed, on January 20, 2025, the day he was inaugurated, he issued an executive order titled "Ending Radical and Wasteful Government DEI Programs and Preferencing," which terminated all DEI programs and policies in the federal government (White House 2025).

Conservative media, most notably Fox News, played a key role in pushing the anti-Black agenda. Using the TV News Archive from the Global Database of Events, Language and Tone Project, I found major spikes in coverage of DEI, CRT, and wokeness that started during or soon after the summer of 2020. Several notable trends are shown in figure 4.7. First, shown in figure 4.7A, coverage of wokeness rapidly increased in the early months of 2021 and has remained high ever since. Second, shown in figure 4.7B, coverage of CRT spiked in 2021, dominating airtime on Fox News, and then quickly receded less than a year later. Third, shown in figure 4.7C, coverage of DEI started slowly rising in 2021 and then spiked in

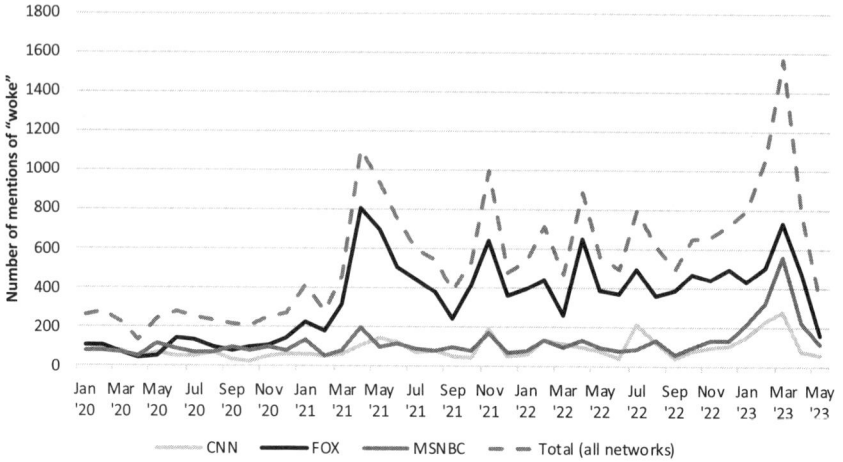

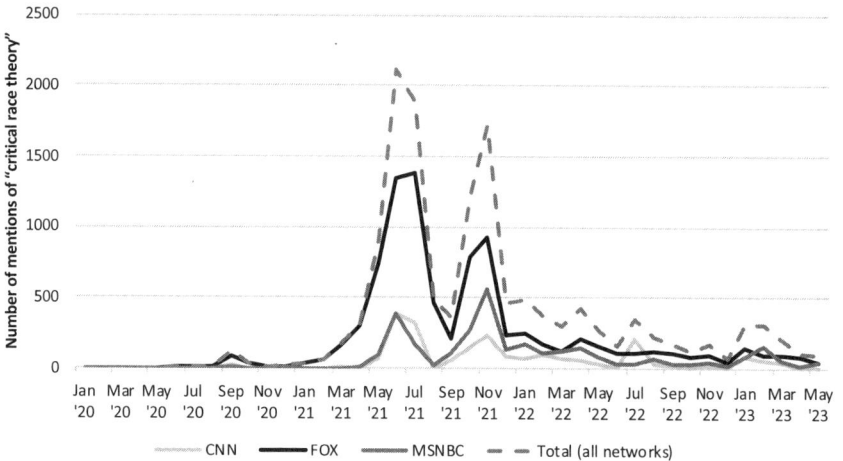

FIGURE 4.7. Fox News, CNN, and MSNBC coverage from 2020 to 2023 of (*top*) wokeness; (*bottom*) critical race theory (CRT); and (*facing*) diversity, equity, and inclusion (DEI). Data from the TV News Archive.

2023. These trends are almost exclusively driven by Fox News. CNN and MSNBC gave some airtime to these topics; but at no point between 2020 to 2023 was their coverage anywhere close to that of Fox News.

These ideas are all part of a backlash agenda against racial progress. Wokeness has been weaponized by the right wing to push back against

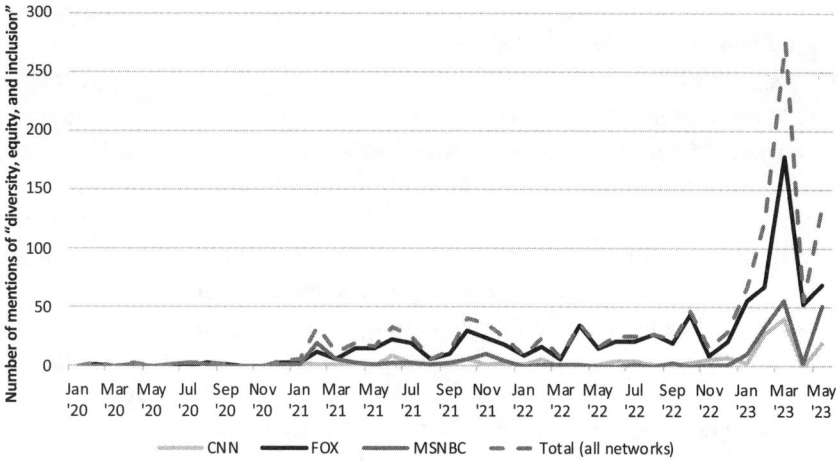

FIGURE 4.7. (*continued*)

what it calls "radical leftism" and to build support for policies that undo any progress made for marginalized communities. Critical race theory and DEI initiatives also became weaponized as boogeymen to stoke fear of status quo loss among white Americans. These ideas are powerful because they prey upon existing fears and allow elites to push an anti-Black and antiminority agenda without being explicit about their intentions. In other words, elites can avoid violating the norm of racial equality and maintain plausible deniability about racism while still activating animus from many of their supporters.

All of this contributed to a quick reversal in public opinion gains made by BLM and allies during the 2020 protests. By summer 2021, white Americans and Republicans had become less supportive of BLM than they had been at the beginning of 2020, prior to the massive protests (Chudy and Jefferson 2021). Of course, much of this reversal is due to the fleeting effects of any event on public opinion (see Zaller 1992). As media attention to the murders of Floyd and Taylor and the resulting protests waned, these events likely also receded from the minds of many Americans. Any progress made by BLM in changing the hearts and minds of people who tend to be staunchly opposed to racial equality, like many white people and Republicans, was always going to be difficult to maintain. However, this is not the only reason for the reversal in public attitudes. The gains in movement support among white individuals and Republicans had not just disappeared: These groups were now less supportive than they had been prior to 2020's racial reckoning.

Moreover, as of October, 2024, the GOP had introduced 861 anti-CRT bills, resolutions, executive orders, and other measures in 247 local, state, and federal legislatures since 2020.[17] During that same time period, at least twenty-eight state legislatures had introduced eighty-six anti-DEI bills and fourteen had already been signed into law.[18] As it has throughout most of US history, anti-Blackness is playing a central role in the conservative agenda. The attacks on Black rights, democratic norms, and education regarding historical and contemporary racial inequality came on the heels of the massive 2020 protests that shone a light on anti-Blackness. Despite broad rejection of overt anti-Black messaging, coded attacks on Black rights remain pervasive and are highly effective in activating racial animus among large segments of the population.

Conclusion

The findings in this chapter show that overt anti-Black racism continues to be unpalatable to the American public. Overwhelmingly, respondents rejected openly racist campaign appeals from candidates and overtly racist policies. Republicans are more supportive of candidates who use explicit anti-Black appeals than Democrats and Independents but will still reject these candidates in favor of opponents who avoid overt racism. It is no coincidence that elites tend to shy away from being openly anti-Black. When politicians do cross the line, such as former Representative King in 2019, they face negative repercussions. The findings also show that acceptance of overt anti-Black messaging is conditioned by social norm adherence. Respondents who adhere to inegalitarian norms as measured by the SNI were far more likely to support anti-Black candidates than respondents who adhere to egalitarian norms. These findings provide evidence for my assertion that a norm of racial equality in principle continues to guide messaging targeting the Black community.

However, many politicians also face incentives to appeal to the anti-Black sentiments of their constituents. They do this through coded messages about wokeness, CRT, DEI, and other veiled attacks on Black rights and racial progress. Politicians also do this through "racial distancing," or conveying to key constituents that will not do anything to disrupt the racial status quo (Stephens-Dougan 2020). As long as racial animus is pervasive in society and the party system is based on a racial cleavage, appeals to anti-Blackness will be used by political elites. If the norm of racial equality continues to hold, these appeals will remain coded.

There is also evidence that the norm of racial equality in principle is destabilizing within the GOP. Old-fashioned racist beliefs like opposition to interracial relations and belief in Black intellectual inferiority have become more closely tied to Republican identification and support for Republican candidates (Tesler 2013) and recent survey data show that Republicans find the *n*-word less offensive than they did ten years earlier (Tesler 2018). The results presented in this chapter show that, in some cases, 30%–40% of Republicans support candidates who are openly racist. The majority of Republican still rejected overtly anti-Black candidates in nonpartisan, primary, and partisan general elections; and rejected an openly anti-Black policy. But, given the direction of public opinion and the dynamics of the Republican Party, this may soon change.

There is also some evidence that the principle-implementation gap is closing within the Democratic Party. Democratic support for government interventions aimed at developing racial equality has risen substantially in recent years. Democrats are now more supportive of governmental efforts to improve the economic positions of Black people and of Black people receiving preferences in hiring and promotion than they were in past years. Democrats are bridging the principle-implementation gap at least partially due to decreased levels of racial resentment within the party, which is an attitude that has long been associated with opposition to pro-Black policies (e.g., Sears et al. 1997; Jardina and Piston 2019). This emerging norm of racial equality in practice within the Democratic Party has the potential to push both political messaging and policy making in a racially egalitarian direction.

This chapter has focused on a minority group for whom a norm of equality in principle exists. The next chapter examines messaging targeting a group that tends to be perceived as high threat among much of the American public and for whom I argue a norm of equality is absent. In the following chapter, I argue that a norm of inequality has developed instead which guides messaging targeting the Muslim community.

CHAPTER FIVE

Anti-Muslim Messaging and Political Evaluations

Donald J. Trump is calling for a total and complete shutdown of Muslims entering the United States until our country's representatives can figure out what is going on. —Donald Trump (Trump 2015)

During his rise to political power, Donald Trump both capitalized on existing anti-Muslim public sentiment and exacerbated the force of these attitudes on political decision-making. At a rally on September 30, 2015, Trump pledged to kick out all Syrian refugees, saying, "They could be ISIS" (J. Johnson 2015a). Over the next two months, he talked about closing mosques in the US and creating a database of all US-based Muslims, and he falsely claimed that thousands of Arabs in New York City cheered as the World Trade Center came down on 9/11 (Patel and Levinson-Waldman 2017). A timeline of Trump's comments put together by the *Washington Post* shows frequent and explicit derogation of Muslims and Muslim Americans (J. Johnson and Hauslohner 2017).

Trump's explicit anti-Muslim rhetoric is at odds with previous Republican presidents and presidential candidates. In a speech at the Islamic Center of Washington, DC on September 17, 2001, President George W. Bush said, "The face of terror is not the true faith of Islam. That's not what Islam is all about. Islam is peace." (White House 2001). Many of Bush's policies curtailed the rights of Muslims and Muslim Americans, but in his rhetoric, he was careful to not overtly attack the community. Mitt Romney, the 2012 Republican presidential nominee, condemned Trump's proposed Muslim ban, saying: "This is not who we are as a party or a country" (Hensch 2015). Although Republican and Democratic politicians alike have supported many policies that harm Muslims, prior to Trump in 2016 it was rare to see a serious presidential candidate so overtly denigrate the group. Moreover, it was not just Trump who was openly signaling his opposition to equal rights for Muslims in 2016. Trump's main opponents in the GOP primary race did so as well. Ben Carson invoked the Islamophobic idea of "civilization jihad" during a presidential debate (*New York Times* 2016), and Ted Cruz advocated for law enforcement officers to "patrol and secure Muslim neighborhoods" (Pilkington 2016). Nevertheless, Trump was the most forceful in his anti-Muslim rhetoric. Islamophobia was one of the defining characteristics of Trump as a presidential candidate and of his administration.

Despite pervasive negative stereotypes and feelings of threat, attitudes about Muslims and Islam did not have a strong influence on partisanship, presidential approval, or other measures of political attitudes prior to Barack Obama's 2008 presidential campaign (Tesler and Sears 2010). Obama's candidacy brought anti-Muslim attitudes to bear on political decision-making, such as voting and party preference (see Tesler 2022). A significant portion of the public held mistaken beliefs about his religious identity and upbringing. Public opinion polls conducted in 2008 showed that between 10% and 20% of the public believed Obama was a practicing Muslim, and more than 25% of registered voters believed Obama was raised Muslim. Importantly, more than 40% of registered voters who had an unfavorable opinion of Obama said his "Islamic faith" was the reason for their negative attitudes toward him. As Tesler and Sears (2010, 141) persuasively demonstrated, Obama's candidacy "made attitudes about Muslims a more central component of political decision-making." Trump was able to capitalize on this by activating festering anti-Muslim attitudes that had become connected to partisan politics to build support for his presidential campaign.

His strategy seems to have worked. Not only did voters not reject Trump for his explicit anti-Muslim sentiment, this rhetoric appeared to help his bid for the presidency. Among respondents in the Democracy Fund's Views of the Electorate Research Survey who had the least favorable views of Muslims, about 60% supported Trump over the other Republican primary candidates (Sides et al. 2018). Anti-Muslim sentiment continued to boost Trump in the general election. Across four survey samples, Lajevardi and Abrajano (2019) found that Muslim American resentment was associated with an 8- to 16-percentage-point increase in the probability that an individual supported Trump in the general election. Moreover, data from the RAND Presidential Election Panel Survey and the American National Election Survey showed that people who had very unfavorable views of Muslims were more than 30 points more likely to support Trump than those who had very favorable views of Muslims.[1] These studies provide compelling evidence that the activation of anti-Muslim attitudes among voters was a winning strategy for Trump in 2016.

In the years since, anti-Muslim rhetoric has become even more hostile and widespread. A report commissioned by Muslim Advocates (2018) found that Islamophobia was a prominent part of many candidate's messaging strategies during the 2018 midterm elections. The report showed that these candidates propagated harmful stereotypes and bigoted conspiracy theories, endorsed known anti-Muslim hate groups or activists, and advocated for policies that would strip constitutional rights and protections from Muslim Americans. Islamophobic campaign rhetoric became so intense and widespread that at least one news outlet referred to the 2018 election cycle as the "most Islamophobic election ever" (Aziza 2018). The trend continued in 2020, even in an election largely defined by a global health pandemic. According to a database of campaign ads compiled by America's Voice (2021), Islamophobic ads were featured in state and congressional races in at least eight states. In turn, the salience of anti-Muslim attitudes for determining vote choice (Tesler 2016; Lajevardi 2020), policy preferences (Lajevardi 2020) and partisanship (Tesler 2022) increased significantly. Negative portraits of Muslims have increasingly shaped partisan preferences: Attitudes about the group were one of the strongest predictors of vote choice in the 2008, 2012, and 2016 presidential elections (see Sides et al. 2018; Lajevardi and Abrajano 2019) and now has a "remarkably consistent and considerable effect" on the political evaluations of white Americans (Jardina and Stephens-Dougan 2021, 10).

The tenor and overtness of anti-Muslim rhetoric is also at odds with most anti-Black rhetoric coming from political elites, which is often coded in opposition to the Black Lives Matter movement, wokeness, critical race theory, and diversity, equity, and inclusion programs. Both anti-Muslim and anti-Black appeals are prominently featured in contemporary political rhetoric; the main difference is that anti-Blackness is generally communicated through coded language to avoid social censure while Islamophobia is often communicated explicitly.

This is because, as I argued in chapter 4, a set of factors highlighted by the groundswell of activism during the BLM movement has helped maintain a norm of racial equality in principle. Congruent survey findings indicate that the public at large does not accept overt anti-Black political messaging. In contrast, I demonstrate in this chapter that the factors that would predict the development of a norm of equality for Muslim Americans are largely absent. Instead, a major exogenous shock, the 9/11 terrorist attacks, shaped public views of Muslims and Islam and provided an opportunity for elites to leverage the raw negative emotions of the public for their own political gain. Furthermore, prominent signals of commitment to inequality from the media, pop culture, political institutions, and rightwing activists reinforced negative sentiments and feelings of threat from much of the American public, helping to develop a norm of inequality.

The existence of a norm of inequality means overt anti-Muslim political rhetoric should be accepted at higher rates than similar rhetoric targeting a group for whom a norm of equality is in place. This is exactly what I found. The results of two original survey experiments, one conducted in 2017 and the other in 2023, show respondents are much more supportive of candidates who overtly disparage Muslim people than they are of similar candidates who overtly disparage Black people. Another experiment conducted in 2023 shows respondents support a policy that is overtly discriminatory against Muslim people more than a similar policy that overtly discriminates against Black people.

The theory of differential norms also posits that norms of acceptable political rhetoric have developed differently within the Republican Party than within the Democratic Party. Norms tend to be less egalitarian within the GOP, and Republicans should, on average, be more accepting of antiminority messaging. This again is exactly what I found. Survey findings show that Republicans are more likely than Democrats to view it as acceptable to discriminate against Muslims, to say they are threatened by Muslims, and to have colder feelings toward Muslims. In the experiments discussed above, Republicans were far more supportive than Democrats of the anti-Muslim candidates and the anti-Muslim policy. Another survey conducted in 2018 found that candidates who use explicit anti-Muslim campaign appeals garner substantial support from Republican respondents in primary election contexts. Republican respondents also support these candidates over Democratic opponents in general election contexts.

Using an original measure of social norm adherence, I then empirically tested the effects of adherence to inegalitarian norms on support for candidates who make anti-Muslim statements. I find the social norms index (SNI), developed in chapter 3, predicts support for candidates who use explicit anti-Muslim and anti-Black campaign appeals. Moreover, the measure is useful for explaining differing levels of support for candidates based on their use of explicit anti-Muslim or anti-Black messages. In sum, the findings in this chapter show that overt Islamophobia is accepted by large portions of the American public, particularly Republicans, and individual reactions to this messaging are conditioned by social norm adherence.

Hypothesis Development

Anti-Muslim Political Messaging

The theory of differential norms, discussed in detail in chapter 2, argues that norms of acceptable political rhetoric vary based on the subject group. One reason for this variance is that the factors that lead to the development of egalitarian norms—strong commitments to equality from influential actors such as political institutions and social movements—are not equally present for all groups. The conditions for developing a norm of equality for Muslim Americans appear to be absent. There have been no major efforts from the Supreme Court, US Congress, or other major political institutions to protect the rights of Muslims. Although there have been impactful social actions taken to protect the rights and freedoms of Muslims—notably, the protests against Trump's Muslim ban—none of these actions have been sustained and developed into a social movement anywhere near the scale of the civil rights movement or Black Lives Matter movement.

To the contrary, political and social leaders have demonstrated a commitment to inequality. Anti-Muslim attitudes have been observed in US society for decades (e.g., Kalkan et al. 2009), aided by the dissemination of anti-Muslim and anti-Arab stereotypes from influential media and cultural elites. For decades, the news media have used frames like threat, extremism, and fundamentalism when discussing Muslims and Islam (Esposito 1999); associated the group with harmful stereotypes like terrorism and violence (Nacos and Torres-Reyna 2007); and contributed to a vision of Muslims as culturally inferior (Said 1979). For example, a 1967 story in *Time* about the Six-Day War referred to the "Arab enemy" (Rothman 2017). Shaheen's (2001) work on stereotypical portrayals of minority groups in Hollywood found that, from 1949 to 2001, at least forty-five films portrayed Palestinians as terrorists. Events such as the oil embargo and Iran hostage crisis of the 1970s and the September 11, 2001, terrorist attacks further engrained negative stereotypes about Muslims and Arab Americans that linked these communities to terrorism, violence, and anti-

American sentiments. Indeed, news media coverage of these events and popular culture narratives drawn from them have shaped how Americans view the Middle East and Islam (McAlister 2005).

Responses to the 9/11 terrorist attacks in particular shifted the norm environment. Many of the same tropes that painted Muslims as culturally inferior, uncivilized, and opposed to democratic norms were amplified in media portrayals, political cartoons, and political rhetoric during the subsequent global war on terror (see Dabashi 2017). Media coverage of Muslim groups (including Muslim Americans, Middle Eastern Americans, and Arab Americans) increased after 9/11 and the framing of these groups was largely negative (Lajevardi 2020). This "brown threat" now permeates the public imagination (Rivera 2014) and leads to members of the group being viewed as national security threats and destructive to American culture. Abdo (2005) argues that pervasive negative media and political attention to Muslims and Muslim Americans that link the group to terrorism has perpetuated a cycle of fear, distrust, and alienation among the public. Indeed, studies show that reliance on the media for information about Muslims is associated with more negative attitudes toward the community, belief in negative stereotypes, and support for discriminatory policies (Saleem et al. 2016).

The US government leveraged public fear and anger after 9/11 to enact several measures that curtailed the rights of Muslims. These measures included passing the USA PATRIOT Act, opening the Guantanamo Bay prison, and implementing a special registration program designed to collect information from foreign visitors who were "identified as presenting an elevated national security concern or who are from Iran, Iraq, Libya, Sudan, and Syria" (Jachimowicz and McKay 2003). In 2017, Trump issued Executive Order 13769 to ban travel from seven majority-Muslim countries and suspended resettlement of Syrian refugees. Although this original order was successfully challenged, the Supreme Court allowed the third iteration of Trump's Muslim ban to take force. These measures indicated to the public that major political institutions in the US do not support equal rights for Muslim Americans and legitimized the curtailment of the group's civil rights. These signals from political institutions helped shape the public's understanding of status quo support for the group, thereby influencing the development of social norms (see Tankard and Paluck 2017).

Another way that political leaders have stoked fear of Muslims has been through the constructed myth of the spread of Sharia law. Despite the absence of any evidence of Sharia law in America, stopping its spread became a focus of state legislatures in the 2010s. According to a report by the Southern Poverty Law Center (SPLC), more than two hundred anti-Sharia bills were introduced in forty-three states between 2010 and 2017 (Shanmugasundaram 2018). Fourteen of these bills were enacted. The model for these bills was developed by a network of anti-Muslim, right-wing activists and organizations who also spread conspiracy theories about radical Muslims infiltrating the US government (Gardiner and Olalde 2019). Anti-Muslim hate groups like ACT for America contributed to the fear of Sharia law by organizing the March against Sharia in at least twenty-eight cities in 2017 (Hatewatch 2017). Fox News amplified the message by mentioning Sharia 4,955 times between 2010 and 2017, with the vast majority of mentions coming from popular shows *Hannity* and *The O'Reilly Factor*.[2] Not coincidentally, a national poll conducted during this period found 37% of Americans were worried Sharia law could be applied in the US (Smietana 2015).

The way that Muslims have been constructed as threats in US society is especially relevant for understanding the development of norms of inequality for the group. Politicians took advantage of these frames to build support for policies that restrict group rights, such as Trump's Muslim ban, and signaled to voters that they are taking the threat of Islam seriously (Mendelberg 2018). Indeed, the global war on terror created a "state of exception" in which the rights of groups who were seen as terrorist threats could be curtailed using the justification of public safety (Alsultany 2022, 546). Alsultany eloquently argued that popular culture contributed to this logic of exception:

> The most popular post-9/11 TV drama, *24*, involved Central Terrorism Unit agent Jack Bauer, who repeatedly had to torture suspects, not because he wanted to but because, if he didn't, we would all die. Under the circumstances, he had no choice. He was filled with remorse and regret for the choices he had to make, emotions that also helped justify the use of torture. The logic of exception as articulated in terrorism-themed TV dramas ran thus: Racial profiling and torture are wrong, except during *exceptional* times of crisis, and during such times it is regarded as terrible and regretful but necessary to protecting the larger good, thus ultimately restoring the US to its ethos of democracy, freedom, and equality for all. (2022, 546)

Essentially, the logic of exception allows discriminatory and prejudicial actions against groups that are viewed as societal threats because of larger concerns about public safety and protecting American values (Alsultany 2022). Thus, an individual can support prejudice directed at a group that is operating under the logic of exception without feeling they are compromising their personal values.

The logic of exception created by 9/11 provided an opportunity for elites, particularly conservative elites, to shape the norm environment. But these inegalitarian signals were so effective largely because they arrived on the backdrop of preexisting negative sentiments and feelings of threat toward the Muslim community from much of the public. Studies conducted post-9/11 found that much of the American public viewed Muslims and Arab Americans negatively and felt high levels of threat from both groups. For example, one study showed that mean feeling thermometer scores of Muslims, which are standard survey items used to measure the public's general favorability of a group, dropped by 10 percentage points between 2002 and 2004 (Panagopoulos 2006). Another study found that the percentage of Americans who said that Muslims "do not at all agree with my vision of American society" was similar to that for atheists and the LGBTQ+ community and significantly higher than for other racial, ethnic, and religious groups (Edgell et al. 2006, 218). Similarly, Sides and Gross (2013) found in an examination of stereotype evaluations that Muslims are rated more negatively than other groups on trustworthy–untrustworthy and peaceful–violent scales. Several studies also found that the 9/11 attacks increased the public's sense of threat (Davis 2006; Kam and Kinder 2007) and that the heightened threat levels may have made people more supportive of restricting civil liberties (Davis and Silver 2004) and supportive of more aggressive antiterrorism policies (Huddy et al. 2005).

Negative public sentiment also bred harmful actions against Muslim and Arab Americans. Hate crime statistics compiled by the Anti-Defamation League show that reported hate crimes categorized as anti-Muslim or anti-Islamic skyrocketed after 9/11.[3] During this same time period, an organized network of anti-Muslim hate groups started developing (SPLC 2023). These groups disseminated prejudicial ideas and hostile conspiracy theories such as *civilization jihad*, which accuses Muslims of working to undermine democracy and Western civilization with Islamic despotism. They did this by organizing public demonstrations and events, writing and publishing Islamophobic content for public audiences, and working with politicians to develop and pass anti-Muslim legislation. These groups also developed and fortified political ties with prominent Republican members of Congress, helping legitimize their aims. Anti-Muslim networks helped undermine rights for the Muslim community and legitimized inegalitarian norms by showing that there is a groundswell of support for the curtailment of Muslim rights and by disseminating and popularizing anti-Muslim ideas. More recently, opposition to Muslim rights has played out through hundreds of antimosque demonstrations across the country[4] and large increases in hate crimes (Lichtblau 2016).

Contemporary US politics is fraught with signals that Muslims are undeserving of equal rights. Media coverage of Muslims and Muslim Americans has become more frequent and more hostile in recent decades. An organized network of hate groups targeting the community is spreading Islamophobic ideas and conspiracy theories and partnering with politicians to enact anti-Muslim legislation. Major political institutions including the Supreme Court, US Congress, and the president have legitimized the curtailment of Muslim rights by introducing anti-Muslim legislation and by enshrining anti-Muslim acts into law. All of this is set against a backdrop of public fear, resentment, and threat toward the Muslim community from much of the public. These factors have created a hostile and sometimes threatening environment for many in the Muslim American community who are targeted by vitriolic actions and hate crimes (e.g., Kalin and Lajevardi 2017; Calfano et al. 2019; Lajevardi 2020). Recent survey data found that many respondents make "blatantly racist evaluations" of Muslim Americans and rate the group as least "evolved" (Lajevardi and Oskooii 2018).

Although many minority groups are viewed negatively and face public hostility, pervasive threatening frames constructed for Muslims make this group a particularly effective boogeyman in contemporary US society. As such, political candidates are sometimes incentivized by their constituencies to overtly express hostility to Muslims and Islam. In sum, salient signals of commitments to norms of inequality from elites, institutions, and organized social groups, along with constructed narratives of threat, have led to rhetoric targeting this group to be guided by a norm of inequality. It follows from this that overt anti-Muslim political messaging is likely to be accepted, along with the messenger, by the general public at higher rates than antiminority messaging targeting a group like Black Americans for whom a norm of equality has, at least in principle, been developed and maintained.

Hypothesis 5.1. Candidates who use explicit anti-Muslim appeals will receive more support from voters than candidates who use explicit anti-Black appeals.

Partisan Polarization

The first prong of the theory of differential norms is that norms of acceptable political rhetoric vary based on the subject group of the message. The second prong states that the specific norm developed among the target audience of the antiminority message is crucial to understanding whether the message will be accepted or rejected. An individual's decision-making process is most likely to be influenced by what people in their reference group do. As discussed in detail in chapter 2, norms develop within groups when there are opportunities for communication, group uniformity, and when the norm is important to the group. I have established that these factors have led to norms of acceptable political rhetoric developing differently within the Republican and Democratic Parties. In chapter 4, I showed that these factors explain partisan differences when examining reactions to overt anti-Black political messaging. In this section, I argue that these factors also help us understand partisan differences in the acceptability of Islamophobia.

The factors that lead to the development of a norm of inequality and the perception of threat from Muslims and Islam, are most prevalent within the Republican Party. First, through established communication avenues, Republicans are receiving far more anti-Muslim messages than Democrats. As established in previous chapters, Republicans and Democrats often live in different media environments. While most major news networks air negative content focusing on Muslims and Islam (see Lajevardi 2020), anti-Muslim content is featured on conservative networks more than others. Fox News is one of the main culprits. Mobashra Tazamal (2019), associate director of the Prince Alwaleed Bin Talal Center for Muslim–Christian Understanding, called Fox News "a megaphone for anti-Muslim hatred." Tazamal pointed out that Fox News has pushed anti-Muslim conspiracy theories such as the spread of Sharia law in the US and has provided a platform for prominent anti-Muslim activists like Brigitte Gabriel and Frank Gaffney. According to my own analysis of the Global Database of Events, Language and Tone Project's TV News Archive, between 2010 and 2017, Fox News mentioned Sharia almost 5,000 times, while CNN and MSNBC mentioned it 1,620 and 1,058 times, respectively.[5]

It is no surprise then that 76% of those who most trust Fox News supported congressional hearings into alleged Muslim extremism, according to a poll conducted by the Public Religion Research Institute (R. Jones and Cox 2011). In that poll, 59% of those who most trust Fox News

believed Muslims had not done enough to oppose extremism, 35% believed Muslim Americans wanted to establish Sharia law in the United
States, and only 16% believed Muslim Americans had been unfairly targeted by law enforcement. Respondents who trusted Fox News had substantially more anti-Muslim attitudes than respondents who trusted other
news sources, like CNN, MSNBC, broadcast network news, or public television. Republicans, the primary audience of Fox News, are receiving a
plethora of signals from conservative mainstream media that influential
leaders are committed to inequality for Muslims.

Second, the GOP has become relatively homogeneous in its anti-
Muslim animus. Across many studies, Republicans consistently have
significantly more negative attitudes toward Muslims than Democrats do.
For example, Republicans consistently score higher on the Muslim American resentment scale (MAR), a measure that captures public perceptions
of how the public perceives Muslim Americans and how the public thinks
the government should treat the group, than Democrats and Independents (Lajevardi 2020) and assign lower favorability scores to Muslims
than Democrats do. Higher levels of resentment toward the group as measured by the MAR is also predictive of support for Trump (Lajevardi and
Abrajano 2019). The 2022 Critical Issues Poll conducted by the University of Maryland (Telhami and Rouse 2022) asked respondents whether
they would vote for a Muslim presidential candidate if they agreed with
the candidate's policy positions. Among Republican respondents, 30%
said they would and 44% said they would not. Democrats and Independents were much more likely to say they would support the candidate.[6]
In the same poll, respondents were asked whether the number of Muslim Americans in the country strengthens, weakens, or has no impact on
American society. There again were major partisan splits in the responses:
21% of Republicans said strengthen and 32% said weaken; 66% of Democrats said strengthen and 5% said weaken; and 37% of Independents
said strengthen and 18% said weaken. Similarly, Republicans are more
threatened by Muslims and Islam than Democrats are. In a Pew Research
Center survey (2017), respondents were asked how concerned they were
about extremism in the name of Islam. Among Republicans, 67% were
concerned about extremism around the world and 64% were concerned
about extremism in the US. The percentages of Democrats who were concerned about extremism were much lower (40% and 30%, respectively).

Third, a norm of inequality for Muslims appears to be beneficial to the
GOP. Donald Trump's successful presidential campaign in 2016 utilized

anti-Muslim rhetoric to attract voters. Since then, Islamophobia has become an important messaging strategy for many Republican candidates. Almost all the candidates who were found to have utilized Islamophobic campaign appeals in the America's Voice report on the 2020 election and the Muslim Advocates report on the 2018 election were Republicans. Many Republican elected officials have also aligned themselves with anti-Muslim hate groups. For example, Senator Cruz (R-TX) and Representative Louie Gohmert (R-TX) are public allies with groups the SPLC (2023) has categorized as anti-Muslim hate groups. In 2021, Representatives Lauren Boebert (R-CO) and Marjorie Taylor Greene (R-GA) were pictured with a prominent anti-Muslim activist at an event hosted by ACT for America, a nativist and anti-Muslim hate group (SPLC n.d.). Islamophobia has also become a useful mobilizing tool for far-right groups to attract people to demonstrations and grow their ranks.

In sum, there are many reasons to believe that norms of acceptable political rhetoric regarding Muslims and Islam have developed in distinct ways within the two major political parties. Conservative news media frequently spreads anti-Muslim sentiment through endorsing harmful stereotypes and conspiracy theories. Anti-Muslim hate groups have grown in size, have developed connections to right-wing politicians, and are now a prominent part of the far-right movement. Republicans are relatively homogeneous in their negative views of the community and are more likely than Democrats or Independents to perceive Muslims and Islam as threatening. Finally, the GOP stands to benefit from the development and maintenance of inegalitarian norms. Consequently, we would expect norms of inequality targeting Muslims to have developed and become engrained within the GOP more strongly than within the Democratic Party or among Independents. Thus, Republicans should be more likely to accept overt anti-Muslim messages, along with the messengers, than Democrats or Independents.

Hypothesis 5.2. Candidates who use explicit anti-Muslim appeals will receive more support from Republicans than from Democrats or Independents.

Social Norms

Hypothesis 5.1 posits that norms of acceptable political rhetoric have developed differently for Muslims than for Black people. Hypothesis 5.2 posits that norms have developed differently within the Republican Party than within the Democratic Party. In other words, norms are the mechanism that determines public reactions to political messages that target minority groups. This should be the case when measured at the individual level as well. Support for candidates who use explicit prejudicial appeals should be highest among individuals who adhere to inegalitarian rather than egalitarian norms.

Hypothesis 5.3. Respondents who score high on the SNI (i.e., adhere to inegalitarian norms) will be most likely to support candidates who use explicit anti-Muslim appeals, and those who score low on the SNI (i.e., adhere to egalitarian norms) will be least likely to support these candidates.

Hypothesis Testing

Public Responses to Explicit Anti-Muslim Messaging

To test hypothesis 5.1, I conducted multiple survey experiments in which respondents were randomly assigned to read about a fictional candidate who used either an overt anti-Black message or an overt anti-Muslim message. Then, respondents were asked how likely they were to vote for the candidate they were assigned to. This allowed for a direct comparison of the likelihood of the public to support a candidate whose main campaign rhetoric was overtly anti-Muslim relative to a candidate whose main rhetoric was overtly anti-Black. Table 5.1 provides basic information about the three survey experiments I conducted to test the first hypothesis. As shown in more detail in chapter 4, respondents tended to reject the candidates who used overt anti-Black messaging. Conversely, across a series of survey samples and experiments, I found the public tended to accept overt anti-Muslim political messaging.

In the first survey, conducted in August 2017 on Amazon's Mechanical Turk (MTurk) and described in more detail in chapter 4, respondents were randomly assigned to one of two experimental conditions.[7] Each group was shown a biography of a fictional candidate running for a seat in the US House of Representatives and then asked how likely they would be to vote for the candidate. The biography described Mark Williams as a moderate who wants to "rebuild crumbling infrastructure" and "bring jobs back to the district." Each treatment group read the biography with one of the following explicit antiminority messages added: "Candidate Williams will work hard to protect the community by increasing spending for law

TABLE 5.1 **Anti-Muslim messaging experimental design information**

Treatment	Description	N
August 2017 MTurk survey		
Treatment 1	Anti-Black campaign appeal	399
Treatment 2	Anti-Muslim campaign appeal	401
March 2023 Lucid survey		
Treatment 1	Anti-Black campaign appeal	744
Treatment 2	Anti-Muslim campaign appeal	752
March 2023 Lucid survey		
Treatment 1	Anti-Black policy	596
Treatment 2	Anti-Muslim policy	600

enforcement to crack down on [violent Black criminals / violent Muslim extremists.]" Then, respondents in each treatment group answered a series of questions about Mark Williams to gauge support for the candidate. The results are presented in figure 5.1.[8] While only about 10% of respondents said they were very or somewhat likely to vote for the candidate who used the overt anti-Black message, about 57% of respondents said they were very or somewhat likely to vote for the candidate who used the overt anti-Muslim message. The substantial 47 percentage point difference in vote likelihood is statistically significant at the $p < .001$ level according to a two-sample t-test.

In a survey conducted March 2023 through Lucid and described in more detail in chapter 3, I included another fictional candidate experiment in which respondents were assigned to a candidate who used either an explicit anti-Black message or an explicit anti-Muslim message.[9] The treatment was as follows:

> In a recent interview with the Associated Press, Senate candidate Kyle Anderson was asked about the country's system of administration. "It is true that [Blacks/Muslims] are more violent and choose to get involved with [crime/terrorism]," he said. "[Blacks/Muslims] have to stop being [criminals/terrorists]. Stiffer penalties will act as a deterrent to [crime/terrorism]."

The setup of this experiment was similar to the one found in Bonilla et al. (2022). An overt antiminority message was paired with a congruent group

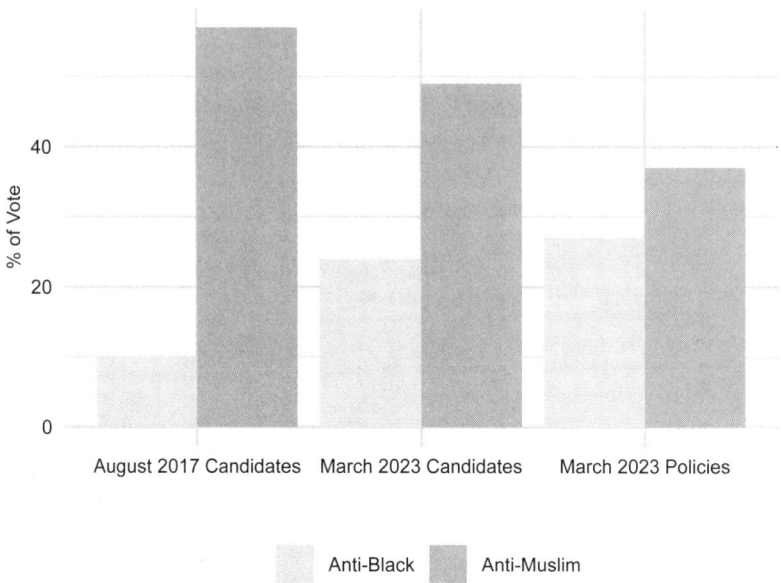

FIGURE 5.1. Support for anti-Black and anti-Muslim candidates and policies. Data from August 2017 MTurk survey and March 2023 Lucid survey.

stereotype. The congruency of the message is important for two reasons. First, it is more realistic, which helps improve the external validity of the results. In other words, experiments that do a good job of mimicking real-world phenomena are more likely to also mimic real-world results. Second, the intent of the message is more likely to be recognized by the audience when the issue and group in a message are congruent (see Reny et al. 2020), thereby presenting a better experimental test of an overt message. Respondents were then asked how likely they would be to vote for the candidate if the election were held today. These results are also presented in figure 5.1. Although only 24% of respondents said they were very or somewhat likely to vote for the anti-Black candidate, roughly 49% of them said they would vote for the anti-Muslim candidate. These differences are statistically significant at the $p < .001$ according to a two-sample t-test. In two survey experiments conducted six years apart, the fictional candidate who used an explicit anti-Muslim campaign appeal received far more support than the one who used an explicit anti-Black campaign appeal.

In the same March 2023 Lucid survey, respondents were asked how much they would support or oppose a fictional piece of legislation. The experimental treatment was based on the special registration program that was set up to gather information on foreign visitors from designated countries following the 9/11 attacks (Jachimowicz and McKay 2003). The treatment was as follows:

> A proposed legislative bill would create a special registration program to collect information on [Blacks/Muslims]. Proponents of the bill say that the group is a threat to the American way of life and need to be put under surveillance. Opponents say the bill would violate the group's civil liberties.

Respondents were asked how much they supported or opposed this bill. As shown in figure 5.1, 27.5% of respondents said they strongly or somewhat supported the bill when it was framed around collecting information on Black people. When the bill was framed around collecting information on Muslims, 37% of respondents said they supported the bill at some level. This difference is statistically significant at the $p < .01$ level according to a two-sample t-test.

In sum, across a series of survey samples using different experimental treatments, candidates and policies that were explicitly anti-Muslim garnered substantially more support from the general public than otherwise identical candidates and policies that were explicitly anti-Black. The results indicate that the subject group of an antiminority political message influences the likelihood that the message will be accepted or rejected by the public. The results provide evidence in support of hypothesis 5.1, which posits that candidates who are explicitly anti-Muslim will receive more support from voters than candidates who are explicitly anti-Black.

The Role of Partisan Identification

All respondents in the October 2020 survey conducted on YouGov (discussed in more detail in chapter 3) were asked whether it is acceptable or unacceptable to discriminate against a set of groups.[10] Figure 5.2 shows more than 35% of Republicans said it is "always acceptable" or "acceptable in some situations" to discriminate against Muslims, and about 18% said the same about Black people. About 7% of Democrats said it was acceptable to discriminate against Muslims, and roughly the same percentage said it was acceptable to discriminate against Black people. About 14% of Independents said it was acceptable to discriminate against Muslims and 9% said the same about Black people.

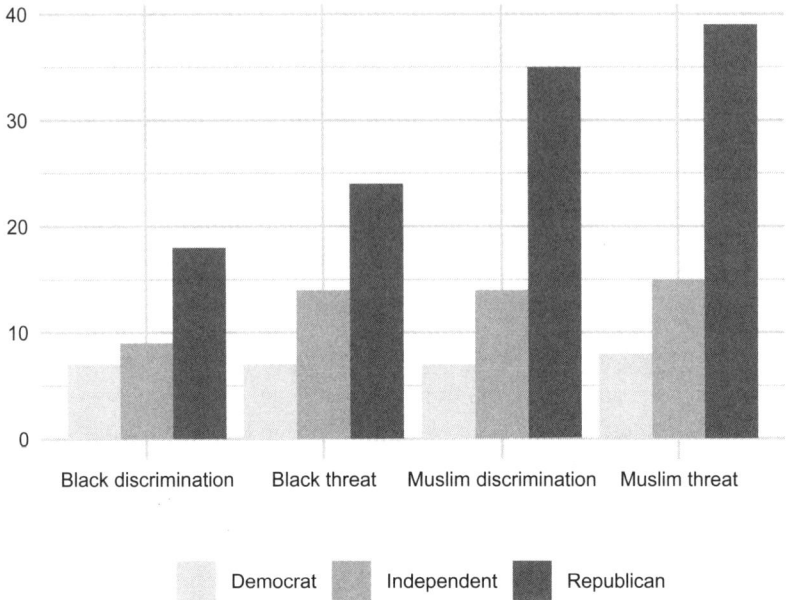

FIGURE 5.2. Partisan differences in the percentage of respondents who believe it is acceptable to discriminate against Black/Muslim people and the percentage of respondents who feel threatened by Black/Muslim people. Data from the October 2020 YouGov survey.

Respondents were also asked how often they felt threatened by various groups. Among Republicans, roughly 39% reported feeling threatened by Muslims "often" or "sometimes," which was the highest of any group asked about in the survey and almost 15 percentage points higher than the proportion who said they felt threatened by Black people. Just under 8% of Democrats reported feeling threatened by Muslims and 7% said they felt threatened by Black people. About 15% of Independents reported feeling threatened by Muslims and 14% by Black people. Republican respondents are more threatened by Muslims than by other groups and feel that it is more acceptable to discriminate against Muslims than it is to discriminate against other groups. Moreover, relative to Democrats and Independents, Republicans are more threatened by Muslims and feel it is more acceptable to discriminate against them.

Feeling thermometer scores also provide some indication of the public's view of Muslims relative to other groups. Figure 5.3 displays feeling thermometer scores over time for African American, gay and lesbian, Muslim, and white people among respondents in the American National Election

Study (ANES).[11] Respondents were asked to evaluate each group on a scale from 0 (cold feelings toward the group) to 100 (warm feelings toward the group). Republicans rated Muslims substantially colder than African Americans or white people, and somewhat colder than gay and lesbian people, and had substantially colder views of Muslims than Democrats did. Similar measures asked in original Lucid surveys suggest the ANES results are robust to different specifications and different time points.[12]

These findings track with scholarship that shows people are less hesitant to express negative feelings about Muslims than other groups. Lajevardi (2020, 34) found similar results using her MAR scale, which consists of nine statements that "capture particularized attitudes toward Muslim Americans." The mean MAR score for Republicans across ten survey samples was about .5 out of 1, while resentment scores for Democrats ranged between .24 and .36 (47). The MAR is a useful scale because it captures the particular ways Muslims have been racialized in the US. Tesler (2016) showed that a substantially larger portion of the American public admitted they were less

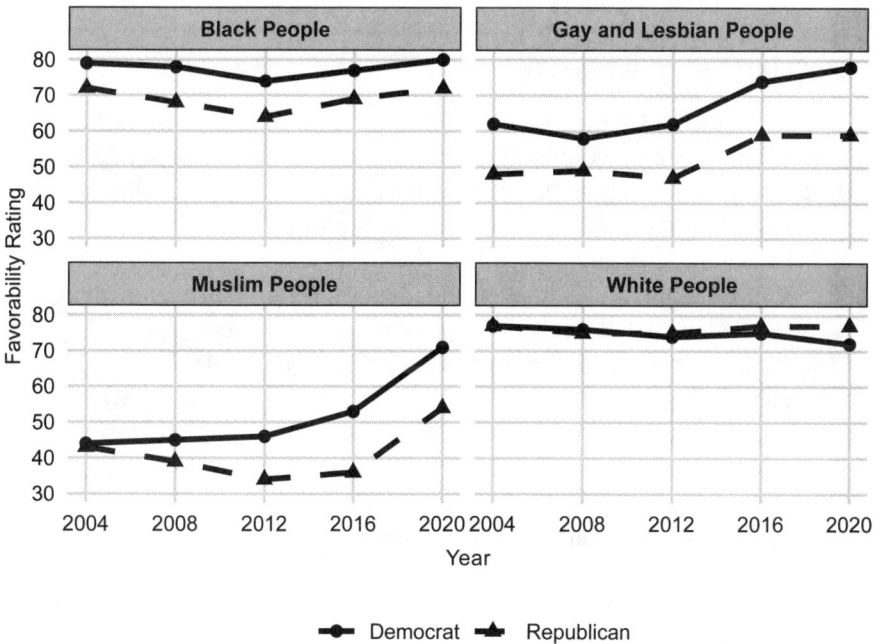

FIGURE 5.3. Favorability measures of groups over time by party. Data from American National Election Studies 2004–2020.

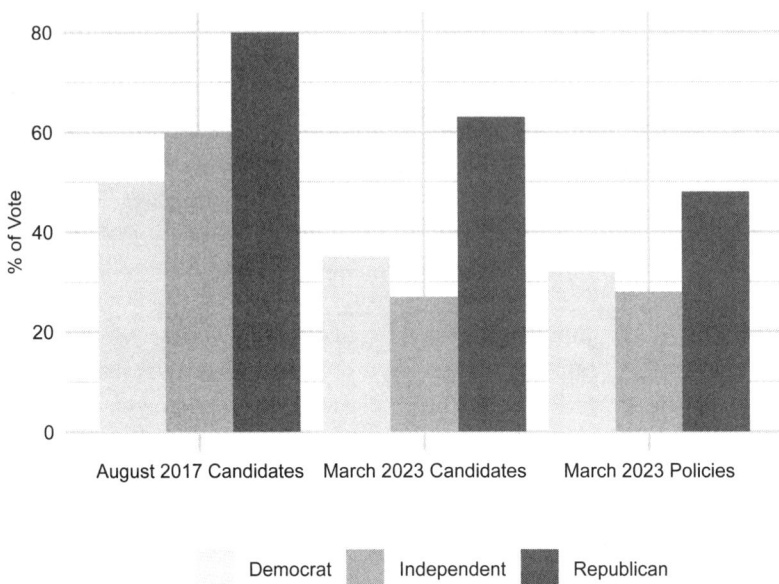

FIGURE 5.4. Partisan differences in support for anti-Black and anti-Muslim candidates and policies. Data from the August 2017 MTurk survey and March 2023 Lucid survey.

likely to vote for Obama because of his religion (presumably believing him to be Muslim) than because of his race. Similarly, in a June 2015 Gallup Survey, less than half of Republicans reported they would vote for an otherwise qualified Muslim presidential candidate (Newport 2015).

Earlier in the chapter, figure 5.1 showed that in the 2017 MTurk survey, 57% of respondents said they would vote for Mark Williams, a fictional candidate for the US House of Representatives, after he signaled his opposition to "violent Muslim extremists." Figure 5.4 displays the results by partisanship and shows that support for the candidate was fairly high among Democrats and Independents. Almost 50% of Democrats said they would vote for the candidate, as did almost 60% of Independents. However, almost 80% of Republicans said they would vote for the candidate, showing again that Republicans support overt anti-Muslim political messaging more than others do.

Support for the overtly anti-Muslim candidate in the March 2023 Lucid sample is even more segmented by partisan identity. Among the full sample, 47% reported they would vote for him. Figure 5.4 shows that among Republicans, 63% said they would vote for him, which is 28 percentage points higher than support among Democrats. Support for the candidate among Independents was even lower: Only 27% said they would vote for the anti-Muslim candidate. Figure 5.4 also shows that almost 50% of Republicans supported a special registration program to collect information on Muslims. Support for the policy among Democrats and Independents was almost 20 points lower. The partisan differences shown in the figure are all statistically significant to at least the $p < .05$ level according to two-sample t-tests.

In sum, Republicans are more likely than Democrats and Independents to support political candidates who explicitly signal their anti-Muslim stances and to support a policy that curtails the civil rights of Muslim Americans. Republicans are also more threatened by Muslims and more likely to believe it is acceptable to discriminate against Muslims. These results provide clear evidence for hypothesis 5.2, which says political candidates who use explicit anti-Muslim appeals will receive more support from Republicans than from Democrats or Independents. The next subsection will further analyze the primary election scenarios presented in chapter 4 to better understand how overt anti-Muslim political messaging functions in GOP primary election contexts relative to anti-Black messaging.

Election Tests

PRIMARY ELECTIONS.   Another way to test the first two hypotheses is by examining reactions to overt antiminority messaging in election contexts—first in primaries and then in general elections. The results in this subsection are from primary election scenarios that were included in the July 2018 and October 2018 Lucid surveys.[13] Respondents who self-identified as Republican were shown a matchup between two Republican candidates for the US House of Representatives. In each election scenario, the fictional candidates had the same stances across a range of typical Republican policies. The only difference between the anti-Black or anti-Muslim candidate and his opponent was that he used an overt antiminority campaign appeal while his opponent did not. The anti-Muslim candidate in the first election used an Islamophobic campaign appeal ("Muslim extremists"), and his opponent did not. In the second election, the anti-Black candidate made an openly racist campaign appeal ("Black gang members"). In each scenario, the candidate named the group he was targeting and invoked a congruent and threatening stereotype ("extremists" for Muslims and "gang members" for Black people).

The following is an excerpt of a media article written about a Republican primary election to fill a seat in the US House of Representatives from your state. After reading the excerpt, you will be asked to evaluate the candidates in the election.

Kyle Anderson and Peter Miller, the two candidates in the Republican primary election, have similar views on most important policy issues. Both have promised to repeal Obamacare, simplify the tax code, and decrease entitlement spending. The two candidates differ slightly in their policies and rhetoric on law enforcement. While both candidates are supportive of law enforcement, Anderson has made it a central campaign promise to "empower law enforcement agencies to crack down on [Black gang members / Muslim extremists]."

If you lived in this district, which candidate would you vote for?

Respondents were then asked who they would vote for: the candidate who used the racist or Islamophobic appeal, the opponent who did not use a prejudicial appeal, or neither. This was the primary dependent variable used in the analysis. Figure 5.5 presents percentage-point differences in candidate support in the fictional Republican primary elections. The Republican candidate who used an overt anti-Muslim appeal garnered about 54% of the vote—about 28 percentage points more than his opponent in the July 2018 survey—indicating that overt Islamophobia can have a strong mobilizing effect on Republican voters. Support for the candidate using the anti-Muslim appeal was lower in the October 2018 survey (45%), but was still 15 points higher than his opponent. In contrast, the candidate who used an overt anti-Black appeal received only 29% of the vote in the July 2018 survey and 27% in October 2018—much lower than the Islamophobic candidate in both surveys. In a real election, both anti-Black candidates would have been soundly defeated by their opponents while both anti-Muslim candidates would have sailed to victory. Results from two-sample *t*-tests indicate that mean differences between vote intention for the antiminority candidates and their opponents were statistically significant in all the election scenarios to at least the $p < .05$ level.

Explicit prejudicial campaign appeals targeting Muslims, and the candidates who utilize them, are much more acceptable to Republican voters than explicit anti-Black appeals. This finding further bolsters support for hypothesis 5.1, showing that anti-Muslim political messaging is more acceptable than anti-Black messaging. The candidates who used overt anti-

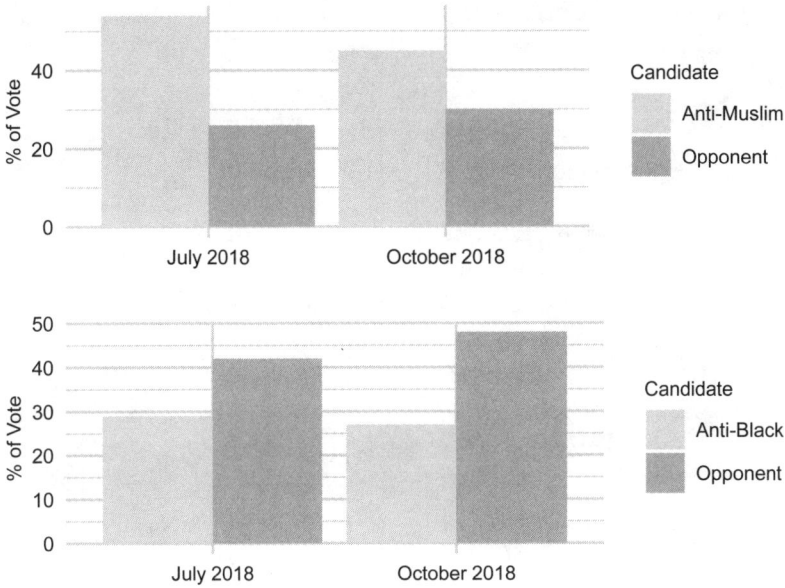

FIGURE 5.5. Percentage of Republican identifiers who supported the candidates who used overt anti-Muslim and anti-Black campaign appeals and percentage who supported the non-racialized opponent in two fictional Republican primary elections. Data from the July 2018 and October 2018 Lucid surveys.

Muslim campaign appeals won their election matchups against similar opponents, which provides evidence that overt Islamophobia might be not only acceptable but also mobilizing to large portions of the Republican base. This finding bolsters support for hypothesis 5.2, showing that Republican voters are likely to accept Republican candidates who use Islamophobic campaign appeals. This idea is further interrogated in the next subsection, which focuses on general election matchups.

GENERAL ELECTION. In two national samples, Republicans supported a primary election candidate who used an overt anti-Muslim campaign appeal over an otherwise identical opponent. What happens when that candidate moves on to the general election to face a Democratic opponent? Will the anti-Muslim message carry any cross-party appeal? How will Independents react? To answer these questions, respondents in the October 2018 Lucid survey were asked to choose between fictional candidates in general election contests. Respondents were randomly

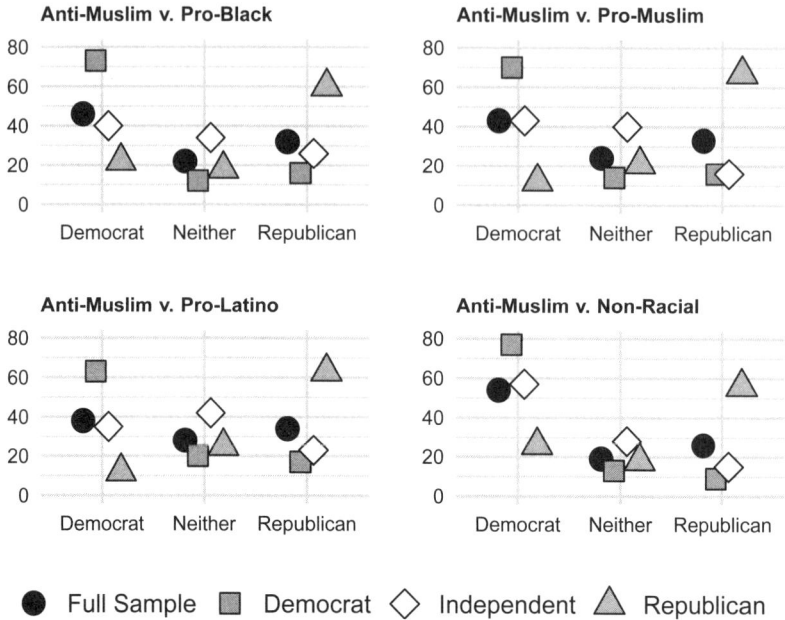

FIGURE 5.6. Percent support for anti-Muslim Republican candidates in four different fictional general election scenarios. Data from the October 2018 Lucid survey.

assigned to an election scenario featuring a Republican candidate who used an overt anti-Muslim campaign appeal or one who used an overt anti-Black campaign appeal. Within each scenario, the Democratic opponent used a pro-Black, pro-Latino, or pro-Muslim appeal, or advocated a reduction in crime rates without naming a specific minority group. Respondents were then asked which candidate they would vote for: the Republican candidate, the Democrat, or neither. This test helped illuminate two aspects of the use of anti-Muslim messaging. First, it addressed whether anti-Muslim messaging by Republican candidates is electorally viable in a general election context. Second, it shed light on which general election contests increase or decrease the viability of anti-Muslim messaging.

The results for the anti-Black candidate were discussed in chapter 4. There was very little support for the anti-Black candidate across any of the general election scenarios. Figure 5.6 displays the results of all four general election matchups that featured the anti-Muslim candidate, and breaks down candidate support by full sample, Democrats, Independents, and Republicans. The results indicate that the Republican candidate would lose all four election matchups. Support for the Republican candidate was between 32% and 34% in each scenario, except for the matchup that pitted the candidate against the Democrat who did not openly appeal to pro-minority sentiments. In that matchup, support for the Republican dropped to 26%. In general, the GOP candidate fared better when pitted against a Democrat who made pro-minority campaign appeals. Although the overt anti-Muslim message helped the candidate in a primary election context, he fared poorly in a general election context.

The partisan breakdowns show that the anti-Muslim candidate enjoyed majority support from Republican respondents in all four scenarios. Between 56% and 67% of Republicans said they would vote for the anti-Muslim candidate. That is a higher level of support than the anti-Black candidate received from Republicans. In other words, Republican candidates who make overt anti-Muslim comments will receive more support from their base in general election matchups than Republican candidates who explicitly disparage Black people. However, it is still far below the level of support the candidate would need from copartisan voters to win a real election. The anti-Muslim candidate also did not receive much support from Democrats or Independents. Indeed, a substantially higher percentage of Independents supported the Democratic opponent over the anti-Muslim Republican in all four election scenarios.

Based on these results, the viability of explicit anti-Muslim campaign appeals is nuanced. In multiple survey experiments, overt Islamophobia seemed to boost a candidate's electoral chances in a GOP primary. However, across several different general election contexts, that same candidate was soundly defeated by a Democratic opponent. Strikingly, the anti-Muslim Republican candidate was unable to garner significant support from Independents in any of the general election scenarios and only received slightly higher support from their base than the similar Republican candidate who used an overt anti-Black appeal. Over the last decade, GOP candidates have increasingly used overt Islamophobia in their election campaigns. The results presented in this chapter indicate that while that may be a sound strategy in a primary race, it may not be a winning strategy in a general election.

The Role of Social Norms

The results in this chapter so far show that overt anti-Muslim political messaging is generally acceptable to large portions of the American public. Republicans in particular are open to anti-Muslim campaign appeals.

In primary election contexts, overt Islamophobia may even benefit Republican candidates. Across several different tests, the public supported candidates who were openly anti-Muslim at much higher rates than candidates who were openly anti-Black. This is not to say that Islamophobia is more pervasive or more deeply held among Americans than anti-Black racism. Survey data presented in chapter 4 demonstrated that anti-Black attitudes are widespread, are deeply held, and powerfully shape political decision-making. Instead, I argue that norms guiding anti-Black political speech are closer on the spectrum to egalitarianism than norms guiding anti-Muslim political speech.

In this subsection, I used the SNI to empirically test the role of social norm adherence in guiding reactions to anti-Muslim messaging. I also used the SNI to analyze the differences in acceptability of Islamophobia and racism. I found that respondents who adhere to egalitarian norms rejected candidates who used overt anti-Muslim messaging and policies. Respondents who adhere to inegalitarian norms tended to support these same candidates. I also found that respondents who adhere to egalitarian norms were much less likely to reject anti-Muslim messages than anti-Black ones, while respondents who adhere to inegalitarian norms were more likely to accept anti-Muslim messages than anti-Black ones. In other words, both ends of the social norm spectrum, measured through the SNI, help explain why overt Islamophobia is more acceptable to the public than overt racism.

Figure 5.7 presents results of OLS regressions that analyzed the effect of the SNI on support for the fictional anti-Muslim candidate and the fictional anti-Black candidate presented in the March 2023 Lucid survey. Both models control for party identification, gender, education level, age, and racial resentment. The SNI had a powerful independent effect on voter intention among both treatment groups even after accounting for these other variables. The dotted line shows that respondents who were closest on the scale to inegalitarian norms were 40 percentage points more likely to support the anti-Muslim candidate than those who were closest to egalitarian norms. The solid line shows that the SNI had an even larger 78-point effect on support for the anti-Black candidate. Substantially greater support for the anti-Muslim candidate from the most egalitarian voters explains why that candidate fared so much better in the election scenario than the anti-Black candidate. Indeed, among the most egalitarian respondents, 48% said they would vote for the anti-Muslim candidate, compared to only 12% who would vote for the anti-Black candidate.

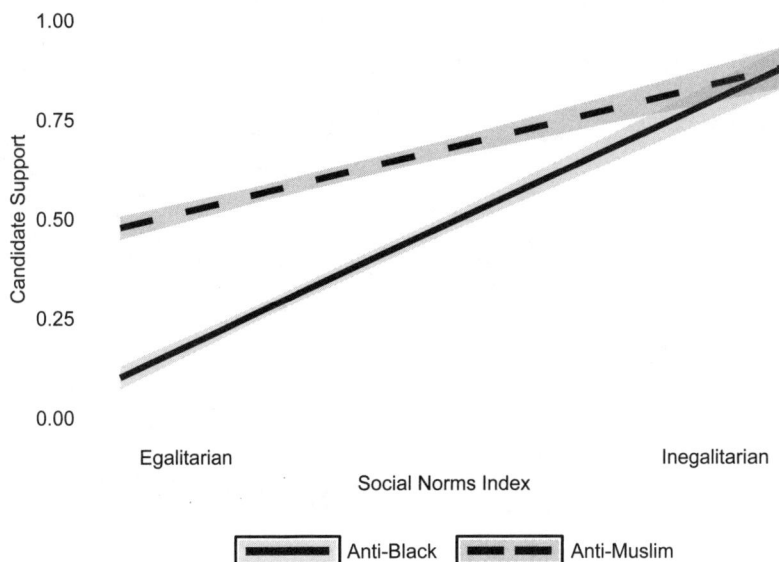

FIGURE 5.7. Marginal effects of the SNI on support for the anti-Black and anti-Muslim candidates. Data from the March 2023 Lucid survey. The dependent variable in each model is stated intention to vote for either an anti-Black political candidate or anti-Muslim political candidate. Response options for the dependent variable in each model range from 0 to 1. Both models control for party identification, gender, education, age, and racial resentment. See appendix table A.5 for full model results.

Respondents at the midpoint of the SNI scale were also more likely to support the anti-Muslim candidate than the anti-Black candidate by over 20 points.

Figure 5.8 displays the relationship between the SNI and support for the Republican candidates presented in the primary election scenarios in the October 2018 Lucid survey.[14] The dependent variable in each model is a dummy variable in which 1 represents choosing to vote for the candidate who used the antiminority appeal and 0 represents choosing not to vote for that candidate (either choosing his opponent or neither candidate).[15] Both models control for gender, education level, age, and racial resentment. Adhering to inegalitarian norms predicts an increase in support for the anti-Muslim and anti-Black candidates among Republicans. Moving from most egalitarian to most inegalitarian on the SNI leads to a 39-percentage-point increase in likelihood of voting for the anti-Muslim candidate after accounting for the control variables. Moving from egalitarian to inegalitarian norms predicts a 35-point increase in support for

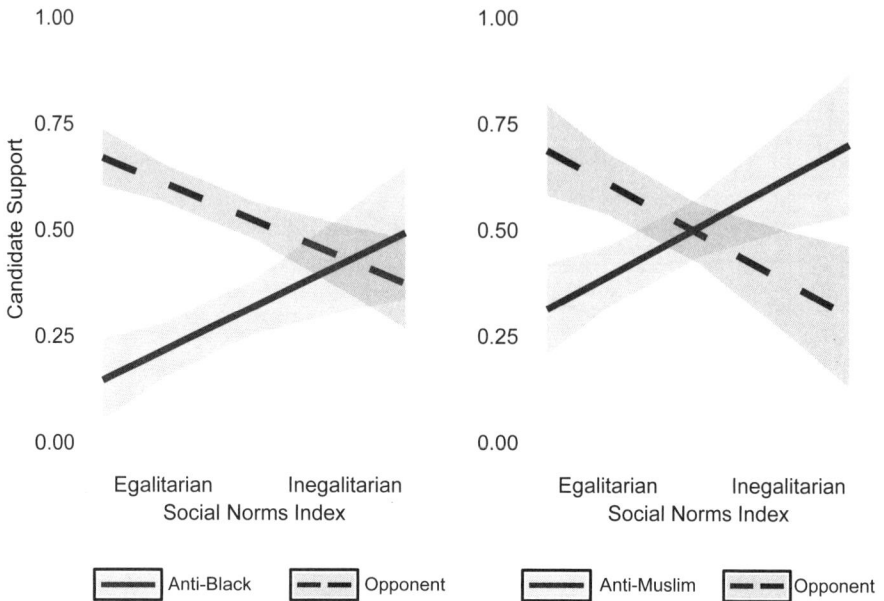

FIGURE 5.8. Marginal effects of the SNI on support for the anti-Black and anti-Muslim candidates and their opponents across two fictional Republican primary elections. Data from the October 2018 Lucid survey. Response options for the dependent variable in each model range from 0 to 1. Both models control for gender, education, age, and racial resentment. See appendix for full model results.

the anti-Black candidate. In both cases, the SNI helps explain support for the antiminority candidates.

The SNI also helps explain why the anti-Muslim candidate received so much more support from Republican voters than the anti-Black candidate. Among the most egalitarian Republicans, 16% said they would vote for the anti-Black candidate, while almost 32% said they would vote for the anti-Muslim candidate. On the other end of the spectrum, 51% of the most inegalitarian respondents said they would vote for the anti-Black candidate compared to 71% who said they would vote for the anti-Muslim candidate. In other words, the anti-Muslim candidate received higher levels of support across the full social norms spectrum than the anti-Black candidate.

In sum, social norms, as measured through the SNI, help explain who supports overt anti-Muslim appeals and who does not. In accordance with hypothesis 5.3, I found that respondents who adhere to inegalitarian norms are much more likely to support Islamophobic candidates than those who adhere to egalitarian norms. The results also explain why explicit anti-Muslim appeals and their messengers are more acceptable to Republican voters than candidates who use explicit anti-Black appeals. Figures 5.7 and 5.8 both show that respondents on the egalitarian end of the scale were far more likely to vote for the anti-Muslim candidates than the anti-Black candidates. Even though these respondents adhere to egalitarian norms, it does not appear that they view overt Islamophobia as a violation of these social norms as consistently as they view anti-Blackness as a norm violation. These findings bolster the assertion that Islamophobia has become normalized in contemporary US politics.

Conclusion

In the current political climate, salient minority groups are being rhetorically targeted frequently and overtly. Muslims in particular have become one of the most common targets of this messaging, which has led to more hate crimes targeting group members (Abdelkader 2016), increased fear and anxiety among Muslims (Lajevardi 2020), avoidance of public spaces among many in the community (Hobbs and Lajevardi 2019), and other harmful outcomes. The theory of differential norms shows that the factors necessary for the development of a norm of equality are missing. Furthermore, prominent inegalitarian signals from political institutions, social movements, and influential leaders in politics and the media, in conjunction with existing negative sentiments and feelings of threat from much of the public, have shifted the norm environment in an inegalitarian direction. Meanwhile, the norm of racial equality, however superficially held, continues to dictate norms of acceptable rhetoric toward Black Americans. Consequently, empirical findings show the public is more willing to accept overt Islamophobia and its messengers than overt racism and its messengers.

This is particularly true within the Republican Party and among individuals who adhere to inegalitarian norms. Indeed, Republican elites, conservative media, and right-wing activists have pushed norms in an inegalitarian direction. Experimental results provide evidence that Republicans are substantially more supportive of candidates who overtly derogate Muslims than they are of candidates who openly appeal to anti-Black sentiments. Republicans also accept overt Islamophobia more than

Democrats or Independents do. Moreover, respondents who subscribe to inegalitarian norms are substantially more likely to support candidates who utilize explicit prejudice than those who subscribe to egalitarian norms, and those who subscribe to inegalitarian norms find explicit Islamophobia more acceptable than explicit racism.

It is important to note that egalitarian norms can be developed. Evidence presented in this chapter shows that a norm of equality may be slowly developing within the Democratic Party. Indeed, I found that attitudes toward Muslim have become more positive in recent years among Democrats, Democratic elites are at times signaling support for equal rights for Muslims, and there has been some large public demonstrations opposing GOP efforts to restrict Muslim rights. Moreover, findings in chapter 7 show bipartisan messages condemning prejudice can neutralize Islamophobic messages in some situations. But in the long term, targeted elite messages, institutional support for groups' rights, and strong social movements are needed to develop a more stable norm of equality for Muslims.

This chapter showed that overt prejudicial political messages about a group for whom a norm of equality has not been developed will be accepted by the public. In several experimental tests, most Republican respondents supported the candidate espousing overt Islamophobia. Moreover, a policy that went so far as to say that Muslims are a "threat to the American way of life and need to be put under surveillance" received a great deal of support from Republicans. Although these candidates and policies received lower support from Democrats and Independents, support was still much higher than it was for similar candidates and policies that used overt anti-Black messaging. The next chapter examines a group, the LGBTQ+ community, for whom social norms of acceptable political rhetoric appear to be highly stratified and in flux.

CHAPTER SIX

Anti-LGBTQ+ Messaging and Political Evaluations

For many religious and political conservatives, the same-sex marriage issue has been largely decided—and for the American public, absolutely. That's not true when it comes to these transgender issues. Americans are much more divided, and this is an issue that can gain a lot more traction. —Kelsy Burke[1] (Nagourney and Peters 2023)

On June 26, 2015, the Supreme Court ruled in *Obergefell v. Hodges* that the fundamental right to marry is guaranteed to same-sex couples. The marriage equality decision enshrined a basic civil right for gay and lesbian couples and signaled to the American people that major political institutions value and seek to protect the community's rights. Millions across the country cheered the decision as a major step toward justice and equality for the LGBTQ+ community. *Obergefell v. Hodges* was the pinnacle of a slate of victories pro-equality activists and their allies had won in the Supreme Court and state and city legislatures in prior years. The decision was also partly the result of a rapid sea change in public opinion on marriage equality, which had shifted from being a minority position in the mid-2000s to a majority position (Michelson and Harrison 2020). Support for equal rights was rapidly increasing across most segments of society. Indeed, even within the Christian community, most Catholics and white mainline Protestants supported marriage equality (Pew Research Center 2019). During this period, support for gay and lesbian rights was being communicated not only by political institutions but also by prominent political elites, societal leaders, and the media (Garretson 2018; Kuhnhenn and Lerer 2015). Moreover, the Supreme Court had not only enshrined same-sex marriage but also legitimized it in the eyes of the public, making it riskier for groups to oppose it (see Tankard and Paluck 2017).

Yet, some influential groups balked at the Supreme Court's decision and vowed to continue opposing same-sex marriage and other LGBTQ+ rights. For example, a coalition of evangelical leaders issued a joint statement condemning the decision: "As evangelical Christians, we dissent from the Court's ruling that redefines marriage. The state did not create the family, and should not try to recreate the family in its own image. We will not capitulate on marriage because biblical authority requires that we cannot. The Supreme Court's actions pose incalculable risks to an already volatile social fabric by alienating those whose beliefs about marriage are motivated by deep biblical convictions and concern for the common good" (*Tampa Bay Times* 2015). Religious groups, particularly evangelical ones, were especially upset with the turn of events. For years, these groups had used the issue of same-sex marriage to galvanize supporters to vote, donate, and organize for socially conservative political candidates and causes. The decision also posed a major problem for the GOP as the evangelical voting bloc has been one of the most important interest groups in the party since the 1980s (see Balmer 2021). The Supreme Court had essentially removed from political contention a central mobilizing issue that evangelical groups and the GOP had long relied on to rally the base.

Evangelical and right-wing organizations were forced to search for a new cause to rally around. They needed an issue that would galvanize social conservatives without violating increasingly egalitarian social norms. As Terry Schilling, president of the right-wing super PAC American Principles Project put it: "We knew we needed to find an issue that the candidates were comfortable talking about. And we threw everything at the wall" (Nagourney and Peters 2023). To adapt to the new norm environment, they had two options. One option was to change the way they communicated their opposition to gay rights, akin to the way opponents of racial equality transitioned to more coded language to appeal to the anti-Black sentiments of their constituents following the civil rights movement. The second option was to find a new issue or group to demonize that was less protected by egalitarian norms. They found this new cause in opposition to transgender rights.

Modern opposition to transgender rights started with bathroom access and has morphed into an all-out assault on medical treatment, discussion of gender in public spaces, sports participation, and the very right for transgender people to exist. At least twenty states, all controlled by the GOP, have battled Democratic opposition and passed laws that restrict transgender rights since 2020. Prominent Republican leaders like Donald

Trump and Ron DeSantis have overtly and intensely supported these efforts. Indeed, this debate has become a central issue for evangelical groups and the GOP and a rallying cause for social conservatives in the ongoing culture war. Meanwhile, the Democratic Party, at least to an extent, has worked to defend LGBTQ+ rights. Democratic elites have rhetorically signaled their support for equal rights, blocked anti-LGBTQ+ bills in states they control, and tried to stop similar bills in states where they are in the minority. At the federal level, President Joe Biden signed the Respect for Marriage Act in 2022, which granted federal protections to same-sex and interracial couples. Every Democrat in the House and Senate supported the bill. This support is likely to continue: A record number of Democrats who identify with the LGBTQ+ community ran and won election in 2022 and 2024 (LGBTQ+ Victory Fund 2024).

The previous case studies presented in this book examined a group that had a developed norm of equality in principle (Black Americans) and a group that had a developed norm of inequality (Muslim Americans). I argue that there are so many competing signals of egalitarianism and inegalitarianism that the norms guiding messaging about the LGBTQ+ community are in a transitionary phase. The norm of equality, which was painstakingly won through the hard work of LGBTQ+ activists and their allies, is actively being destabilized. This norm also likely never internalized within large segments of the population who continued receiving signals of opposition to equal rights. Moreover, it is likely that egalitarian norms did not fully extend to all members within the broader LGBTQ+ community.

This leads to five related empirical expectations. First, similar to previous case studies, I expect norms to vary by political party. The GOP and conservative media are some of the primary drivers of anti-LGBTQ+ ideas and content, so I expect norms to be more inegalitarian within the GOP. Second, I expect norms to vary by religious group. Evangelical leaders are on the forefront of the anti-LGBTQ+ agenda, so I expect norms to be most inegalitarian within evangelical communities. Third, I expect variation among age cohorts. In this chapter, I trace the recent history of the factors that influence social norm development. After decades of political messaging being guided by a norm of inequality, factors that help develop norms of equality emerged in the 2000s and 2010s. The first few years of the 2020s have seen a reversal. Essentially, people in different age cohorts have received very different signals during their most impressionable years. For example, someone who was in school during the 1980s grew up in a much more overtly anti-LGBTQ+ environment than someone who was in school during the 2010s. Therefore, I expect younger people to be guided by more egalitarian norms than older people. Fourth, similar to previous chapters, I expect variance in support for anti-LGBTQ+ rhetoric across adherence to egalitarian/inegalitarian norms. Fifth, I expect antitransgender messaging to be more acceptable to the public than antigay or antilesbian messaging. Most of the political gains in recent decades, such as marriage equality, have furthered gay and lesbian rights specifically. Moreover, the primary focus of recent attacks from right-wing and religious groups has been on demonizing the transgender community.

Testing these hypotheses leads to six sets of empirical findings. First, results from a series of survey experiments show that, on average, the public accepts overt anti-LGBTQ+ campaign appeals and the candidates who use them. Second, Republicans support these messages more than Democrats and Independents. Third, evangelicals support candidates who use overt anti-LGBTQ+ messaging more than other religious respondents—and much more than nonreligious respondents. Fourth, there is some evidence of age variation, with older cohorts supporting anti-LGBTQ+ candidates somewhat more than younger cohorts. Fifth, respondents who adhere to inegalitarian norms are substantially more supportive of anti-LGBTQ+ candidates than respondents who adhere to egalitarian norms. Finally, antitransgender messaging is accepted at only slightly higher rates than antigay messaging. Antigay messaging is largely accepted, particularly among Republican, evangelical, and older respondents. I conclude the chapter with a discussion of the ways in which the effects of intense antitransgender opposition are spilling over into norms for the broader LGBTQ+ community.

Historical Development of Social Norms

High Levels of Threat and a Norm of Inequality

In 1977, the Dade County (Florida) Commission passed an antidiscrimination ordinance to protect gay and lesbian people. In reaction, Anita Bryant, a singer and born-again Christian, led a campaign to collect the signatures needed to put a repeal vote on the ballot. Five months after the ordinance passed, voters repealed it by a vote of almost two to one. Bryant used this momentum to create Save Our Children, a coalition that claimed to protect children from the alleged threat posed by gay and lesbian people. The coalition's central argument was: "Homosexuals cannot reproduce, so they must recruit. And to freshen their ranks, they must recruit the youth of America" (Duncan 2022). Buoyed by the success of Bryant's campaign in Miami, antigay activists worked to repeal similar antidiscrimination laws in cities across the US.

Bryant's campaign took place in a political and social atmosphere in which opposition to LGBTQ+ rights was commonplace. Police regularly raided gay and lesbian bars. Popular press referred to gay and lesbian people as "freaks" and "perverts," and movies and television shows either presented negative stereotypes of homosexuality or ignored the community altogether (see Steiner et al. 1993). The national news media described gay and lesbian people as threats to national security and public safety (see Bennett 1998). Politicians openly signaled their opposition to the community during this period, and state and federal legislation discriminated against LGBTQ+ Americans in employment, education, and health care. Government departments rooted out and fired gay and lesbian staff members as part of the so-called lavender scare (Domonoske 2017). Congress made its position clear when it published *Employment of Homosexuals and Other Sex Perverts in Government*, a report that urged the Civil Service Commission to root out and fire "moral perverts" from government positions (*PBS Frontline* n.d.).

The antigay movement intensified in the 1980s with the arrival of the AIDS epidemic. Organizations like the National Gay and Lesbian Task Force documented widespread violence and harassment targeting gay and lesbian individuals. A survey conducted in 1984 found that 94% of the 2,074 gay and lesbian people in the sample had experienced some form of physical or verbal abuse (Berrill 1990). The groundswell of fear and hatred toward the community was spurred on by influential right-wing leaders. In 1983, President Ronald Reagan's communications director, Pat Buchanan, referred to AIDS as "nature's revenge on gay men." Paul Cameron, an antigay extremist, suggested in remarks at the 1985 Conservative Political Action Conference that "the extermination of homosexuals" might be necessary to combat the AIDS epidemic. In 1989, Republican US Representative William Dannemeyer published *Shadow in the Land: Homosexuality in America*, which called gay and lesbian people "the ultimate enemy." Other members of Congress and the Reagan administration made remarks casting AIDS as a "gay disease" that people contracted because of immoral lifestyle choices (Green 2011).

Right-wing affiliated antigay groups began playing a larger role in politics during this period as well. Moral Majority, an organization founded by

Jerry Falwell, worked to elect right-wing Christian politicians and made a "declaration of war" against homosexuality. Other organizations like the Coalition on Revival and the American Center for Law and Justice were founded to oppose gay rights. Political institutions also continued to curtail the rights of gay and lesbian people. In 1982, the Department of Defense removed thousands of gay troops from service because of its stance that homosexuality was incompatible with military service. A few years later, the Supreme Court held that state antisodomy laws were constitutional in *Bowers v. Hardwick*. In sum, prominent elites, political institutions, the media, and organized social groups were sending clear signals of opposition to equal rights for gay and lesbian people and constructing narratives of threat. In *The Homosexual in America*, one of the most influential works of the gay rights movement, Donald Webster Cory (1951, 15) aptly summed up the pervading norms of inequality: "It is apparent that condemnation of homosexuality is today almost universal. . . . Occasionally one encounters an attitude not so much of tolerance but of actual acceptance, but this is rare. . . . The basic problem is the hostile spirit pervading even the more permissive of modern people."

The Push for Equality

Although a norm of inequality was pervasive, the modern gay rights movement also got its start during this period as gay rights activists mobilized in response to rampant injustice. For example, historian Julio Capo Jr. said this about the influence of Anita Bryant's campaign on LGBTQ+ activism: "It was transformative. It got people to see themselves as a voting bloc" (Eugenios 2022). Gay and lesbian advocacy organizations like the Mattachine Society and the Daughters of Bilitis formed in the 1950s. They were followed by many similar organizations across the country that organized know-your-rights trainings, demonstrations, and lectures in support of gay rights; and provided safe spaces at a time when homosexual activity was illegal in most states. The mobilization and activism of these organizations helped start the nationwide movement for gay rights.

The Stonewall Uprising in 1969 was a watershed moment for the movement. A routine police raid of the Stonewall Inn, a gay bar in New York City's Greenwich Village, turned into a multinight uprising. Bar patrons and allied community members resisted police action by chanting, singing, and throwing pennies and beer bottles at police vehicles. The revolt lasted six nights, with thousands of activists and allies participating. Although earlier acts of resistance garnered little media attention, the events at Stonewall were covered in *The New York Times*, *New York Post*, and *Daily News*. Though not the first instance of resistance to police action, Stonewall served as a catalyst for the movement. Many gay rights organizations were created soon after, and America's first gay pride parade was held on the one-year anniversary of the uprising. Prominent activist Frank Kameny said this about its legacy: "By the time of Stonewall, we had fifty to sixty gay groups in the country. A year later there was at least fifteen hundred. By two years later, to the extent that a count could be made, it was twenty-five hundred. And that was the impact of Stonewall" (NYC LGBT Historic Sites Project 2021).

This rise in activism was accelerated by the growing AIDS crisis in the 1980s. While conservatives and the religious Right were using the epidemic to openly express bigotry and hostility, gay rights activists and organizations pressured the media to cover the crisis and pressured the government to respond appropriately to it. This laid the groundwork for a period during which the gay rights movement precipitated major changes in public attitudes toward the community, achieved prominent political victories, and transformed the media and political environment.

Indeed, media representation of the community increased dramatically in the 1990s and 2000s, highlighted by popular shows like *Ellen*, *Will and Grace*, and *Queer Eye for the Straight Guy*. Exposure to these shows and other on-screen depictions of gay and lesbian characters is associated with support for equal rights (see Bond and Compton 2015). The news media also began covering LGBTQ+ issues more frequently than in the past (see Bennett 1998; Chomsky and Barclay 2013). Media portrayals of a community, however imperfect, can make audiences more familiar with it and allay feelings of threat toward the group.

Politicians and political institutions, pressured by gay rights activists, began supporting equal rights efforts. In 2003, the Supreme Court deemed sodomy laws unconstitutional in *Lawrence v. Texas*. At the time, such laws were in place in fourteen states. Several prominent politicians overtly signaled their support for marriage equality, including some who had previously been opposed. In his 2004 senatorial run and 2008 presidential run, Barack Obama opposed same-sex marriage. But in 2012, Obama made it clear that he fully supported marriage equality for gay and lesbian Americans, becoming the first sitting president to publicly do so. Similarly, Hillary Clinton, who in 1996 had supported the Defense of Marriage Act (DOMA), said in 2011, "Gay rights are human rights, and human rights are gay rights" (Kuhnhenn and Lerer 2015). Many other prominent Democrats, including Joe Biden, Bill Clinton, Jimmy Carter, Al Gore, and Michelle Obama, also publicly supported marriage equality. Almost every Democrat in the US Senate endorsed marriage equality, and so did several Republican senators. During the 1990s and 2000s, Americans received signals of support for gay rights from a robust social movement, political institutions like the Supreme Court and Congress, prominent politicians, and the media. In short, many of the factors necessary to shift norms in an egalitarian direction were present.

Consequently, public support for gay rights increased dramatically from the late 1980s to the 2010s. For example, 65% of parents in 1985 said they would be very upset if their child said they were lesbian or gay and only 8% said they would not be upset. By 2013, only 19% of parents said they would be very upset and a majority said they would not be upset (Garretson 2018). Another measure found that support for allowing a book about homosexuality in one's community library increased from 58% in 1988 to 78% in 2012 (Garretson 2018). A variety of opinion polls show similarly large increases in support for employment nondiscrimination, equal employment opportunities, and same-sex adoption rights. Indeed, public support for political, economic, and civil rights for gay and lesbian people improved across the board over those decades.

Same-sex marriage is one of the clearest examples of increased public and institutional support for equality. In the 1990s, many gay rights activists and organizations coalesced around marriage equality as a central cause. The movement dramatically increased public support for the issue. Only 27% of the public supported same-sex marriage when DOMA, which restricted the definition of marriage to exclude same-sex couples, was enacted in 1996. Nationwide support surpassed 50% in 2011 and increased further to 70% by 2021, according to Gallup polls (Brenan 2024). The movement won a major institutional victory in 2003 when Massachusetts became the first state to legalize same-sex marriage. Over the next twelve years, thirty-five states and Washington, DC legalized same-sex marriage through court rulings, legislation, referenda, or ballot initiatives. In 2013, the US Supreme Court struck down DOMA in *United States v. Windsor*. Finally, in 2015, the Supreme Court ruled that same-sex couples have the same fundamental right to marriage as do opposite-sex couples in *Obergefell v. Hodges*. Much of the egalitarian shift in norms can be attributed to these wins for the movement, particularly the landmark 2015 Supreme Court case. Indeed, the ruling is associated with a significant increase in perceived support for gay marriage among the American public and the belief that support for gay marriage in the US will continue to increase in the future (Tankard and Paluck 2017). These shifts matter because perceptions of social norms influence behavior. In other words, if an individual believes support for gay rights is high, then their behavior is likely to conform to that norm regardless of their actual attitudes toward the group. Over time, the norm can internalize within individuals and change mass attitudes.

Garretson (2018) argued that the massive attitude change over this time period was caused by a multistep process precipitated by the concerted efforts of gay rights activists. First came increased activism in response to the AIDS crisis. Gay rights activists and organizations strategically targeted key political and media elites to gain institutional support for gay and lesbian rights and to normalize media coverage of the AIDS crisis and other issues affecting the community. These institutional changes "encouraged lesbians and gays to 'come out' en masse" (6). As a result, much of the public had greater exposure to gay and lesbian people through the media and interpersonally. Garretson further argued that signals supporting gay and lesbian rights from political elites and greater media exposure directly caused some of the attitudinal shifts in support for the community; but it was increased interpersonal exposure to gay and lesbian people that was the primary cause of the broad, rapid, and durable support for equal rights. In short, the push for equality was mass driven; but it was the mutually reinforcing efforts of activism and elite signals that transformed the landscape of gay and lesbian rights.

In other words, a norm of equality for gay and lesbian people developed through a mutually reinforcing relationship between gay rights activists, influential elites, and mass attitudes. Gay rights activists buoyed support for equal rights and led more gay and lesbian people to come out publicly. As members of the community came out "en masse," interpersonal exposure to gay and lesbian people greatly increased, which further improved public attitudes toward the community. The work of activists and advocacy organizations also influenced political, media, and cultural elites, and political institutions, to signal commitments to gay and lesbian rights, which helped mainstream support for the community and develop a norm of equality.

Reversion to Inequality

Though support for gay rights increased dramatically in the 1990s and 2000s, opposition remained strong among some segments of the population, most notably among Republicans and conservative Christians. Soon after *Lawrence v. Texas*, President George W. Bush publicly opposed marriage equality and endorsed a proposed constitutional amendment that would have defined marriage as between a man and a woman. Bush's sentiments were echoed throughout the GOP. In 2014, just one year before the Supreme Court's decision on marriage equality, only four of the 234 Republicans in the House of Representatives endorsed same-sex marriage (Garretson 2018). After *Obergefell v. Hodges*, right-wing Christian groups worked to pass religious freedom laws to allow Christians to refuse services to same-sex couples and allow certain forms of discrimination against members of the LGBTQ+ community (see Wilcox 2020). Even during a period that saw important advances in equal rights, the public was receiving mixed signals from leaders and institutions regarding their support for gay rights. Thus, it is likely that egalitarian norms never internalized within groups like the GOP and the evangelical community.

Moreover, after settling on opposition to transgender rights as a new central issue, the political prominence of anti-LGBTQ+ opposition increased dramatically. Similar to how the marriage equality movement pushed norms in an egalitarian direction, the current anti-LGBTQ+ movement is destabilizing this norm by signaling intense public opposition to equality. Across several measures, the LGBTQ+ community, particularly the transgender community, has again become a primary target of the right wing in recent years. Anti-LGBTQ+ demonstrations doubled in 2022 from 2021, and politically violent acts targeting the community more than tripled (S. Jones and Kishi 2022). Much of the rise in anti-LGBTQ+ mobilization has been led by far-right militia groups like the Proud Boys and Patriot Front. Indeed, anti-LGBTQ+ mobilization was the second biggest focus of far-right protest activity in 2022, after white supremacy / white nationalism (Armed Conflict Location and Event Data Project 2022). This trend shows no sign of abating. Anti-LGBTQ+ demonstrations continued in 2023 and 2024, targeting drag queen story hours, drag shows, and other similar events.

Fox News, one of the primary influencers of Republicans, strongly and frequently denigrates the LGBTQ+ community. For example, Fox News anchors verbally attacked the community at least once on 106 of the first 181 days of 2022, including twenty-six of the thirty days during Pride Month in June, according to a report published by Media Matters (Paterson 2022). The attacks focused on the transgender community, referring to gender-affirming health care as "child abuse," misgendering transgender people, and pushing the grooming theory. Fox News is able to influence the norm environment for several reasons. First, Fox News has a large platform. Fox News regularly and decisively outpaces CNN and MSNBC in average viewers and viewers during prime time (T. Johnson 2023). Second, Fox News has a dedicated audience that tends to be influenced by the content it receives.[2] Consistent signals of support for inequality from Fox News hosts contributes to the destabilization of any existing norm of equality for the LGBTQ+ community.

The villainization of the transgender community is part of a broader pattern of anti-LGBTQ+ messaging coming from right-wing media. Following a mass shooting at a school in Tennessee in March 2023, right-wing media used the shooter's reported transgender identity to create a narrative that transgender people are a threat to society. Tucker Carlson, who at the time was still a Fox News host, reported a conspiracy theory that "trans radical activists" were planning violence against Christian people. Members of other right-wing media outlets like The Daily Wire, Newsmax, and Infowars, as well as right-wing activists and podcast hosts joined in the attack on the transgender community (Kleefeld and Hagle 2023). One of the most direct statements came from Benny Johnson (2023), a conservative news columnist and chief creative officer at the right-wing organization Turning Point USA: "One thing is *very* clear: the modern trans movement is radicalizing activists into terrorists." This is far from an isolated incident (see Nirappil 2023). Right-wing media, political, and cultural leaders have a history of villainizing and dehumanizing members of the LGBTQ+ community, particularly transgender people. Right-wing elites have, without any evidence, blamed several other mass shootings on transgender people and encouraged their audiences to harass healthcare workers for providing gender-affirming care and to disrupt drag shows (Knefel 2022).

Republican politicians have also signaled their opposition to equality by communicating harmful stereotypes and endorsing antitransgender legislation. In the final weeks before election day in 2022, Republican candidates, party organizations, and affiliated political action committees spent more than $50 million on political ads and direct mail that included antitransgender messaging in at least twenty-five states (HRC 2022a). One of these ads, run by the American Principles Project, showed transgender people's surgery scars and accused Democrats of "pushing transgender drugs and surgeries on kids." It was not just fringe candidates who used such rhetoric. Mainstream Republican candidates have also been using explicit antitransgender messaging. Senator Marco Rubio, a prominent

Republican and former presidential candidate, spent more money on anti-transgender campaign advertising than any other candidate, according to a report from the Human Rights Campaign (HRC 2022a). Some states, like Texas, even included this rhetoric directly in their party platforms. The GOP doubled down on this strategy in 2024, spending tens of millions of dollars on antitransgender ads in the presidential race and in key Senate and House races in more than a dozen states (Goldmacher 2024). Indeed, an enduring image of the election is Trump's ad "Kamala is for they/them, President Trump is for you," which accused Harris of supporting government-funded gender-affirming care for prisoners.

Not only have right-wing elites rhetorically signaled their antitransgender stances, but Republican lawmakers have also targeted the community through legislation. Republicans in thirty-five state legislatures have introduced more than eight hundred bills since 2022 aimed at curtailing the rights of the transgender community. Many of these bills were enacted, and many more are working their way through the legislative process. These include laws that prohibit gender-affirming care for adolescents and adults, bathroom bans, restrictions on changing birth certificates, and laws that rigidly define sex in a way that erases transgender people from legal codes (Reed 2023a). The number of anti-LGBTQ+ bills introduced in state legislatures has increased every year since 2018, when a relatively low forty-one such bills were introduced.

The same process that can help develop a norm of equality can also push norms in an inegalitarian direction. Some of the most influential right-wing elites are spreading antitransgender tropes and conspiracy theories and even promoting violence toward the community. An increasingly active antitransgender movement forcefully signals opposition to equal rights from a large and vocal segment of the public. Moreover, the plethora of antitransgender legislation being introduced and passed in states across the country signals institutional opposition to equal rights.

As discussed in chapter 4, modern objections to Black rights tend to be coded. Rather than being overt, anti-Blackness is generally expressed as opposition to the Black Lives Matter movement and wokeness, and through anti-CRT and anti-DEI efforts. In contrast, modern opposition to LGBTQ+ rights is very explicit. This is particularly true of antitransgender messaging coming from Republican elites, conservative activists, and right-wing media. Anti-LGBTQ+ mobilization efforts from far-right groups are overt in their attacks on the community on the basis of sexual orientation and gender identity rather than being filtered through coded issues.

Findings from the 2022 US Transgender Survey, conducted by the National Center for Transgender Equality, capture many of the detrimental effects of the antitransgender movement (see Murib 2024). Among the 92,329 people in the sample, 44% said they had experienced "serious psychological distress in the last thirty days." Of sixteen- and seventeen-year-old respondents, 60% said they had been mistreated at school including verbal and physical harassment and online bullying. Almost half of the respondents in the survey (47%) said they had considered moving to another state because of the discriminatory actions of their state legislatures; 5% had actually moved. The actions of politicians, political institutions, right-wing media, and anti-LGBTQ+ activists are having clear, disastrous effects on the health and well-being of transgender people.

Despite the onslaught of the antitransgender movement, efforts to promote and reinforce norms of equality continue. These actions help counter the overt attacks on the transgender community. In 2023, thousands of people gathered in almost two hundred events across the US on Transgender Day of Visibility (TDOV). According to a report from the Crowd Counting Consortium, an organization that tracks political demonstrations in the US, it was "almost certainly the largest and broadest celebration of TDOV in history" (Ulfelder 2023b). Other nationwide events like Trans Day of Resistance and the March for Queer and Trans Youth Autonomy brought thousands to the streets to resist the attacks on LGBTQ+ rights. These events are part of a larger wave of pro-LGBTQ+ activism. According to another report from Crowd Counting Consortium, there were more than 160 pro-LGBTQ+ demonstrations nationwide per month during the twelve-month period from March 2022 through February 2023 (Ulfelder 2023a).

This timeline indicates that decades of intense and widespread opposition to gay and lesbian rights were followed by a period of advancement in equal rights. Then, during the last several years, right-wing Christian groups and the GOP have again made the LGBTQ+ community a primary political target, with a particular focus on opposing transgender rights. Consequently, there are several reasons to expect identifiable variation in norms of acceptable political rhetoric targeting the LGBTQ+ community. First, clear battle lines have been drawn. Republican elites, conservative media, far-right activists, and right-wing evangelical leaders are actively working to destabilize recently developed egalitarian norms and move them in an inegalitarian direction. Similar to discussions in previous chapters, these groups meet the criteria for group norm development. One, Republicans and evangelicals have established communication avenues that they have leveraged to signal opposition to LGBTQ+ rights. Two, both groups are relatively cohesive and members of both groups have maintained negative views of the LGBTQ+ community, even in times of egalitarian norms. Three, inegalitarian norms are clearly important to both groups as tools to mobilize their bases. Meanwhile, Democrats are following the lead of LGBTQ+ activists in resisting the right-wing campaign against transgender rights. The Democratic Party also has established communication avenues and its membership is relatively cohesive in their support of LGBTQ+ rights. There are also signs that a norm of equality is growing in importance for the party—particularly with LGBTQ+ individuals becoming a larger proportion of the party's voting base and elected officials.

Second, socialization is likely playing an important role in the fractioning of the norm environment. Younger people, who grew up in a political environment that saw important gains in gay and lesbian rights, are more likely to have internalized egalitarian norms than older people, who grew up in an environment that was more overtly hostile to the LGBTQ+ community. Third, norms may be stratified within the broader LGBTQ+ community. The major victories for equality discussed in this chapter have centered on gay and lesbian rights. In contrast, the current onslaught of anti-LGBTQ+ attacks has been primarily focused on the transgender community. Thus, it is possible that norms of acceptable rhetoric are different when transgender people are the subject of the antiminority message than when gay and lesbian people are its subject. Alternatively, the effects of antitransgender attacks may be spilling over into the norms that guide all forms of anti-LGBTQ+ rhetoric. In the next section, I formalize these theoretical expectations into empirical hypotheses.

Hypothesis Development

Partisan Variations in Norm Adherence

Resistance to egalitarian norms is taking place almost exclusively within the Republican Party and right-wing politics. Erin Reed, an independent journalist and prominent activist, constructed a legislative risk map that tracks the introduction and passage of antitransgender legislation in state legislatures (Reed 2023a). Her map shows a stark partisan split. Fourteen states were categorized as "worst states" or "high-risk states" because they had already passed harmful antitransgender laws and were likely to pass additional discriminatory legislation. Thirteen of the fourteen states were under full Republican control, while Kansas had split government. Meanwhile, fourteen other states and Washington, DC were categorized as "most protective" because they had "safeguarded the rights and well-being of transgender individuals." All these states except Vermont were under full Democratic control. Democrats are passing legislation in states where they have majorities to protect transgender rights and using tactics like the filibuster to block antitransgender legislation in GOP-controlled states like Nebraska. As of October 2024, 673 anti-LGBTQ+ bills had either passed into law or were advancing through state legislatures during the 2024 legislative session.[3] Almost all these bills were coming from Republican-led legislatures. In short, there are clear partisan differences: The Republican Party is leading the charge to curtail LGBTQ+ rights, and Democrats are generally working to protect the community's rights.

While Republican elites across the country are using antitransgender rhetoric in their campaigns and introducing antitransgender legislation, Democrats are taking a different tack. The LGBTQ+ community gained major victories in the 2022 midterm election, including electing the first out lesbian governors and the first out transgender man to win a state legislative race (Chen 2022). Each of these candidates ran as a Democrat. Indeed, a report from the LGBTQ+ Victory Fund found that at least 1,065 LGBTQ+ individuals ran for office in 2022 from all fifty US states. More than 89% of these candidates ran as Democrats; only 4.5% ran as Republicans (LGBTQ+ Victory Fund 2022). In sum, we should expect Republicans to be much more open to anti-LGBTQ+ messaging than Democrats.

Hypothesis 6.1. Candidates who use explicit anti-LGBTQ+ campaign appeals will receive higher levels of support from Republicans than from Democrats or Independents.

Religious Variations in Norm Adherence

In March 2023, *Mother Jones* published a report describing leaked emails from a secret group behind many of the antitransgender laws being introduced in state legislatures across the country (Pauly 2023). The group consisted of legislators, doctors, and members of various right-wing anti-LGBTQ+ organizations. A notable aspect of the emails was their religious overtones. Many of the emails included phrases like "under His wings," "praise God," and "the Devil never sleeps." Thomas Lecaque, an expert on apocalyptic religion and political violence, said after reading the emails: "It is the language of Christian nationalism. It is the language of those who very much believe they are doing God's will, and it is the language of people who very much believe they are engaged in a holy war" (Zoledziowski 2023). Religious leaders, particularly evangelical leaders, are at the forefront of contemporary opposition to transgender rights.

This is a recent example in a long history of religious-based opposition to LGBTQ+ rights. Christian right-wing groups have long been on the forefront of the anti-LGBTQ+ movement through groups like the Moral Majority and Focus on the Family. For example, the Alliance Defense Fund, a coalition of thirty-five Christian right-wing groups, has led legal challenges to LGBTQ rights to military service, marriage, adoption, foster parenting, and domestic partner benefits (SPLC 2005). Right-wing Christian groups have also been central to political actions opposing the extension of hate crime laws, public health initiatives, and many other rights to the LGBTQ+ community (see Sherkat 2019). Even during periods of advancing rights, many religious leaders have continued to oppose equality, particularly leaders within the evangelical Christian community. Opposition from religious leaders likely wields enormous influence on the views of their congregants and on the social norms within their congregations. Thus, I expect evangelicals to be much more accepting of anti-LGBTQ+ messaging than nonevangelicals.

Hypothesis 6.2. Evangelical respondents will be more likely to accept overt anti-LGBTQ+ political messaging than respondents who identify with other religious denominations or who identify as nonreligious.

Age Variation in Norm Adherence

Another way of viewing differences in norm adherence is by age. The recent advances in rights following a long period of inegalitarian norms placed norms in a transitionary phase. As the norm environment shifted for the LGBTQ+ community, the perception and internalization of the norm among individuals shifted along with it. But this process does not happen at the same rate for all people in society. Young people are generally most receptive to shifts in norms for several reasons. First, young people have spent less time in the old norm environment, so the old norm is less likely to have internalized for them. Second, young people's political and social attitudes tend to be less crystallized than those of older people, so their attitudes are more receptive to change. Third, young people often have high needs of social acceptance, which can lead them to follow social norms more closely (e.g., Zhang et al. 2016). Fourth, childhood is a crucial period of identity development for most people, which can strongly influence both intergroup attitudes and norm adherence (e.g., Henry and Sears 2009). For example, white people who grew up during the civil rights movement more strongly supported interracial marriage and desegregation than their counterparts who grew up prior to shifts in racial norms (Schuman et al. 1997). Over time, racial norms internalized for the entire population, but it happened more quickly for young people.

In the 2000s and 2010s, a strong social movement signaled deeply held support for LGBTQ+ rights. Prominent institutional decisions like *Lawrence v. Texas* and *Obergefell v. Hodges* showed that political institutions were invested in expanding equal rights. News and entertainment media provided more frequent and more positive portrayals of the LGBTQ+ community. Political elites, particularly Democrats, overtly signaled their support for equal rights. These factors combined to shift social norms in an egalitarian direction. There is some evidence that the shift in norms influenced young people more than older people. For example, from 2005 to 2015, as the movement for marriage equality heated up, support for same-sex marriage increased much more quickly among younger generations than among older generations (Pew Research Center 2019). Moreover, younger people are substantially more likely to identify as members of the LGBTQ+ community than older people and are more likely to interact with LGBTQ+ individuals (Doherty 2022). I argue that egalitarian norms have internalized among young people, for whom these events are more central to their socialization, more strongly than among older people. This should lead younger people to be less accepting of the overt anti-LGBTQ+ messaging that has dominated the political landscape in recent years.

Hypothesis 6.3. Younger people will be less accepting than older people of overt anti-LGBTQ+ political messaging.

Social Norms

Each of the hypotheses presented so far posit variance in the extent to which egalitarian/inegalitarian norms have engrained in various groups. I hypothesized that norms regarding the LGBTQ+ community have developed in a more inegalitarian way within the Republican Party and the evangelical community compared to the Democratic Party and other religious/nonreligious communities. Moreover, I hypothesized that egalitarian norms have internalized within younger generations more so than older generations. Similarly, we should see variance in acceptance of anti-LGBTQ+ messaging at the individual level across levels of adherence to generalized egalitarian/inegalitarian norms.

In previous chapters, I argued that the social norms index (SNI) should be applicable to antiminority messaging regardless of subject group because of the strong tendency for an individual who is prejudiced against one group to be prejudiced against other groups as well. Though the process of othering is unique for each minority group, as should be evident by the processes detailed in each of the case study chapters, the underlying mechanisms of out-group animus may be similar, and political messaging about each group is likely guided by a similar set of egalitarian/inegalitarian norms.

Hypothesis 6.4. Respondents who score high on the SNI (i.e., adhere to inegalitarian norms) will be most likely to support candidates who use explicit anti-LGBTQ+ appeals, and those who score low on the SNI (i.e., adhere to egalitarian norms) will be least likely to support these candidates.

The T in LGBTQ

The first four hypotheses posit identifiable variation in norm adherence among the public. I also argue that there are likely separate norms guiding rhetoric about different segments of the community. In examining the advances in equal rights for the LGBTQ+ community, it is important to note that some constituents have benefited more than others. Movements to combat the AIDS epidemic, repeal sodomy laws, and pass marriage equality centered on gay and lesbian rights. In other words, the factors that develop egalitarian norms discussed earlier in the chapter are both recent and not equally applicable to all segments of the LGBTQ+ community. These rights can spill over to other members of the broader LGBTQ+ community but, other segments of the community, like transgender people, have seen fewer advances in rights that are specific to them. As such, egalitarian norms guiding rhetoric for transgender people probably did not develop as strongly as they did for gay and lesbian people.

It is also true that many of the political attacks in recent years have targeted transgender people. The American Civil Liberties Union's report on the dramatic rise in anti-LGBTQ+ legislation shows that most of these bills target the transgender community. Many of the bills restrict transgender athletes from participating in sports that are consistent with their gender identities. The public seems to support these bans. A poll conducted in May 2021 by Gallup found that 62% of US adults, including 86% of Republicans, believed transgender athletes should only be allowed to play on sports teams that match the gender assigned to them at birth and not be allowed to play on teams that match their gender identity (McCarthy 2021). Other bills aim to deny gender-affirming care for transgender youth and ban transition care for transgender adults.

Right-wing activists are also targeting the transgender community in ways that are overtly hostile. For example, Michael Knowles, a conservative commentator with The Daily Wire, said, "Transgender people . . . is not a legitimate category of being" (Media Matters for America 2023). This kind of openly discriminatory rhetoric is coming from fringe members of the far right, like Pastor Mark Burns who said, "There's no such thing as trans kids, only abusive parents [who should be] in jail for abusing their child's minds" (Padgett 2023). It is also coming from more mainstream members of the Republican Party, like Candace Owens, who called transgender people "hateful, narcissistic human beings" (Drennen 2023b), and Charlie Kirk, who has called for violence against transgender people (Reed 2023b). It is possible that separate norms are emerging, or have already emerged, for transgender people and other groups within the LGBTQ+ community. Indeed, transphobia appears to be driving much of the rise in anti-LGBTQ+ political behavior.

Fox News has been one of the primary drivers of transphobic rhetoric. Using the Global Database of Events, Language, and Tone Project's TV News Archive, I analyzed the use of "transgender" and related search terms in Fox News broadcasts from June 5, 2009, to April 25, 2023.[4] Prior to 2022, there were only four months when the search terms were used more than 200 times in broadcasts. Starting January 2022, almost every month reached at least 200, topping out at 951 in April 2023. The vast majority of these mentions came from *Tucker Carlson Tonight*, *The Ingraham Angle*, and *Hannity*, all prime-time shows that were among the most highly rated on the network. This trend is also different from Fox News coverage of other groups within the LGBTQ+ community. The terms "gay," "lesbian," "bisexual," "queer," and "homosexual" had very little airtime over the last five years.[5] Indeed, in March 2023 when transgender and related search terms were used 788 times, these other terms were only used 132 times combined. Figure 6.1 displays these results. It is reasonable

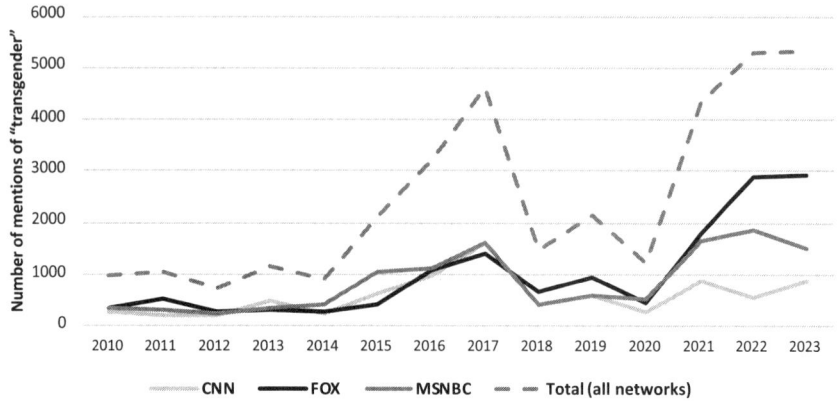

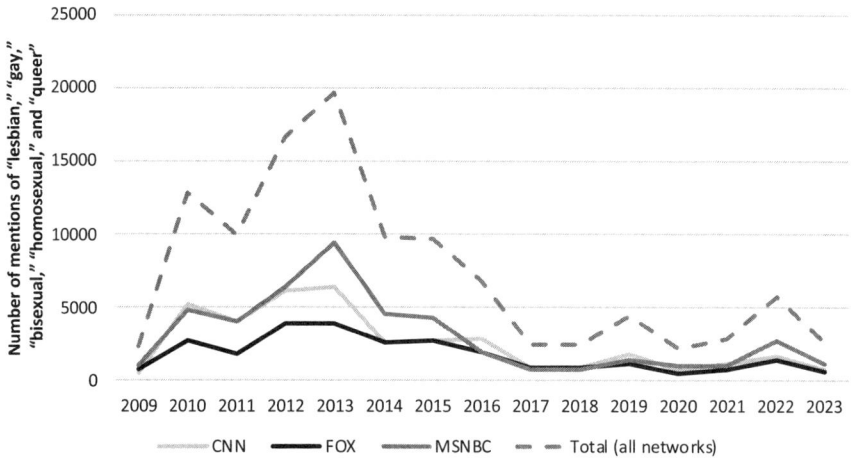

FIGURE 6.1. Fox News, CNN, and MSNBC coverage from 2009 to 2023 of *(top)* transgender mentions; and *(bottom)* lesbian, gay, bisexual, homosexual, and queer mentions. Data from the TV News Archive.

to conclude from this evidence that antitransgender messaging during this political moment is likely more acceptable to the public than antigay messaging.

Hypothesis 6.5. Antitransgender political messaging will be accepted at higher rates than antigay political messaging.

Hypothesis Testing

Testing Variation in Public Responses to Anti-LGBTQ+ Messaging

Hypothesis 6.1 posits that norms have developed within the GOP differently than within the Democratic Party. As one piece of evidence for this, a plethora of survey data show that Republicans are much less supportive than Democrats of LGBTQ+ rights. A survey conducted by YouGov in April 2022 asked 1,000 US adult citizens a series of questions about their views of components of Florida's "Don't Say Gay" law (YouGov 2022). Figure 6.2 shows the partisan differences in responses to these questions. Republican respondents were much more supportive (61%) than Democrats (35%) of banning public school teachers from providing classroom instruction on sexual orientation and gender identity. Republicans were also much more supportive (75%) than Democrats (29%) of allowing parents to sue a school district if they believe instruction on sexual orientation and gender identity is not age appropriate.

The survey also asked respondents their views about a set of hypothetical classroom scenarios. Among Republicans, 67% thought it was inappropriate for a teacher to display a photo of their same-sex spouse on their desk, 78% thought it was inappropriate for a teacher to tell students they recently married someone of the same gender, and 84% thought it was inappropriate for a teacher to read students a book about a child who has a crush on another child of the same gender. Democrats were 38 to 53 percentage points less likely to deem each of these scenarios inappropriate. Some of these results are likely driven by belief in the unfounded school grooming theory. Indeed, 48% of Republican respondents in the survey thought it was definitely or probably true that "Gay and lesbian public school teachers are trying to recruit children to the gay and lesbian lifestyle and prey on them sexually." Only 20% of Republicans said this was definitely false. In comparison, 16% of Democrats believed the grooming conspiracy to be definitely or probably true.

Across all the measures presented, Republicans were much less supportive than Democrats of LGBTQ+ rights and much more likely to believe a prominent anti-LGBTQ+ conspiracy theory. My expectation is that Republicans should also be more supportive of candidates who engage in anti-LGBTQ+ campaign messaging. To test this hypothesis, I collected a sample of 4,074 adult US residents in June 2023 through the survey firm

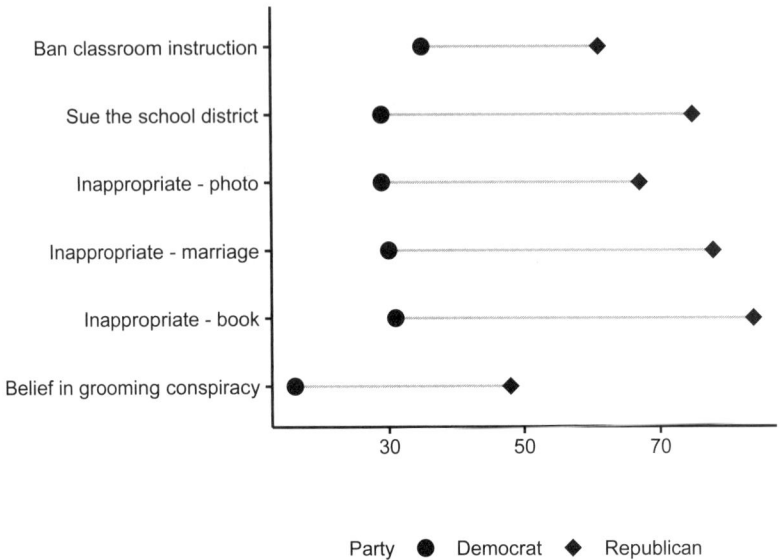

FIGURE 6.2. Partisan differences in support for LGBTQ+ rights. Data from the 2022 YouGov survey.

Lucid.[6] I embedded an experiment in the survey to test the effect of overt antigay and antitransgender campaign appeals on voters' evaluation of political candidates and public policies. Respondents in the control condition were shown this information about Peter Miller, a fictional member of the US House of Representatives:

> Next, you will be shown information about a member of the US House of Representatives and asked to evaluate the politician. Representative Peter Miller has proposed the Protect Parental Rights in Education Act. The bill would require school districts to notify parents of all reading material used in classroom instruction and allow parents to opt their child out of any reading material that the parent believes is "age-inappropriate" for their child. In support of his bill, Miller said, "We will stand up for the rights of parents and the fundamental role they play in the education of their children."

Respondents in the first treatment condition (T1), which I will refer to as the antitransgender condition, were shown the same information, but with an overt antitransgender framing substituted at the end:

In support of his bill, Miller said, "We will stand up for the rights of parents and the fundamental role they play in the education of their children by helping them protect their children from the immorality of transgenderism."

In treatment 2 (T2), "transgenderism" was replaced by "homosexuality," allowing me to test the difference between antigay and antitransgender political messaging. I will refer to this as the antigay treatment condition.

Respondents in each experimental condition were then asked a series of questions about the proposed policy and the politician. First, respondents were asked how much they supported or opposed the Protect Parental Rights in Education Act. Second, they were told Representative Miller was up for reelection in 2024 and asked how likely they would be to vote for him if they lived in his district. Third, they were asked how much Representative Miller represented their interests.

Figure 6.3 shows that, overall, there was no statistically significant difference in support for the policy when it was framed as antitransgender (T1) or antigay (T2) rather than framed around parental rights (control). However, there were large differences in policy support within partisan groups. Among the 499 Republicans in the antitransgender condition, 77% said they supported the policy. Among the 521 Republicans in the control group, 71% supported the policy. This difference is statistically significant at the $p < .05$ level according to a two-sample t-test. Among the 493 Republicans in the antigay condition, 75% reported that they supported the policy, which is also statistically significantly different from the control group ($p < .05$). Republican identifiers supported the Protect Parental Rights in Education Act more when it was framed as antitransgender or antigay.

Among Independents, there was no difference in support between the control group and T1, the antitransgender condition. About 49% of Independent respondents supported the policy in each. However, 43% of Independents supported the policy in T2, the antigay condition, which is a statistically significant decrease from the control and antitransgender groups ($p < .05$). The framing of the policy as antitransgender or antigay also seemed to bifurcate Independents. In the control group, only 15% of Independents opposed the policy. Opposition increased to 19% in T1 and 23% in T2. Democrats were least supportive of the policy in each experimental group. However, there was no statistically significant difference in their support for the policy based on how it was framed: 44% of Democrats in the control group, 42% of Democrats in T1, and 43% of

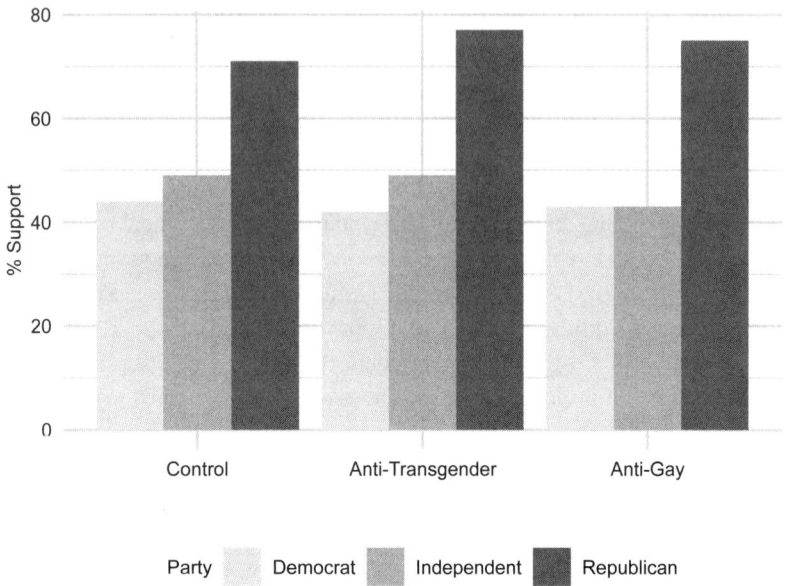

FIGURE 6.3. Partisan differences in support for the Protect Parental Rights in Education Act. Data from the June 2023 Lucid survey.

Democrats in T2 supported the policy. Like Independents, framing the policy as antitransgender or antigay enflamed opposition: 34% of Democrats in the control group opposed the policy; opposition rose to 39% in T1 and 41% in T2.

Respondents were then told the representative was running for reelection in 2024 and asked how likely they would be to vote for him if they lived in his district—very likely, somewhat likely, neither likely nor unlikely, somewhat unlikely, or very unlikely. The top chart in figure 6.4 shows that Republicans were more likely to say they would vote for the candidate in T1, the antitransgender condition (65%), than in the control group (59%) or in T2, the antigay condition (61%). The differences are statistically significant at the $p < .05$ level. Similarly, as shown in the bottom chart in figure 6.4, a higher proportion of Republicans in T1 viewed the congressperson as representing their interests (54%) than in the control (49%) and T2 (48%) conditions. Republicans were more supportive of the candidate and more likely to say he represents their interests when he used an overt antitransgender campaign appeal (T1) than when his campaign message was about parental rights (control) or was openly antigay (T2).

Support for the representative among Democrats and Independents was low across both variables—likelihood of voting for the candidate and how much he represented the respondents' interests.[7] There was also little change across experimental conditions in terms of percentage of Democrats or Independents who said they supported the candidate. However, there was notable change on the other end of the scale. For example, 40% of Democrats in the control group said they would be unlikely to vote for the representative if he ran for reelection in 2024. This number jumped to 48% in both T1, the antitransgender condition and T2, the antigay condition. Similarly, 35% of Independents in T2 said they would not vote for the candidate, compared to 25% who said that in the control group.

Several important conclusions can be drawn from this first set of experimental results. First, Republicans responded positively to antitransgender

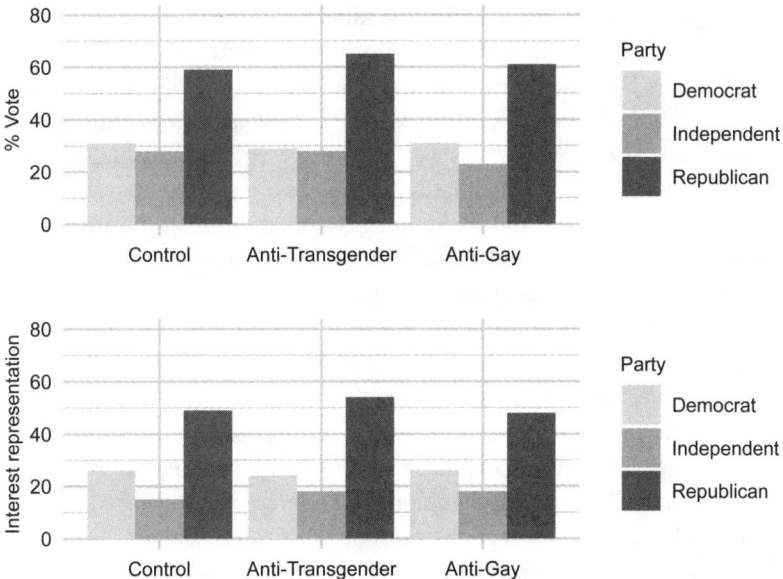

FIGURE 6.4. Partisan differences in electoral support for the fictional representative and perceptions of interest representation across three experimental conditions. Data from the June 2023 Lucid survey.

and antigay messaging. They supported the politician and the policy more when anti-LGBTQ+ messaging was present than when it was absent. This finding supports the assertion in hypothesis 6.1, that political messaging regarding the LGBTQ+ community is not guided by a norm of equality within the GOP. Second, Republicans respond slightly more positively to antitransgender messaging than to antigay messaging. This finding will be revisited later in the chapter. Third, Independents are not mobilized by overt anti-LGBTQ+ messaging. Less than one-third of Independents showed support for the representative across any of the experimental conditions. The findings for Democrats are less clear. It is possible that Democratic respondents inferred the partisan identity of Representative Peter Miller from the vignette they were presented with. If so, the findings simply show that Democrats are generally opposed to a politician they believe is Republican, regardless of their messaging strategy. Yet, if this is true, it also means the Republican Party is associated with anti-LGBTQ+ rhetoric while the Democratic Party is not. Either way, the results provide evidence in support of hypothesis 6.1, that politicians who use explicit anti-LGBTQ+ campaign appeals will receive higher levels of support from Republicans than from Democrats or Independents.

The next set of results examine the same experiment by religious identity and are depicted in figure 6.5.[8] Once again, there are several important findings. First, evangelical respondents are consistently the most supportive of candidates who use anti-LGBTQ+ appeals and policies framed as anti-LGBTQ+. Evangelicals were between 8 and 17 percentage points more supportive of the candidates and policies in treatments 1, the antitransgender condition and 2, the antigay condition, than the next most supportive group. Second, religious respondents were much more supportive of the candidates and policies than nonreligious respondents were across each scenario. Third, there was very little difference in support for a candidate and policy when an antitransgender message was used versus an antigay message. This finding will be discussed later in the chapter. Overall, the results show strong support for hypothesis 6.2, which posits that evangelicals will support anti-LGBTQ+ messaging more than members of other religious denominations and nonreligious people.

Hypothesis 6.3 posits that older respondents will accept anti-LGBTQ+ messaging more than younger respondents. To test this assertion, I examined support for the Protect Parental Rights in Education Act and for the candidate in treatments 1 (antitransgender condition) and 2 (antigay condition) across the following age groupings: eighteen to twenty-nine,

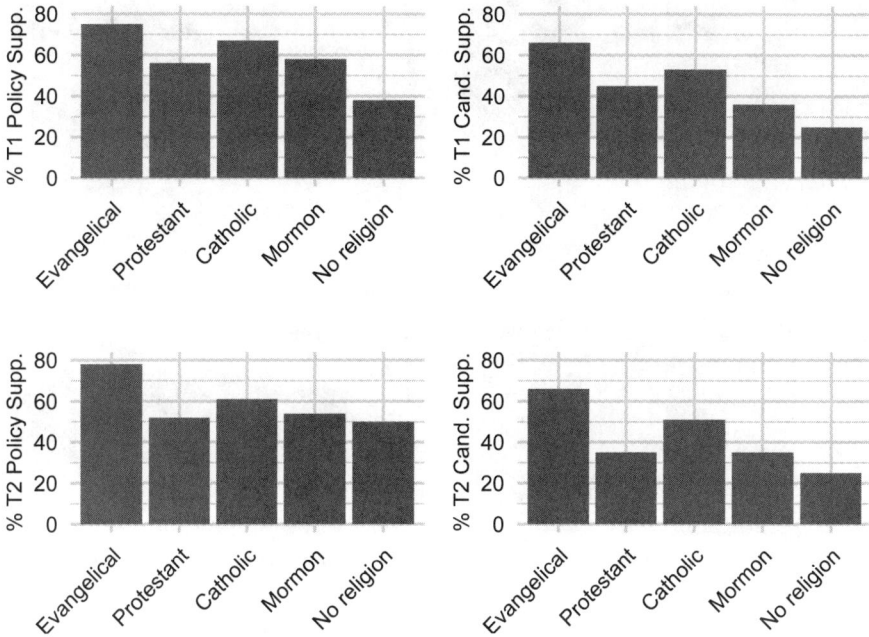

FIGURE 6.5. Policy and candidate support in antitransgender (T1) and antigay (T2) treatment conditions by religious identity. Data from the June 2023 Lucid survey.

thirty to thirty-nine, forty to forty-nine, fifty to sixty-four, and sixty-five and older. These are standard age groupings that provided roughly equal numbers of respondents. Figure 6.6 displays the results by age cohort in two ways. The top four panels of the figure show the percentage of respondents in each age group who were very or somewhat likely to support the candidate and policy in each treatment group. The results show that younger respondents were no more or less likely to support the policy than older respondents. However, the results also show that eighteen- to twenty-nine-year-olds were less likely to support the candidate in both treatments. The difference was largest in T1, as eighteen- to twenty-nine-year-olds were more than 10 percentage points less likely to support the candidate than any other age group. These differences were statistically significant, according to two-sample t-tests ($p < .05$).

The bottom four panels of figure 6.6 display the percentage of respondents across each age group who said they were very likely to support the policy and candidate. Here there are much larger differences across age groups. Eighteen- to twenty-nine-year-olds were substantially less likely to

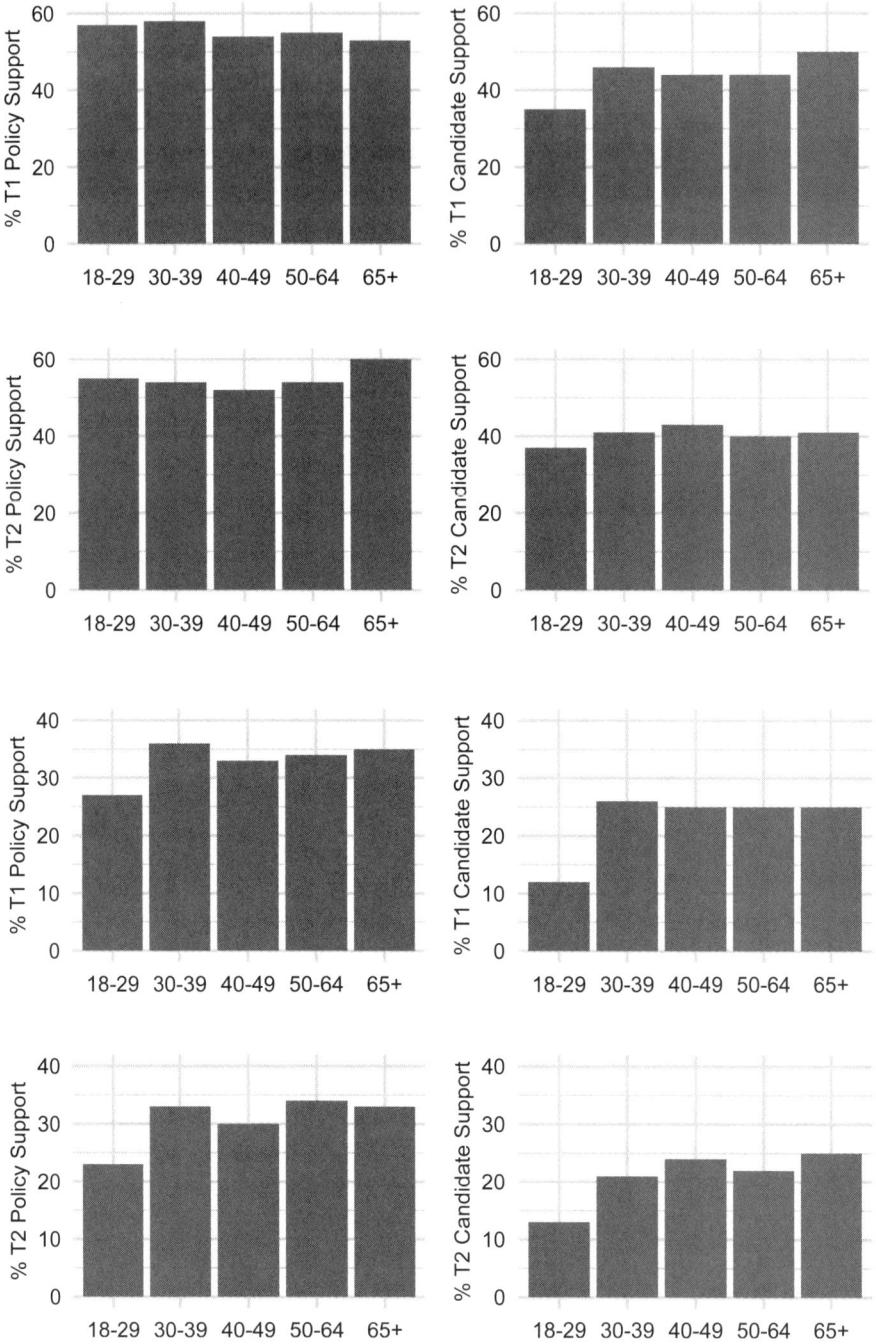

FIGURE 6.6. Policy and candidate support in antitransgender (T1) and antigay (T2) treatment conditions by age. *Top four panels*: Very or somewhat likely. *Bottom four panels*: Very likely. Data from the June 2023 Lucid survey.

be very supportive of the policy and candidate in both treatment conditions than their older counterparts. Indeed, eighteen- to twenty-nine-year-olds were almost 15 points less supportive of the candidate in T1 than any other age group and more than 10 points less supportive of the policy and candidate in T2 than any other age group. All these differences are statistically significant to at least the $p < .05$ level according to two-sample t-tests.

This has several important implications. First, there is no overall difference in support for a policy framed as antitransgender or antigay across age cohorts. There is, however, some evidence that younger respondents are less enthusiastic about policies framed as anti-LGBTQ+: Fewer of them reported they would be very likely to support the policies than older respondents. Second, younger respondents are much less supportive than older respondents of a candidate who openly signals an antitransgender stance. Third, there is little evidence that younger respondents support a candidate who is overtly antigay less than older respondents do. The overall differences in support for this candidate across age groups are not statistically significant, though far fewer eighteen- to twenty-nine-year-olds were very likely to vote for the candidate. Moreover, these differences are exclusively among eighteen- to twenty-nine-year-olds. Other age groups like thirty- to thirty-nine-year-olds, who grew up during a time when egalitarian norms were being constructed were similarly likely to support the candidate and policy as their older counterparts. In sum, the only clear evidence for hypothesis 6.3, that norms of equality are more internalized within younger people, is the lack of support for candidates who are explicitly antitransgender among eighteen- to twenty-nine-year-olds.

The Role of Social Norms

Similar to the previous case study chapters, I used the SNI to test the effect of norm adherence on reactions to anti-LGBTQ+ messaging. Figure 6.7 presents results of OLS regressions that analyzed the effect of the SNI on support for fictional candidate Peter Miller in the control, antitransgender (T1), and antigay (T2) experimental conditions.[9] All three models controlled for party identification, gender, education, age, and racial resentment. The SNI had a substantial effect on voter intention among respondents in both anti-LGBTQ+ conditions even after accounting for these control variables. In the antitransgender condition (T1), the SNI predicted a roughly 41-percentage-point increase in support for the candidate. In the antigay condition (T2), the SNI predicted a 27-point increase. Respondents who adhere to inegalitarian norms were much more supportive of candidates

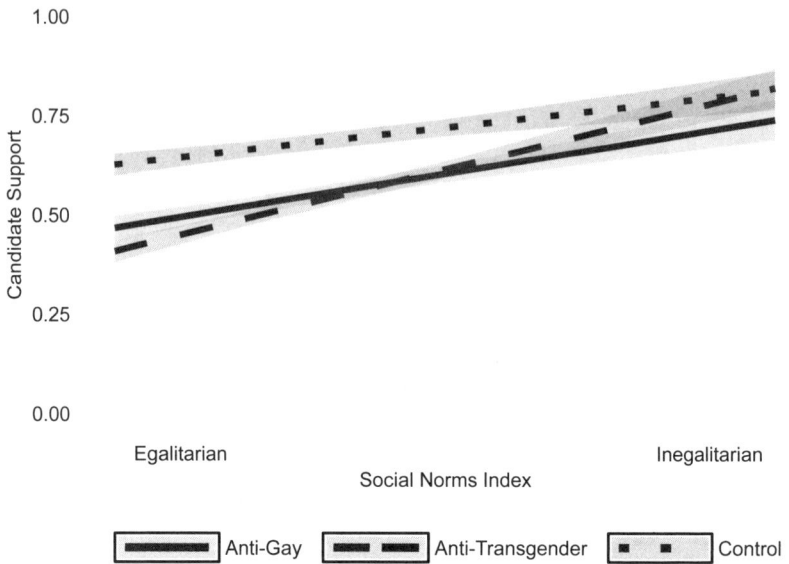

FIGURE 6.7. Marginal effects of the SNI on support for candidate Peter Miller in the control, antitransgender (T1), and antigay (T2) experimental conditions. Data from the June 2023 Lucid survey.

who use anti-LGBTQ+ messaging than respondents who adhere to inegalitarian norms.

Interestingly, among the most inegalitarian respondents, support for the candidate in all three experimental conditions was roughly the same. But the most egalitarian respondents were much more supportive of the candidate when he campaigned for parent's rights than when he made an overt appeal to antitransgender or antigay sentiments. Indeed, the most egalitarian respondents were 32 points more supportive of the candidate in the control condition than in the antitransgender condition (T1); and 28 points more supportive of the candidate in the control condition than in the antigay condition (T2). Thus, the SNI is a useful measure for understanding who is most likely, and who is least likely, to support candidates who make anti-LGBTQ+ appeals. These results provide clear evidence in support of hypothesis 6.4.

The Connection Between Antitransgender and Antigay Messaging

Hypothesis 6.5 posits that antitransgender messaging should be more acceptable to the public than antigay messaging. Yet, I find very little empirical support for this assertion. Figure 6.8 displays the percentage of respondents in my June 2023 Lucid survey who supported the Protect Parental Rights in Education Act, the percentage who said they would vote for Representative Miller, and the percentage who said Miller represented their interests across all three experimental groups. Overall, there were only minor differences in support across any of the three measures regardless of whether the candidate used a parental rights frame, an antitransgender frame, or an antigay frame. The anti-LGBTQ+ frames did not increase or decrease overall support for the candidate or policy, and there was no meaningful difference in overall support when the candidate used an antitransgender frame relative to an antigay frame.

Moreover, the subgroup analysis presented earlier in this chapter indicates only small differences in support for the antitransgender and antigay messages within partisan groups, religious groups, or age cohorts. Republicans and evangelicals, the two groups driving the acceptance of anti-LGBTQ+ messaging, support candidates who are explicitly antigay just as much as those who are explicitly antitransgender. They also support policies framed as antigay as much as those framed as antitransgender.

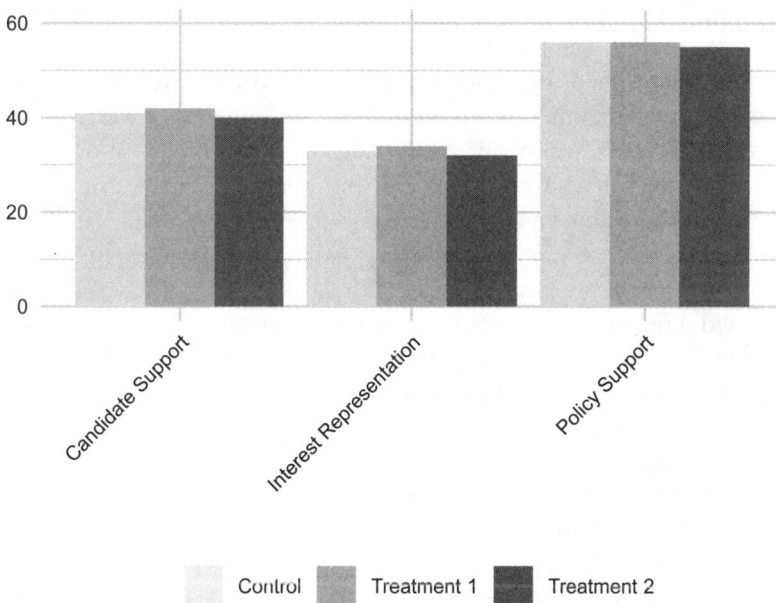

FIGURE 6.8. Policy and candidate support in the control, antitransgender (T1), and antigay (T2) experimental conditions. Data from the June 2023 Lucid survey.

These findings appear to contradict the way norms have developed for the community. Earlier in the chapter, I discussed the many influential signals of support for gay and lesbian people in recent decades, particularly between 2003 and 2015. I also showed that, across many different indicators, support for gay and lesbian rights increased dramatically from the 1980s to the 2010s. Moreover, the vast majority of anti-LGBTQ+ elite rhetoric, policies, media coverage, and right-wing demonstrations in recent years has specifically targeted transgender people. Thus, there was good reason to expect that overt antitransgender messaging would be more socially acceptable than overt antigay messaging.

One explanation for why this is not the case may be that frequent, intense signals of antitransgender prejudice by influential leaders and institutions are eroding norms for the entire LGBTQ+ community. I tested this assertion through an experiment embedded in a June 2023 survey conducted through Lucid centered on the boycott of Bud Light that began earlier that year over the company's partnership with transgender influencer Dylan Mulvaney on a social media promotion campaign. A random sample of roughly half the respondents were asked: "How much have you heard or read about boycotts of Bud Light over a transgendered spokesperson?" The other respondents did not see this question. All respondents were then asked a series of questions to gauge their support of LGBTQ+ rights. The Bud Light experiment was used as a subtle prime to move thoughts of the antitransgender boycott to the top of people's minds. I found that the 2,029 respondents who were primed were, on average, less supportive of gay and lesbian rights across several different measures than the 2,045 respondents who were not primed. Primed respondents were about 2 percentage points more likely to believe that gay and lesbian relations are morally wrong and 2 points less likely to believe that marriages between same-sex couples should be recognized by the law as valid. Primed respondents were also 2 points less supportive of laws that would protect gay, lesbian, bisexual, and transgender people against discrimination in jobs, public accommodations, and housing. All these differences are statistically significant to the $p < .05$ level according to two-sample t-tests.

Although the differences are fairly small, this test is important to understanding the relationship between antitransgender norms and broader norms for the LGBTQ+ community for two reasons. First, the question specifies that the boycotts were over a transgender spokesperson. At least on their face, the boycotts were about opposition to the transgender community specifically, not about opposition to gay and lesbian people. Yet, primed respondents became less supportive of gay and lesbian rights and of a bill that would protect the broader LGBTQ+ community. These findings suggest the antitransgender campaign has spilled over to norms for the broader LGBTQ+ community. Second, simply asking respondents a question about their exposure to the Bud Light boycotts was enough to, at least temporarily, decrease support for marriage equality and antidiscrimination protections and increase the belief that gay and lesbian relations are morally wrong. This is a conservative test of the ability of antitransgender opposition to erode norms of equality for gay and lesbian people because the prime was so subtle.

Real-world examples also suggest the current intensely antitransgender environment is spilling over into opposition to gay and lesbian rights. Although their primary focus has been antitransgender legislation, Republican-led legislatures are also targeting other members of the LGBTQ+ community through bans on gay and lesbian content in books and public education, religious freedom bills that allow businesses to deny service to LGBTQ+ people on the basis of religion, and banning what they call "adult cabaret performances." Several Republican legislatures are now turning their attention to forced outing bills that would require schools to report any student who shows signs of LGBTQ+ identification to their parents (Sargent 2023). Republicans in some states are even starting to go after marriage equality. Indeed, Tennessee Governor Bill Lee recently signed a bill that allows county clerks to refuse marriage licenses if they disagree with the marriage (Otten 2023). This could set the stage for a potential repeal of marriage equality in the state.

Most anti-LGBTQ+ campaign messaging and advertising in 2022 and 2024 was antitransgender, but Republicans in certain states made their opposition to gay and lesbian rights clear as well. For example, the "Homosexual and Gender Issues" section of the Texas GOP party platform for the 2022 midterm election made it abundantly clear that the party opposes equal rights for the full LGBTQ+ community: "Homosexuality is an abnormal lifestyle choice. We believe there should be no granting of special legal entitlements or creation of special status for homosexual behavior, regardless of state of origin, and we oppose any criminal or civil penalties against those who oppose homosexuality out of faith, conviction, or belief in traditional values. No one should be granted special legal status based on their LGBTQ+ identification" (Republican Party of Texas 2022).

Republicans throughout Texas overtly signaled their opposition to gay and lesbian rights through TV ads, mailers, and other forms of campaign communication (Suarez 2022). The Texas GOP did not face any negative electoral consequences for their overt anti-LGBTQ+ messaging strategy. Republicans in Texas comfortably won the governorship, lieutenant governorship, and the attorney general race; won twenty-five of the thirty-eight US House seats; and increased their margins in each house of the state legislature by one seat (Astudillo 2022). In sum, there is both experimental evidence and evidence from real-world politics that the assault on transgender rights is at least partially eroding the recently constructed norm of equality for gay and lesbian people.

Conclusion

A recent article found that hormone therapy significantly decreased gender dysphoria, depression levels, and suicidality among transgender and gender-diverse adults (Nolan et al. 2023). Despite the mounting evidence that gender-affirming health care is beneficial, Republican legislators across the country are working to ban it. This is just one of the many ways that anti-LGBTQ+ legislation is harming the community. Findings from the Trevor Project's US National Survey on the Mental Health of LGBTQ Young People provide a chilling account of the detrimental effects of recent attacks on the community (Trevor Project 2023). More than 50% of LGBTQ+ youth reported that they experienced symptoms of depression, including about 60% of transgender and nonbinary youth. Even more troublingly, 41% of LGBTQ+ youth said they "seriously considered" committing suicide at least once within the last year. The survey also found that poor mental health was directly tied to legislation. About one in three respondents attributed their poor mental health to anti-LGBTQ+ policies and legislation, and two-thirds of respondents said that just hearing about anti-LGBTQ+ laws harmed their mental health. Clearly, the current political environment is having serious detrimental effects on the health and well-being of LGBTQ+ people.

The electoral effect of anti-LGBTQ+ messaging is less clear. The findings of this chapter show that support for fictional antitransgender and antigay candidates is just over 40%. Rates of perceived interest representation for such candidates are even lower. More than 60% of Republicans say they would vote for such candidates, but Democrats and

Independents reject the candidates wholesale. Moreover, Republicans are only slightly more supportive of these candidates than of similar ones who do not make overt antitransgender or antigay campaign appeals. Support for the candidates is high among evangelical respondents and even among Catholics, but other religious groups and nonreligious respondents have little appetite for either one.

There is also some evidence from the 2022 midterm election that anti-LGBTQ+ messaging is not a productive electoral strategy. For example, a survey conducted by the HRC found that less than 5% of prospective voters indicated they were motivated to vote by issues such as gender-affirming care for transgender youth or the participation of transgender individuals in sports[10]—issues that several Republican candidates and political elites discussed leading up to the election. Electoral results for the most prominent anti-LGBTQ+ candidates in 2022 were also mixed. Florida Governor Ron DeSantis and Oklahoma Governor Kevin Stitt, two politicians who have led the way on anti-LGBTQ+ legislation, won reelection. However, prominent anti-LGBTQ+ candidates like Tudor Dixon, Mehmet Oz, and Doug Mastriano all lost.

Moreover, there is some evidence that the messaging strategy motivated the LGBTQ+ community—a community that strongly opposes the Republican Party. A record 1,065 out LGBTQ+ people ran for office in 2022 and 430 of these candidates were elected. A reported by the LGBTQ+ Victory Institute found that transgender women and gender nonconforming, gender queer, and nonbinary candidates were more likely than other candidates to cite anti-LGBTQ+ legislation as their main motivation for running for office (LGBTQ+ Victory Fund 2023).

The findings from this chapter portray a highly stratified norm environment for the LGBTQ+ community. In chapter 4, the majority of respondents across parties rejected candidates and policies that were explicitly anti-Black. In chapter 5, Republicans were consistently supportive of candidates who were openly Islamophobic. In some circumstances, these candidates garnered significant support from Independents and in one scenario enjoyed support from almost 50% of Democrats. Candidates who used explicit antigay and antitransgender rhetoric were consistently supported by Republicans, though at lower rates than anti-Muslim candidates, and were consistently rejected by Democrats and Independents. Norms for the community may also be in a state of flux as recent intense political attacks on transgender people may be shifting norms for the broader LGBTQ+ community in an inegalitarian direction.

The GOP may be counting on this transitionary phase to help them in future election cycles. Although anti-LGBTQ+ messaging may not currently be a winning strategy, there are other strategic reasons for the Republican Party to make it such a major part of its platform. For years, the GOP has relied on grievance politics to animate their base. A necessary aspect of grievance politics is creating us-versus-them situations. After marriage equality was codified by the Supreme Court, evangelical and Republican leaders sought a new strategy to mobilize social conservatives. A strategic decision was made to go after the transgender community. Curtailment of the community's rights by political institutions and mass antitransgender demonstrations normalize overt prejudice and push social norms in an inegalitarian direction. Republican leaders may be counting on this to make antitransgender messaging and legislation a more effective strategy in future elections. Indeed, Project 2025, a blueprint created by right-wing thinkers, refers to transgender ideology as "pornography" and makes it clear that the GOP should continue to vilify the transgender community.[11] President Trump has heeded this advice, issuing several executive orders during his first few months in office that curtail the rights of transgender people. Moreover, normalization of antitransgender prejudice seems to be spilling over to the rest of the LGBTQ+ community. GOP-led states are already going after marriage equality and other rights for gay, lesbian, bisexual, and queer people.

Many potential strategies could be used to combat this overt prejudice. LGBTQ+ activists and allies are demonstrating some of these strategies in their fight to preserve and advance equal rights. Chapter 7 will discuss these strategies and empirically test the effectiveness of several strategies to counteract and defuse overt prejudicial political messaging.

CHAPTER SEVEN

Countering Explicit Prejudicial Political Messaging

I think the president is using language that emboldens them. He's not creating them. They're out there. That kind of language from the person who probably has the loudest microphone on the planet Earth is hurtful and dangerous and it tends to incite violence. —Tim Kaine (O'Brien 2019)

It required years of labor and billions of dollars to gain the secret of the atom. It will take a still greater investment to gain the secrets of man's irrational nature. It is easier . . . to smash an atom than a prejudice. —Gordon Allport (Allport 1954)

Countering prejudice is difficult but not impossible. In fact, back in October 2017, I interviewed James,[1] a member of the group Life After Hate, an organization that works with people who are transitioning away from a life of prejudice and bigotry. Its membership consists mostly of former white supremacists and neo-Nazis. James narrated a story about a Jewish doctor who saved his life despite his swastika tattoos. This interaction caused him to reject his former life as a white supremacist and move in a more compassionate and open direction. He said he could no longer hate a group when one of its members had saved his life. James told me that most members of Life After Hate had similar experiences of kindness and compassion from a member of a minority community that led them to not only abandon a life of hate but to help others do so as well. This story is congruous with many academic studies: Meaningful contact, under a set of optimal conditions, can be an effective way to tear down harmful stereotypes and repair intergroup relations (see Allport 1954; Pettigrew and Tropp 2006; Broockman and Kalla 2016). These types of interventions can be a crucial component in the long-term strategy to develop and maintain egalitarian norms. However, while powerful, this is not a feasible strategy for countering prejudicial campaign appeals because these kinds of individualized experiences cannot be scaled to the level needed to defuse the effects of antiminority rhetoric.

Yet it is imperative to find effective strategies because of the many harmful effects of overt prejudice in politics. One, general elections increasingly involve candidates who take vastly different positions on issues of race and ethnicity, leading to a more explosive brand of politics. Recent scholarship has demonstrated that public perception that the parties are polarized on race and racial issues contributes to growing affective polarization (Valentino and Zhirkov 2018), which has led to dislike for the opposing party being at its highest levels ever (Iyengar et al. 2012). The erosion of civility, respect, and trust among the public and in politics, as well as of prospects for bipartisanship, is at least partially due to the racially charged nature of US politics.

Two, overt prejudicial campaign rhetoric is having a snowball effect among the public. People tend to take their cues from political elites, so appeals to prejudice often activate antiminority sentiment among many Americans. Indeed, Schaffner (2020) found that people who were exposed to Donald Trump's prejudicial remarks became more likely to make similar hostile comments targeting not just the groups Trump targeted but other identity groups as well. As Senator Tim Kaine put it, the president of the US "has the loudest microphone on the planet Earth" (O'Brien 2019). When he uses his pulpit to attack minority groups, he influences others to do the same. Trump's rhetoric serves as an indicator that it is acceptable for people to be overtly hostile toward groups they dislike. In other words, it helps further shift norms of acceptable rhetoric away from egalitarianism, particularly among his many supporters.

Three, antiminority political speech has led to an increase in hate crimes as people become more emboldened to act on prejudicial ideas. Hate crimes targeting the groups Trump verbally attacked during his 2016 presidential election campaign surged during the year after he took office (Edwards and Rushin 2018). Counties that hosted one of the Trump campaign's three hundred rallies were particularly susceptible to increases in hate-related incidents. Feinberg et al. (2022) found that these rallies, combined with Trump's rhetoric, heightened perceived threat among white Americans, which helped them justify using violent means to address their grievances.

Many perpetrators of violent acts have specifically cited Trump as a reason for their actions. Brenton Harrison Tarrant, a white supremacist who killed fifty people after opening fire at a mosque in New Zealand, called Trump "a symbol of renewed white identity and common purpose" (Davidson 2019). In 2019, Trump released a video associating Representative Ilhan Omar, one of two Muslim women in Congress, with the terrorist attacks on September 11, 2001 (Rosenberg and Epstein 2019). After the release of the video, death threats against Omar increased, and a man was charged with threatening to kill her because of her Muslim faith (Čvorak and Williams 2019). These are just two of many examples of violence that have been directly associated with antiminority rhetoric from Trump and others on the political right.

Four, the rise in overt prejudice is having detrimental effects on the health and well-being of minority communities. A report released by the Southern Poverty Law Center (2016, 4) demonstrated that campaign rhetoric from the 2016 GOP primary was "producing an alarming level of fear and anxiety among children of color and inflaming racial and ethnic tensions in the classroom." Many students were worried about being deported or having a family member deported. Others were emboldened by the rhetoric and lashed out at people whose identities were under attack by the Trump campaign, thereby stoking racial animosity. Another study, which examined the effect of political rhetoric on the emotional responses of Mexican American youth, found exposure to hostile messages increased stress levels, worsened people's self-image and sense of well-being, and even led to deterioration in physical health (see Chavez et al. 2019). The effects of political rhetoric are not merely ensconced in a given election or policy debate. The impact is felt throughout the country in our communities, schools, and homes.

As such, an increasingly urgent question in American politics is: What are effective strategies to counter or neutralize explicit prejudicial rhetoric that is enflaming intergroup tensions, harming the mental and physical well-being of minority populations, and inciting violence? This chapter aims to answer this question. First, I reviewed existing scholarship on norms transformation and countering prejudice. Building from this scholarship, I proposed and tested four strategies that can be used to neutralize prejudicial campaign rhetoric. I found that bipartisan condemnation of an antiminority message was a particularly effective strategy. I also found some evidence that an antiracist counterstrategy and a strategy that involves appeals to people's moral codes can diminish the effects of antiminority campaign appeals. On the other hand, media condemnation was a less effective strategy.

Theories of Prejudice Reduction

Racial prejudice is among the most crystallized attitudes held by the public, making it very difficult to change an individual's stances on race and racial issues (Kinder and Sanders 1996; Kinder and Kam 2010; Tesler 2015). Other forms of out-group animosity are becoming increasingly intractable (e.g., Abrajano and Hajnal 2015; Lajevardi 2020). Consequently, campaign messaging intended to activate antiminority sentiment is effective and difficult to neutralize because of how salient and stable out-group animus is. However, when new considerations are brought to bear on an individual's decision-making, it is possible to change their mind (Zaller 1992). This is particularly true when an individual's perception of societal norms shifts.

According to group norms theory, norms come from group attitudes, so it is more efficient to change group attitudes than to focus on individual attitudes (Crandall et al. 2002). Changing the norm about the expression of prejudice can have a strong effect on people's tolerance for prejudice. Blanchard et al. (1994) found that when a single accomplice expressed antiracist views, there was a significant reduction in tolerance for racist actions among participants in a lab experiment. Conversely, when the same accomplice demonstrated acceptance of racist acts, the participants did too. The manipulation affected attitudes when measured publicly and privately, indicating that the expressed opinions of a single person can strongly influence even the private attitudes of others in the group.

Similarly, scholarship suggests that the perception of norms regarding an out-group can influence the expression of prejudice (see Stangor et al. 2001; Sechrist and Stangor 2001). In one study, when respondents were led to believe that their view of Black Americans was more stereotypic than others, their endorsement of harmful stereotypes was reduced. But when they were told their view was less stereotypic than others, they become more likely to endorse those same harmful stereotypes (Stangor et al. 2001). Thus, when norms surrounding an expression of prejudice change, evaluations of the message and the messenger will too. If a derogatory message is strongly condemned, then it loses its ability to prime antiminority predispositions because the message has been shown to violate a norm of equality. In other words, antiminority campaign appeals lose their power when they are perceived to violate social norms.

The most famous example of this is the influence of the Willie Horton ad on the 1988 presidential election (see Mendelberg 2001; McIlwain and Caliendo 2011). In 1988, supporters of presidential nominee George

H. W. Bush ran a campaign ad that featured Horton's mug shot. Horton was a Black prisoner in Massachusetts who, while released on a furlough program, had raped a woman and stabbed her boyfriend. This incident became a cudgel for Bush's presidential campaign to use to portray his opponent, Massachusetts Governor Michael Dukakis, as soft on crime.

At first, discussion of Horton, particularly when paired with visual cues, appeared to benefit Bush's poll numbers. During this time, messaging regarding Horton was almost exclusively communicated in a nonracial manner by the campaign and the media. Indeed, the ad was effective because it made an implicit appeal to the anti-Black sentiments of many voters while allowing Bush and his allies to maintain plausible deniability about its intent. The Willie Horton ad pushed a racialized "tough on crime" message without the public recognizing that the message was, in fact, racialized. However, once Reverend Jesse Jackson pointed out the racial intent of the ad, it lost its effectiveness. The media then began to frame it as an appeal to anti-Black sentiments and made racial references to the Bush campaign. Once the public was made aware of the racial content and shown that it violated the norm of racial equality, the power of the message was neutralized. As a result, Bush's poll numbers took a hit, though it was too late to affect the outcome of the race. Nevertheless, this is strong evidence that condemning a campaign message as racist can effectively neutralize the message and negatively impact the messenger. This finding has been replicated in controlled experimental settings numerous times (see Mendelberg 2001; Valentino et al. 2002; White 2007; Winter 2008; Tokeshi and Mendelberg 2015).

The example of the Willie Horton ad shows that awareness of the prejudicial content of a message can mediate its impact. This is key to any attempt to neutralize the effects of prejudicial rhetoric. If people adhere to egalitarian norms, then they will reject messaging that violates that norm — but only if they recognize that the message did in fact violate the norm. Thus, each of the strategies I propose for neutralizing prejudice includes making the audience aware of the prejudicial nature of the message.

The manner in which people are told that a message has violated social norms also matters. Even when people recognize political misbehavior, they may still support the candidate or policy for political gain (e.g., Simonovits et al. 2022). However, individuals' prejudiced attitudes and behaviors can be constrained under certain conditions (see Kuklinski and Hurley 1994; Paluck and Green 2009). One condition that can help reduce prejudice is appealing to people's moral codes (see Bicchieri 2016). Many people feel a personal aversion to prejudicial rhetoric but, because of their partisan attachments and their normative expectations of those in their party, they support candidates who use such rhetoric anyway. Making these people aware that prejudicial campaign rhetoric can have negative and sometimes violent consequences that go beyond a campaign may activate their moral codes. Those who would otherwise have supported candidates who used prejudicial rhetoric may no longer do so. One way to do this is to help people understand the perspective of the group being negatively affected by the prejudice. Broockman and Kalla (2016) found that ten-minute conversations in which people were encouraged to take the perspectives of others markedly reduced transphobia. Another strategy is to combat false beliefs or stereotypes about a minority group. For example, Batterham (2001) provided people information that challenged widely held false beliefs about Indigenous Australians. Receiving this information was associated with reduced levels of false beliefs and lower modern racism scores.

Another key component of prejudice reduction tactics is the messenger. Attitudes tend to be influenced most by copartisans (e.g., Zaller 1992; Broockman and Butler 2017), coracial opinion leaders (e.g., Kuklinski and Hurley 1994; Arora and Stout 2019), and experts in a relevant field (e.g., Levy et al. 1998). This is unsurprising because, as discussed in previous chapters, people are most influenced by members of their reference group. A message from someone or from an organization you have no connection to is unlikely to change your mind, especially about a topic you have well-developed opinions on. But a message from a person or organization that you trust is much more likely to influence your decision-making process. Within a reference group, people are generally most likely to be swayed by elites or group leaders. Thus, the most effective prejudice reduction strategies will include a message from a trusted figure or organization condemning a prejudicial campaign appeal for violating egalitarian social norms.

Building on these ideas, I proposed four potential ways to neutralize the effects of antiminority political rhetoric: a bipartisan condemnation, a condemnation coming from the opposition party, a media condemnation, and an appeal to moral codes. The next section describes how I tested those strategies.

Testing Neutralization Strategies

Bipartisan Condemnation

I tested this first strategy—a bipartisan condemnation to neutralize the effects of antiminority political rhetoric—against a real-world Islamophobic campaign advertisement that was used by Republican candidate Duncan Hunter in his 2018 campaign for a seat in the US House of Representatives. Zaller (1992) demonstrated that a one-sided information flow, one in which political elites were unified in support or opposition on an issue, can have a powerful unifying effect on the public's stance on the issue. As discussed in chapter 5, signals of commitment to equality for Muslims are coming from segments of the Democratic Party but not from the Republican Party. If a consensus formed among elites of both parties that Islamophobia violates social norms and this consensus were messaged to the public, it could help develop a norm of equality guiding political rhetoric about Muslims.

The power of the bipartisan message largely comes from including a Republican elite in the condemnation. What is considered racism or prejudice is different in the two major political parties. Republicans tend to be less sensitive to allegations of racism or prejudice than Democrats. This is largely because such allegations tend to come from sources outside the GOP. But if Republican elites join Democrats in condemning a message for its prejudicial content, that can diminish these partisan differences because Republican identifiers are more likely to view their copartisans as credible sources.

My expectation is that the bipartisan condemnation will temporarily shift norms in an egalitarian direction. Given how pervasive Islamophobia has become in society and how engrained it is in many people, it is unlikely that the norm would meaningfully shift in a long-lasting way after just one bipartisan message. However, there is reason to believe bipartisan condemnation can influence the short-term evaluation of a particular politician or candidate. When individuals are aware there is high social consensus, they are likely to process subsequent information in favor of that consensus (see Erb et al. 1998). So, if the public receives a bipartisan message condemning Islamophobia, that may have a downstream effect that influences the public to process information in favor of the bipartisan consensus (i.e., reject an Islamophobic candidate).

In keeping with the scholarship discussed earlier in the chapter, this should be an effective strategy for neutralizing an antiminority campaign appeal, because it makes the audience aware that it violates a social norm. This is especially true in low-information election contexts in which individuals have less countervailing information about the candidate in question. In other words, if an individual has little information about a candidate, then bipartisan condemnation of that candidate's messaging is more likely to affect their support of the candidate. This strategy may be less effective in high-information elections in which the public is receiving copious information about the candidates and attitudes about them are more stable.

To test this strategy, I collected a national sample of 1,010 respondents on October 31 and November 1, 2018, just a few days before election day, using the survey firm Lucid. A detailed discussion of this sample can be found in chapter 3.[2] An experiment embedded in the survey centered on a campaign ad run by Duncan Hunter, the incumbent candidate for California's Fiftieth Congressional District. The experiment tested the effect of (1) an overt Islamophobic campaign advertisement and (2) bipartisan condemnation of the advertisement on support for Hunter. The ad described Ammar Campa-Najjar, Hunter's opponent, as a "security threat" working to "infiltrate Congress" with the help of the Muslim Brotherhood. The ad was strongly condemned for its explicit Islamophobia. *The Washington Post*'s fact checker gave the ad four Pinocchios for its false or misleading claims and its "naked anti-Muslim bias" (Rizzo 2018).

Respondents were randomly assigned to one of three treatment groups. The first group (control) read a short biography of Hunter that detailed his conservative credentials by mentioning his "A" rating from the National Rifle Association, his strong pro-life stance, and his opposition to the Affordable Care Act. These details were taken from Hunter's 2018 campaign website. The second group (treatment 1) read the same biography and then watched the full campaign ad. The third group (treatment 2) read the biography, watched the ad, and then read an excerpt of an article in which a "bipartisan group of dozens of national security veterans" condemned the ad as a "racist and bigoted attack." Respondents were then asked how likely they would be to vote for Hunter if they lived in his district.

Chapter 5 theoretically and empirically showed that egalitarian norms regarding Muslims and Islam are not strongly held by the American public, especially among Republicans. In treatment 2, I manipulated the norm in an attempt to create a temporary norm of equality about Muslims by providing a mainstream effect condemning the Islamophobic ad. Respondents were asked to evaluate Hunter after hearing that a credible group of elites (national security veterans) from both major political parties believed the ad was "racist and bigoted." If social norms are the mechanism for supporting candidates who use overt prejudicial appeals, and if these norms vary by group, then a one-sided information flow condemning the message should lead to rejection of the candidate.

TABLE 7.1 **Bipartisan condemnation experimental design information**

Experimental group	Manipulation	N
Control	Biography of Duncan Hunter	342
Treatment 1	Candidate biography + Islamophobic ad	328
Treatment 2	Candidate biography + Islamophobic ad + bipartisan condemnation article excerpt	340

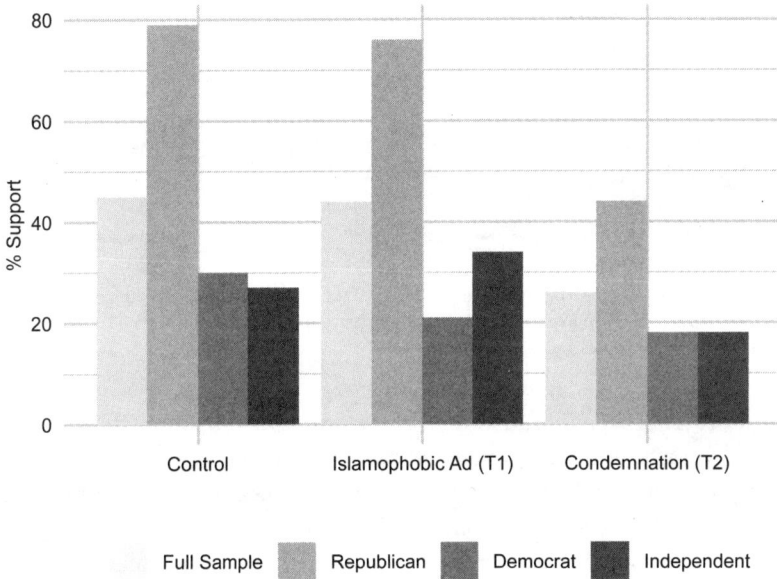

FIGURE 7.1. Percentage of respondents in the full sample and by party identification who were somewhat or very likely to have voted for Duncan Hunter (bipartisan condemnation test). Data from the October 2018 Lucid survey.

Figure 7.1 displays the percentage of respondents who said they were somewhat or very likely to vote for Hunter if they lived in his congressional district by party and across experimental conditions. Three important results are evident in this figure. First, watching the Islamophobic ad had no substantial effect on Republican voters' support for Hunter. The message was not rejected, but it also did not appear to have a galvanizing effect. Second, Hunter faced a backlash from Democrats. Hunter enjoyed 30% support in the control condition and only 21% from Democrats in the Islamophobic ad condition (T1). Third, Hunter received only tepid

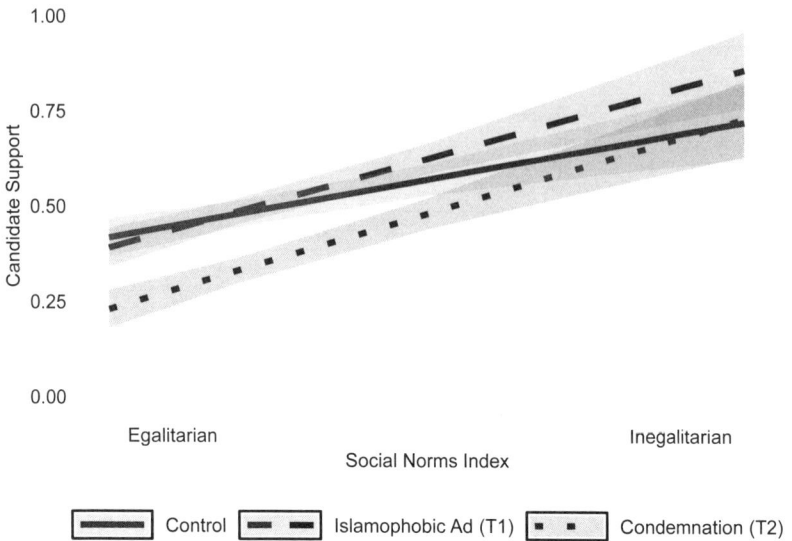

FIGURE 7.2. The relationship between the SNI and reported likelihood of voting for Duncan Hunter across all three experimental groups (bipartisan condemnation test). Data from the October 2018 Lucid survey.

support from Republican voters in the bipartisan condemnation condition (T2) who watched the ad and then read a condemnation of the ad. Only 44% of Republican voters and 18% of Democratic voters supported Hunter in the treatment 2 condition, 35 and 12 percentage points lower, respectively, than in the control condition. Support for Hunter among Independents also dropped in treatment 2. In other words, the condemnation substantially diminished support for the candidate.

To provide further evidence that adherence to norms is driving the effects, I regressed the social norms index (SNI) on support for Hunter among each of the three experimental groups.[3] Each model controlled for partisan identity, gender, education, age, and racial resentment. The SNI, which was developed in chapter 3 and serves as the primary independent variable in the regression models, consists of four questions that gauge respondents' adherence to egalitarian/inegalitarian social norms. Higher scores on the SNI indicate adherence to more inegalitarian norms and lower scores indicate adherence to more egalitarian norms. The dependent variable in each regression model is likelihood of voting for Hunter, which is a five-point Likert scale that ranges from "very likely" (1) to "not at all likely" (0). The marginal effect of the SNI is displayed in figure 7.2.

As shown in the figure, social norms are activated in all three experimental conditions. In the control condition, those who scored highest on the SNI (i.e., most inegalitarian respondents) were about 30 percentage points more supportive of Duncan Hunter than the most egalitarian respondents. In the Islamophobic ad condition (T1), the effect of the SNI increased to 47 points. The Islamophobic ad makes the most inegalitarian respondents more supportive of Hunter without meaningfully decreasing his support among the most egalitarian respondents. This result aligns with the theory and findings from chapter 5. Introducing the bipartisan condemnation leads to meaningful change in support for the candidate from egalitarian respondents. In the control and treatment 1 (Islamophobic ad) conditions, 35% and 33% of the most egalitarian respondents said they were likely to vote for Hunter. But in the bipartisan condemnation condition (T2), support among these respondents dropped all the way to 23%.

Thus, when there was consensus from elites from both major political parties that overt Islamophobia is "racist and bigoted" (i.e., when a mainstream effect was achieved), support for the candidate expressing Islamophobia sharply decreased among those who most strongly adhere to egalitarian norms. The findings from this experiment provide further evidence that a norm of equality is not present for Muslims. The findings also indicate that norms can be manipulated, providing some hope that this norm can be created for Muslims and other groups. In sum, bipartisan condemnation is a very effective strategy for combating overt Islamophobia in short-term, low-information, electoral campaign contexts.

Antiracist Counterstrategy

One issue with the first strategy is that bipartisan messages rarely occur and, due to rising partisan polarization, are becoming increasingly scarce. It is far more likely for prejudicial messaging, which is generally though not exclusively used by Republicans, to be condemned only by the opposing party. One way Democrats can attempt to neutralize the effects of antiminority appeals is to mount an antiracist counterstrategy in which they consistently and forcefully denounce prejudicial campaign messages.

As discussed in previous chapters, the electoral temptation of the Democratic Party for many decades was racial silence in the face of dog whistles from their Republican counterparts (Kinder and Sanders 1996). For a long time, it was believed that discussing race and calling out Republican candidates' messaging as racist were losing strategies for the Democratic

Party (Edsall and Edsall 1992; Kinder and Sanders 1996). Yet, Democrats frequently pointed out the racial connotations of Trump's messages during the 2016 (Banks and Hicks 2019; Stout 2020), 2020, and 2024 elections. Hillary Clinton, Bernie Sanders (Wright 2016), and many others (Lillis 2016) condemned Trump's campaign as racist, prejudiced, and bigoted. The increase in overt prejudicial campaign rhetoric seems to have had an important effect on the news media as well. *The Associated Press Stylebook*, a manual widely used by journalists, has changed its guidelines on race. The stylebook now advises against using ambiguous terms such as "racially charged" and "racially motivated" and instead calls for unambiguous terms such as "racist" and "racism" (Evans 2019). It appears the Democratic strategy, and potentially the strategy of the news media, is in the midst of a transformation away from silence to one of countering overt prejudice by condemning it as a violation of egalitarian norms.

There is scholarship that supports this strategy. Racial priming theory suggests the most effective counterstrategy to dog whistles is to make the audience aware of the racial content of the coded message (Mendelberg 2001). Once voters are made aware that the message was an appeal to racial animus, they should view it as a violation of racially egalitarian norms and reject it. Mendelberg (2001) found that racially resentful white individuals were most affected by this strategy, while Tokeshi and Mendelberg (2015) found that all white people were similarly influenced. More recently, Banks and Hicks (2019) have argued that racially conservative white individuals would not be persuaded by this strategy but racially liberal white people would be, because of motivated reasoning theory, which suggests individuals are motivated toward positions that are in line with their preexisting racial attitudes.

Though these studies examined dog whistles, the theory should hold for more overtly antiminority messaging. It is easier to recognize the racial or prejudicial content of an overt message, but the audience may still need to be told that it violated egalitarian norms. Making voters aware of the norm violation should affect the audience in two ways. One, those who were predisposed to vote for the candidate may decide not to for fear of social censure. This may be particularly impactful because the distribution of the SNI in chapter 3 showed that majorities of both Democrats and Republicans land on the egalitarian end of the scale. Two, it may enflame opposition to the candidate from racially liberal voters. Thus, pointing out that a candidate violated egalitarian social norms should cause decreased support for the candidate.

TABLE 7.2 **Antiracist counterstrategy experimental design information**

Experimental group	Manipulation	N
Control	Biographies of Cindy Hyde-Smith and Mike Espy	498
Treatment 1	Candidate biographies + article excerpt	502
Treatment 2	Candidate biographies + article excerpt + video attack ad	488

I tested this strategy using an incident from the 2018 midterm election. On November 11, 2018, Cindy Hyde-Smith was caught on camera telling one of her supporters that she would "be in the front row" of a public hanging if invited. Hyde-Smith, a white Republican, was competing in a runoff election against Mike Espy, a Black Democrat, for a US Senate seat in Mississippi. Democrats and the media roundly criticized Hyde-Smith's comments as racially charged and violating social norms, particularly given the violent racial history of Mississippi and the prominent role public hangings played in that history. PowerPACPlus, a political action committee supporting Espy, seized upon her comments and released a video attack ad online that showed Hyde-Smith making the controversial comments superimposed on an old photo of a white crowd attending a lynching of two Black men. The ad made it clear that Hyde-Smith's comments were racist and in violation of racially egalitarian norms.

Data for this test came from a survey sample of 1,488 adult US residents collected in May 2019, through Lucid. A detailed discussion of this sample can be found in chapter 3.[4] Respondents were randomly assigned to one of three experimental groups. The first group (control) was told that Hyde-Smith and Espy had competed in a runoff election for the US Senate from Mississippi and read short biographies of both candidates using information taken directly from their campaign websites. The second group (treatment 1) read the same biographies and then read a short excerpt of an article that discussed Hyde-Smith's comment about the public hanging without passing any judgment on the comments or on Hyde-Smith. The third group (treatment 2) read the biographies and excerpt and then watched the campaign video attacking Hyde-Smith for her comments. Treatment 2 served as the test of the antiracist counterstrategy. Respondents in each experimental group were then asked how likely they would have been to vote for Hyde-Smith.

My expectation was that after reading the article, there would be little change in support for Hyde-Smith among Republican voters. Simply reading about the comments without any frame would not increase or

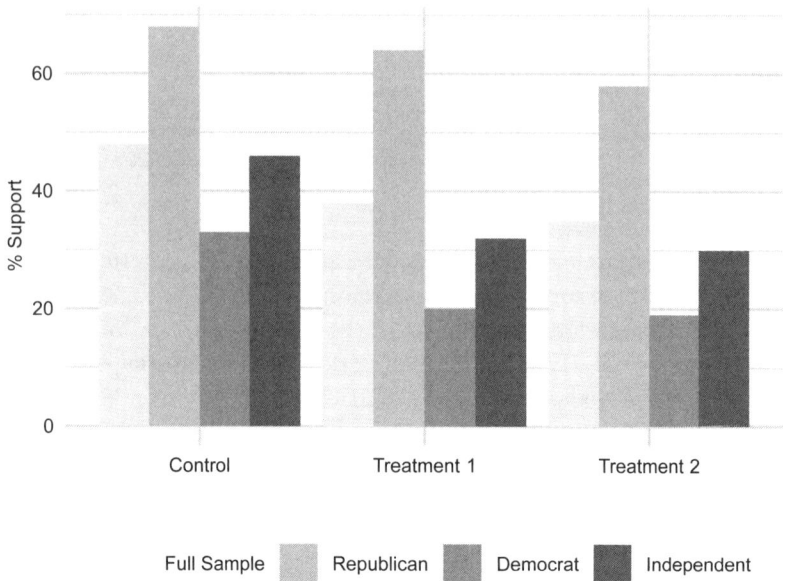

FIGURE 7.3. Percentage of respondents in full sample and by party identification who were somewhat or very likely to have voted for Cindy Hyde-Smith. Data from the May 2019 Lucid survey.

decrease support. However, Republican respondents who watched the campaign video and were told the comments violated social norms should be less likely to say that they would have voted for Hyde-Smith. Democrats and Independents, who were less predisposed to support Hyde-Smith were likely to be influenced by both treatments.

Figure 7.3 shows the percentage of respondents in the full sample and by party who were "somewhat" or "very" likely to have voted for Hyde-Smith if they lived in Mississippi. The figure indicates that 48% of the sample supported Hyde-Smith in the control condition, including 68% of Republicans, 46% of Independents, and 32% of Democrats. In treatment 1, where respondents read about Hyde-Smith's public hanging comments, support for the candidate dropped to 38%. This decrease in support was largely driven by Democrats and Independents and is statistically significant to the $p < .05$ level according to a two-sample t-test. Republican support for Hyde-Smith did not change in a statistically significant way. But in treatment 2, Republican support for Hyde-Smith was a full 10 percentage points lower than in the control condition. Only after hearing that the comments violated social norms did support for the candidate drop among her party base. As predicted, support for Hyde-Smith decreased among Democrats and Independents in both treatment 1 and treatment 2, relative to the control group.

Figure 7.4 displays the relationship between respondents' scores on the SNI and their level of support for Hyde-Smith.[5] Each line represents the marginal effect of the SNI on the reported likelihood of voting for Hyde-Smith after controlling for partisan identity, gender, education level, age, and racial resentment. The figure shows that the relationship between the SNI and support for Hyde-Smith was strong in each experimental group. Moving from most egalitarian to most inegalitarian predicts a 22-percentage-point increase in support among the control group. The strength of the SNI as a predictor increases in treatment 1, as the same movement from most egalitarian to most inegalitarian predicts a 44-point increase, and strengthens even more in treatment 2, as it predicts a 50-point increase in candidate support. Reading about the public hanging comments decreased support for Hyde-Smith among respondents who scored lowest (most egalitarian)

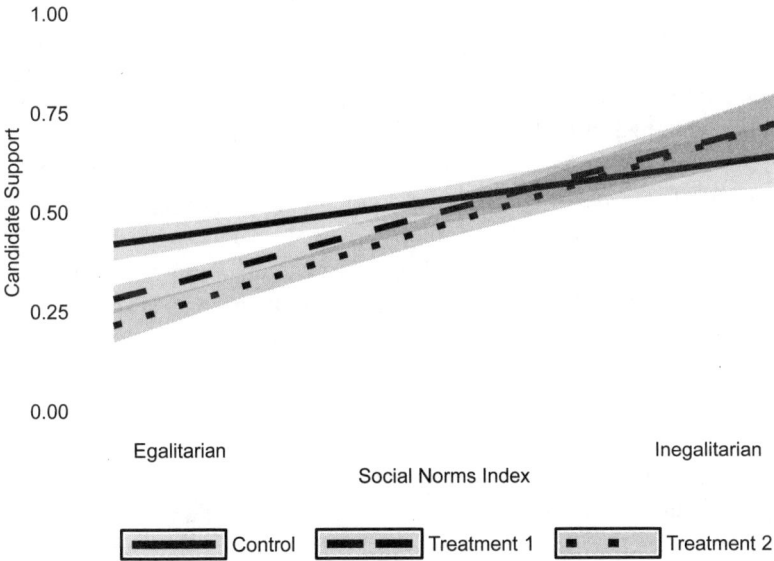

FIGURE 7.4. The relationship between the social norms index and reported likelihood of voting for Cindy Hyde-Smith across all three experimental groups. Data from the May 2019 Lucid survey.

on the SNI. Roughly 46% of the most egalitarian respondents supported Hyde-Smith in the control group, compared to only 29% in treatment 1. But the most inegalitarian respondents were more likely to support Hyde-Smith after reading about her public hanging comments: 72% compared to 65%. This pattern is even starker in treatment 2, where only 22% of the most egalitarian respondents supported Hyde-Smith but 72% of the most inegalitarian respondents did.

It appears that making voters aware that a campaign appeal violated egalitarian social norms can be an effective strategy for decreasing candidate support. It is particularly effective in a low-information context in which voters have received very little additional information about the candidates. This is because egalitarian voters can be persuaded by antiracist messages to not support prejudicial candidates. The most inegalitarian voters became even more likely to support the antiminority candidate but, as shown by the distribution of the SNI in chapter 3, there are substantially more egalitarian voters than inegalitarian voters, at least at the national level.

The effect of this strategy on Democrats and Independents is nuanced. Support for Hyde-Smith among both groups decreased substantially after they read about her public hanging comments (treatment 1) relative to the control group. Support did not further decrease in treatment 2 after watching the attack ad. Thus, Democrats and Independents merely needed to be made aware of the anti-Black prejudicial content to oppose the candidate. This finding nevertheless provides support for the effectiveness of the antiracist counterstrategy. In many cases, prospective voters may not be aware of the prejudicial comment or campaign appeal until they see the condemnation of it. Moreover, this strategy was effective at decreasing support even among Republican voters who were 10 percentage points less supportive of Hyde-Smith after being made aware that her public hanging comments violated egalitarian social norms.

Media Condemnation

The third strategy to combat political prejudice involves media condemnation. The media play an outsized role in shaping and activating public attitudes (see Iyengar and Kinder 1987; Gilliam and Iyengar 2000). As the media are neither neutral nor value free, the way the media frame groups, issues, and events shapes public attitudes. Racial bias and negative reporting about minority groups in the news often activates racial prejudice

TABLE 7.3 **Media condemnation experimental design information**

Experimental group	Manipulation	N
Control	Biography of Duncan Hunter	506
Treatment 1	Biography of Duncan Hunter + Islamophobic ad	496
Treatment 2	Biography of Duncan Hunter + Islamophobic ad + media condemnation article excerpt	486

among viewers and solidifies negative beliefs about out-groups (Dixon 2008; Fiske 1998; Park and Judd 2005). Stereotypic portrayals of minority groups prime racial attitudes, which can influence candidate evaluations (Valentino 1999) and lead to endorsement of antiminority policy positions (Gilliam et al. 2002; Lajevardi 2020).

Media frames can also highlight racial inequality. Arora et al. (2019) found that media attention to policing issues was associated with increased legislative attention to police reform. Moreover, they found that positive media framing of Black Lives Matter activists was associated with the introduction of bills that attempted to increase police accountability. Furthermore, Kellstedt (2000) demonstrated that when media framing of race focused on egalitarianism, there was greater support among the public for active government policies meant to alleviate racial inequality. Given the agenda-setting power and framing power of the news media, its attention to prejudicial messaging and framing those messages as violations of egalitarian norms could lead to rejection of explicit prejudicial campaign appeals.

Data for this test came from a survey sample of 1,488 adult US residents collected in May 2019, through Lucid. A detailed discussion of this sample can be found in chapter 3.[6] Respondents were again randomly assigned to one of three treatment groups. The control group read the same biography of Hunter that was used in the bipartisan condemnation strategy. The treatment 1 group read the biography and watched the same Islamophobic campaign advertisement. In treatment 2, instead of reading an article about bipartisan condemnation of the message, respondents read an excerpt of an article in which members of the media condemned the Islamophobic ad as "racist and bigoted." The wording of the excerpt was exactly the same as in the bipartisan condemnation test. The only difference was, instead of the messenger being a bipartisan group of national security veterans, the messenger was members of the media.

Figure 7.5 displays the percentage of respondents who said they were somewhat or very likely to vote for Hunter if they lived in his congressional

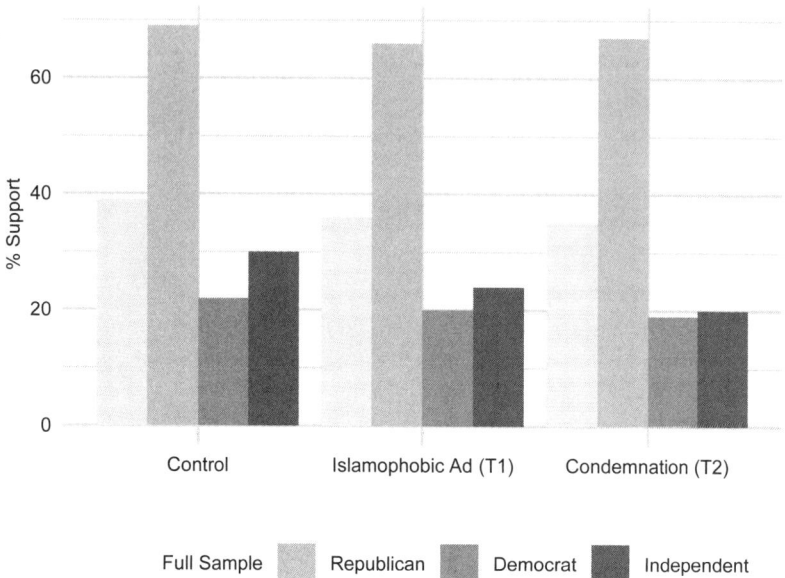

FIGURE 7.5. Percentage of respondents in full sample and by party identification who were somewhat or very likely to have voted for Duncan Hunter (media condemnation test). Data from the May 2019 Lucid survey.

district by party and across the three experimental conditions. Two important results are evident from this graph. First, similar to the bipartisan condemnation test, the overt Islamophobic campaign video did not have any substantial effect on support for Hunter among Republicans. There was, however, a small backlash from Independents. Second, overall support for Hunter was no different in the media condemnation (T2) condition than in treatment 1 or in the control group, showing that media condemnation was unable to neutralize the effect of the Islamophobic campaign appeal. Support for Hunter in treatment 2 was slightly lower among Democrats and Independents relative to treatment 1, but the differences are not statistically significant.

The failure of the media condemnation strategy to neutralize explicit prejudice may be attributed to trust in the media being at historic lows. Gallup polls show that trust in the news media dropped from 54% in 2003 to 32% in 2016 (Knight Foundation 2018). Among Republicans, 94% say their trust in the media has diminished in the last decade, and only 12% say they trust information they receive from national news organizations "a lot" (Gottfried et al. 2018). Only individuals and institutions whom the public trust tend to change public opinion. Thus, as long as people do not trust the media, it is unlikely that the media will be able to effectively neutralize prejudicial campaign messaging. This is particularly true for Republicans, who are most supportive of prejudicial messaging, most likely to receive prejudicial appeals from candidates from within their party, and least trusting of the media. This finding is a major blow to the prospects of neutralizing political prejudice as the media, with its large audience and proven agenda-setting power, could have been a prominent player in the resistance effort.

Activating Moral Codes

The fourth strategy involves appeals to people's moral codes. Numerous social psychology studies show that when people learn about racism and its effects on minorities, their feelings of racial guilt and responsibility are heightened (see Kernahan and Davis 2007) and, in some circumstances, people are more likely to oppose racism (see Hollinsworth 1992; Cross 2003). One way people tend to learn about racism and other forms of prejudice is through diversity trainings. At least one study found that participation in diversity trainings increased interactions with people of other races and led to greater comfort in discussing racial issues (Kernahan and Davis 2009). Given that racial attitudes and other forms of out-group animus tend to be among the most crystallized and stable views people hold, it is remarkable that raising awareness of prejudice and its consequences can have such an effect.

It is thus possible that appealing to people's moral codes could neutralize prejudicial campaign rhetoric by decreasing support for candidates who use that messaging. Many supporters of candidates who make openly hostile remarks about minority groups may be unaware of the dangerous and sometimes violent consequences of these messages. As discussed in the introduction to this chapter, there is a plethora of evidence that prejudicial political rhetoric enflames out-group animus in ways that can have violent consequences. Yet, many who accept prejudicial rhetoric targeting a group may do so for political gain without wishing violent harm on members of that community. Informing respondents of the violent consequences may be an effective strategy for neutralizing these campaign messages because it helps people understand the perspective of the communities under attack, thereby activating feelings of guilt (Kernahan and Davis 2007). As such, if they were made aware of the potentially violent consequences of a prejudicial campaign message, they may reject the candidate who is using that messaging strategy.

I tested this strategy using an experiment embedded in the March 2023 survey collected through Lucid. A detailed discussion of the sample can be found in chapter 3.[7] This sample consisted of 2,994 US adults. Roughly one-third of the sample was randomly assigned to the control group and read a short biography of Kyle Anderson, a fictional US senator who was running for reelection in 2024, including information that the senator had endorsed a bill that would restrict the rights of transgender people:

> Now you will be given information about a Senate candidate and asked to evaluate that candidate. Kyle Anderson is a US senator who is up for reelection in 2024. The senator is a successful former businessman who has promised to simplify the tax code, balance the federal budget, and improve state infrastructure. Senator Anderson has cosponsored a bill to allow private and religious institutions to refuse services to transgender clients.

Another roughly one-third of respondents were randomly assigned to treatment 1, the antitransgender condition. They read the same biography but in this treatment, the candidate's support for the bill was framed using an explicit appeal to antitransgender sentiments.

> In support of his bill, Anderson referred to transgenderism as an "abnormal lifestyle choice" and has promised to do everything he can to "eradicate transgenderism."

The final third of respondents were randomly assigned to treatment 2, the condemnation condition. They were given the same information as the respondents in treatment 1, but were also made aware of the detrimental effects of the antitransgender message on transgender people.

> Anderson was criticized by the CEO of the Human Rights Campaign for his comments about transgender people. The CEO discussed real-world consequences of Anderson's comments, citing a recent report that showed that one in five of any type of hate crime is now motivated by antitransgender bias and that more than 60% of transgender youth said their mental health has deteriorated as a result of recent efforts to restrict their rights.

Respondents in each experimental group were then asked how likely or unlikely they would be to vote for Senator Anderson if they lived in

TABLE 7.4 **Moral codes experimental design information**

Experimental group	Manipulation	N
Control	Biography of Kyle Anderson	743
Treatment 1	Candidate biography + antitransgender appeal	749
Treatment 2	Candidate biography + antitransgender appeal + condemnation	754

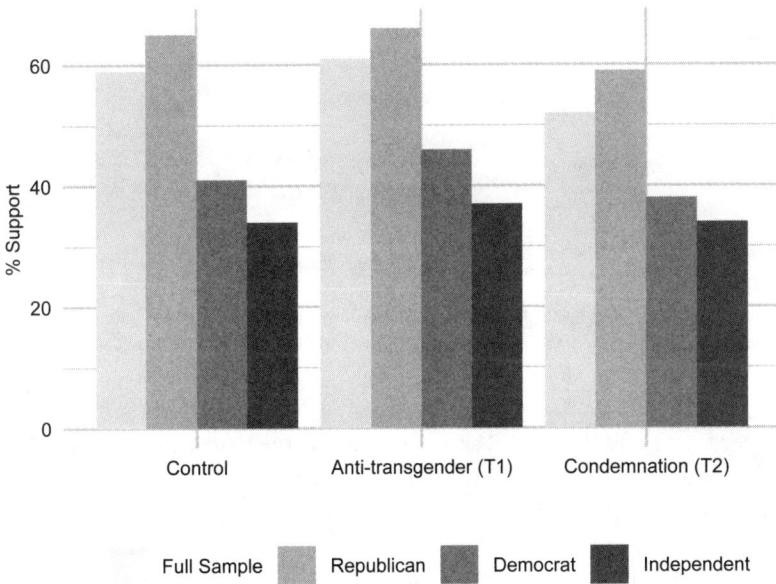

FIGURE 7.6. Percentage of respondents in full sample and by party identification who were somewhat or very likely to have voted for Senator Anderson. Data from the March 2023 Lucid survey.

his state. Response options were "very likely," "somewhat likely," "somewhat unlikely," and "very unlikely." Figure 7.6 displays the percentage of respondents in the three experimental groups who said they were very or somewhat likely to vote for the candidate. There are two notable results. First, support for the senator did not change in the antitransgender (T1) condition relative to the control group. Learning about the senator's overtly antitransgender comments did not increase or decrease his intended vote share among Republicans, Democrats, or Independents in any significant way. Second, support for the senator in the condemnation condition (T2) was 7 points lower than in the control group and 9 points

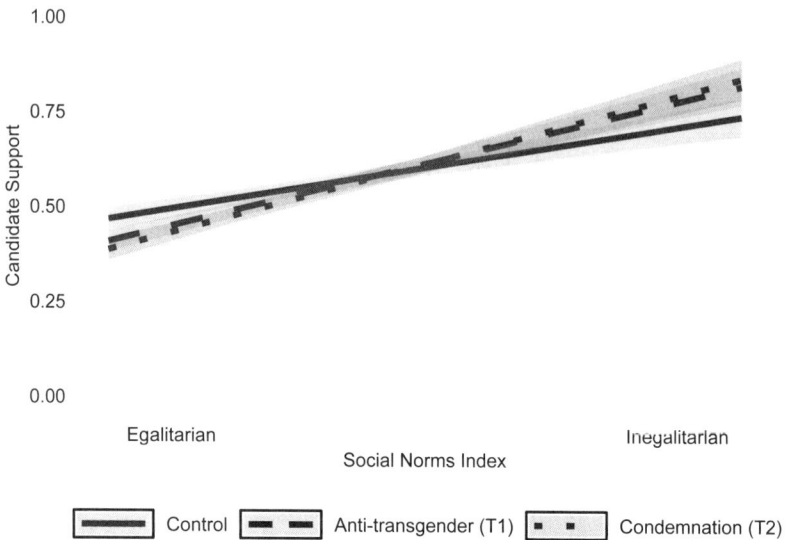

FIGURE 7.7. The relationship between the SNI and reported likelihood of voting for Senator Anderson across all three experimental groups. Data from the March 2023 Lucid survey.

lower than in treatment 1. These differences are statistically significant to the $p < .01$ level according to two-sample t-tests. Appealing to people's moral codes appears to be effective in decreasing support for a politician who is overtly antitransgender. Interestingly, the strategy was effective in reducing candidate support among Republicans and Democrats, but not among Independents. Support for the senator decreased in treatment 2 among Democrats (8 points) and Republicans (7 points)—support among Independents did not change.

Similar to the previous tests, figure 7.7 displays the relationship between respondents' scores on the SNI and their level of support for Senator Anderson.[8] Each line represents the marginal effect of the SNI on the reported likelihood of voting for Anderson after controlling for partisan identity, gender, education level, age, and racial resentment. The findings from this figure are similar to what I have found in the previous tests: The condemnation is most effective in decreasing support among the most egalitarian respondents. In the moral codes condemnation condition (T2), about 37% of the most egalitarian respondents said they would vote for Senator Anderson, which is 7 percentage points lower than stated support from these respondents in the antitransgender condition (T1). Though this is a relatively small change, 7 points among the most egalitarian respondents would be enough in some scenarios to sway the results of a real election and, in this case, stop an overtly antitransgender senator from getting reelected. Overall, the findings are promising. Appealing to moral codes by informing people about the harmful real-world effects of antiminority rhetoric can decrease support for candidates who use such rhetoric. As expected, decreases in support are largest among those who most strongly adhere to egalitarian norms.

Conclusion

There are several notable implications of the four strategies presented in this chapter. First, bipartisan condemnation of an overt anti-Muslim campaign ad was highly effective at reducing support for the candidate who employed that message. Even though chapter 5 showed that overt anti-Muslim prejudice is largely accepted by the American public, bipartisan signals that expressing Islamophobia is a violation of egalitarian norms can have a powerful effect on vote choice in an experimental setting. Second, there is some evidence that an antiracist counterstrategy from Democrats can be effective at the margins. When informed that a candidate violated egalitarian norms, support for the candidate decreased substantially among Democrats and Independents and even decreased among Republicans. The results from this strategy suggest that a foray into identity politics is not only the morally correct strategy but may also be a potentially effective electoral strategy for Democrats because of its potential to, at least somewhat, neutralize the harmful effects of overt prejudice in politics.[9]

Third, there is little evidence that media condemnation can effectively neutralize the effects of an anti-Muslim campaign ad. The media condemnation strategy did not cause any statistically significant change in candidate support. Fourth, the strategy of appealing to people's moral codes showed some promise for reducing support for a candidate who used an overt antitransgender campaign appeal. Support for the antitransgender candidate decreased among Democrats and Republicans after respondents were informed of the harmful real-world consequences of such rhetoric. In each of the tests, the condemnations were most effective in decreasing support for candidates who used antiminority messaging among those who most strongly adhere to egalitarian norms.

The findings show it is very important for Democrats to call out prejudice, whether through bipartisan condemnation or by appealing to the egalitarianism of Independents and weak Republicans. There is evidence that Democrats will do this at increasing rates (see Stout 2020). But the most effective strategy for neutralizing prejudice involved Republicans joining Democrats to condemn a member of their own party. There are some real-world examples of this from recent years. Several prominent Republicans criticized fellow GOP Senator Trent Lott in 2002 for his praise of Strom Thurmond, a prominent segregationist. More recently, GOP Senator Tim Scott and others criticized Steve King, a Republican member of the House, for his endorsement of white nationalism. During his 2016 campaign, and throughout his first term as president, Trump was criticized by fellow Republicans for his overt prejudice. In 2016, Paul Ryan, a Republican and former Speaker of the House, called Trump's comment about a federal judge's Mexican heritage, "textbook racism." One year later, after Trump reportedly referred to several countries in Africa as "shithole countries," Republican and former Ohio Governor John Kasich called his comments "divisive" and "unacceptable."

Yet, these are exceptions to the rule and come with heavy caveats. First, Republican condemnations of their own party members are rare. Marjorie Taylor Greene, Paul Gosar, Lauren Boebert, and many other prominent Republicans frequently make overt antiminority comments without facing any condemnation from within their party. Second, they do not always work. Despite criticism from fellow Republicans, Trump secured the GOP nomination, got elected president, and was subsequently elected again in 2024. Moreover, most Republicans who opposed Trump faced significant backlash from the party and have since faded from any position of prominence that they held. Indeed, the more frequent strategy of the GOP has been to cast Democrats and the media as overly sensitive about racism and prejudice. Either there have to be drastic changes to the internal functioning of the Republican Party or we will have to look elsewhere for methods to combat political prejudice such as an antiracist counterstrategy from Democrats and appeals to people's moral codes that can at least neutralize support for antiminority candidates at the margins.

The strategies tested here do not represent the full universe of potential ways to counter political prejudice. Future studies can test additional ways to signal norm violations. Moreover, strategies that show potential, such as bipartisan condemnation, Democratic condemnations, and appeals to moral codes should be tested in various contexts to discover the conditions under which they are most effective. For example, these strategies are likely more effective in low-information elections than in high-information elections. It is easier to neutralize prejudicial messaging from someone like Duncan Hunter, whom people have less information about, than someone like Trump, who is well known and about whom public attitudes are stable. It is likely also easier to counteract prejudicial messages targeting groups that are closer to the egalitarian end of the social norms spectrum and when condemnations come from trusted sources who have large and influential platforms. The four strategies presented here contribute to the scholarship focused on neutralizing the many detrimental effects of explicit prejudice that have been discussed throughout the book.

CHAPTER EIGHT

Implications of the Normalization of Prejudice

People don't commit violence against other groups—or even condone it—spontaneously. First they must be taught to see other people as pests, vermin, aliens, or threats. Malicious leaders often use the same types of rhetoric to do this, in myriad cultures, languages, countries, and historical periods. We call this Dangerous Speech. —Dangerous Speech Project[1]

On May 14, 2022, an eighteen-year-old white man opened fire in a Tops Friendly Markets in Buffalo, New York, murdering ten people and injuring three more. All of his victims were Black. According to the gunman's manifesto, which he posted online before the attack, he had chosen this location because of its large African American population. The gunman also claimed his motivation for the attack was his belief in a nefarious plot to commit genocide against white people (Abbas et al. 2022). Not coincidentally, this so-called "great replacement" conspiracy theory, which was once a fringe idea among far-right extremists, had recently become mainstream within the Republican Party.

Users of online white nationalist forums like Stormfront had been posting about the great replacement for decades prior to the shooting. These forums served as a breeding ground for this hateful idea by providing a space to develop and sustain a collective identity among white power activists (see Futrell and Simi 2004), and by providing a platform for users to post about the great replacement and other racist ideas in an anonymized fashion. However, the key ingredient was missing: Online posters on Stormfront and other platforms needed someone with a more influential platform to endorse the great replacement theory so it could spread beyond fringe white supremacist communities.

Donald Trump did just this. He weaponized the great replacement theory by making thinly veiled references to it in connection to the 2020 election, blaming his loss on "illegal immigrant voters" replacing lawful white voters (Factbase 2020). Moreover, one year before the mass shooting in Buffalo, Tucker Carlson, who at that time had the most watched show on Fox News, openly embraced the great replacement theory (Petrizzo 2021). The mutually reinforcing effects of far-right online communities laying the initial groundwork, and influential elites like Trump and Carlson endorsing the great replacement theory, provided a runway for a once unacceptable idea to become part of mainstream discourse. The horrific events in Buffalo did not stop the GOP from further embracing the racist conspiracy theory during that year's midterm election. Indeed, a report by America's Voice identified 546 campaign-related tweets, paid political ads, and campaign emails from almost one hundred Republican candidates, elected officials, and party officials that focused on "white replacement" or a "migrant invasion" (Mueller 2022).

What happened in Buffalo was far from an isolated incident. Manifestos published by perpetrators of mass shootings across the world—including a synagogue in Pittsburgh (Lind 2018), a Walmart in El Paso (Arango et al. 2019), and mosques in Christchurch, New Zealand (Iftikhar 2020)—all cited the great replacement theory as at least one of their motives. These manifestos echoed language that is now prominent in right-wing discourse. The acts of violence that the manifestos led to are the horrifying consequences of the normalization of prejudice.

Qualifying the Results

Antiminority Messaging Is Not Only Coming from White Male Republicans

The primary actors who have helped bring this type of antiminority prejudice to the mainstream, like Trump and Carlson, are mostly white, male Republicans. As such, the empirical analysis in this book mostly focused on antiminority messages from white male Republican political elites. However, evidence presented throughout the book shows that the messengers of prejudice and the target audience of these messages are not limited to that group. Republicans, regardless of racial or gender identity, are incentivized in some situations to explicitly signal prejudicial attitudes toward groups for whom a norm of equality has not been developed, such as Muslims and transgender people. Several reports cited throughout the book also show that antiminority messaging in recent election cycles is coming from women Republicans and Republicans of color (see, for example, Mueller 2022). Moreover, Republican women and Republicans of color are often as supportive of antiminority rhetoric as their white male counterparts.

Democrats Are Not Exempt

There are also situations in which Democrats are incentivized to use anti-minority appeals, possibly to pacify voters in their district who think they might attempt to upend the established racial hierarchy. For example, Stephens-Dougan's (2020) racial distancing model argues that Black politicians, including Black Democrats, may need to be even more explicit in signaling their intention to maintain the racial status quo than white politicians because many racially moderate and conservative white voters are predisposed to believe they may disrupt it. Consequently, her experimental findings showed that anti-Black campaign appeals from Black candidates effectively activated negative racial attitudes from many Democratic voters. The findings from this book provide some additional evidence that Democratic voters may be receptive to antiminority messaging in some situations. For example, the experimental results presented in chapter 5 showed that, in some contexts, almost 50% of Democrats supported a candidate who was overtly Islamophobic. The findings in chapter 6 showed that more than 40% of Democrats supported an education bill when it was framed as antitransgender or antigay.

The findings in the case study chapters clearly support the assertion that norms are more inegalitarian within the GOP than within the Democratic Party. And the most prominent purveyors of antiminority prejudice tend to be white men. Still, out-group animus exists within both major political parties and extends to most demographic groups. How that prejudice manifests depends on the social norms that exist within those groups.

Measuring Social Norm Adherence Is Useful but Difficult

Academic studies in a wide range of disciplines from political science and social psychology to legal studies and health sciences have theorized the integral role of social norms on individual attitudes and behaviors. In particular, many previous studies have identified adherence to social norms as the basis for understanding the use of, and reactions to, antiminority messaging. A challenge to this scholarship is the difficulty in measuring individual norm adherence. The social norms index (SNI), detailed in chapter 3, is my attempt to create a generalizable measure. The empirical tests presented in the chapter demonstrate strong internal validity of the SNI. Use of the SNI in subsequent case study chapters established its accuracy in predicting who will accept or reject candidates who use antiminority messaging. Yet, there is much work to be done for it to become a standard measure used in the discipline. The SNI is likely not a perfect measure and may not be applicable to all studies examining reactions to prejudice. But, having a measure is valuable to the hypotheses in this book and to other studies that theorize a relationship between norms and antiminority messaging. Future studies can build from the SNI by varying the subject groups, scenarios, and wording of the vignettes; and testing the effects of the SNI in other experimental and nonexperimental settings.

Geographic Variation Likely Exists

The upshot of many of this book's findings is that primary elections will increasingly be characterized by overt antiminority messaging and general elections will increasingly feature racially polarized candidates. The period of American politics in which prejudice bubbled under the surface and Democrats and Republicans were locked into electoral temptations of racial silence and racial code words seems to have come to an end. Instead, overt prejudice has moved to the forefront of US politics, transforming the electoral incentives of both major political parties.

However, this will not be the case in all circumstances. The effectiveness of antiminority rhetoric depends partially on geography. Support for antiminority messaging among Republican and Democratic voters will likely vary by state and electoral district. Though partisan sorting has led to the parties' bases being increasingly homogeneous on racial attitudes, geographic variation within the parties remains. Moreover, even though attitudes are largely homogeneous, not all Republican voters are mobilized by antiminority messaging to the same extent, and not all Democrats will be turned off by these appeals. For example, Ed Gillespie, the Republican candidate for governor in Virginia in 2017, used numerous explicit anti-Latino and anti-immigrant campaign appeals. But, as I discussed in chapter 3, the general election results demonstrated that an openly antiminority messaging strategy was not effective in that given location. Public opinion polls conducted in Virginia showed that exposure to Gillespie's anti-immigrant advertisements decreased support for the candidate among voters despite opposition to immigration and immigrants' rights being quite high among Republicans and Independents.[2] To more fully understand the changing electoral temptations of political parties, future work can analyze heterogeneity in responses to antiminority rhetoric by geographic region and other salient societal cleavages like gender identity, racial identity, and class.

Prejudice in Politics Will Likely Intensify

Despite the likelihood of geographic variation in response to antiminority messaging, the overall findings are clear. Chapter 5 showed that overt Islamophobia is largely accepted by the public, especially by Republicans. Indeed, overt anti-Muslim campaign appeals benefited Republican candidates in experimental settings and are being widely used in real-world contexts. Sizable portions of Independents and Democrats were also supportive of Islamophobic candidates in some situations. Chapter 6 showed widespread acceptance of overt homophobic and transphobic messaging among Republicans and evangelicals, which corresponds to the current wave of anti-LGBTQ+ rhetoric and legislation. Chapter 4 showed that the norm of racial equality in principle is destabilizing within the GOP. Candidates who made overt anti-Black campaign appeals garnered significant support from Republicans. Moreover, analysis of Fox News coverage demonstrated that the anti-Black agenda is being laundered through opposition to the Black Lives Matter movement and the weaponization of opposition to wokeness, critical race theory, and diversity, equity, and inclusion initiatives. In sum, the case studies present a clear picture of the demonization of minority groups and the growing normalization of antiminority prejudice in politics.

This is not simply a function of the Trump era, either. The roots are far deeper and far older than Trump and will live on after he has left the political limelight. The partisan realignment that sorted racial conservatives into the GOP and racial liberals into the Democratic Party began before Trump was born. Other important factors in shifting the norm environment—like the September 11, 2001, terrorist attacks, the 2008 economic recession, and Barack Obama's election and reelection—also took place before Trump's rise to political prominence. Professor John E. Owens (2021, 32) succinctly described the transformation of the Republican Party: "It's the result of a decades-long process by which the Grand Old Party (GOP) unshackled itself from its core conservative principles, as it harnessed itself to opposition and identity politics, exploited white low-income voters' fears of cultural change and economic displacement, and embraced antidemocratic action. Building on groundwork laid by House Speaker Newt Gingrich's ruthless partisanship and a scorched-earth style of politics in the 1990s, as well as the steady migration of noncollege white male voters to the Republican Party, Trump's nativist, populist appeal and brazen personal style further reinforced this shift."

Trump may not be the root cause, but he is a major catalyst in spreading grievance politics and normalizing prejudice. Trump's candidacy was built on demonizing minority groups and appealing to the prejudicial sentiments of voters. Not coincidentally, hate crimes skyrocketed during his first term in office. White nationalist organizations flourished as their membership grew and their ideas were mainstreamed with the help of Republican elites and conservative media hosts. Republican candidates in each election cycle since 2016 have largely relied on antiminority messaging to mobilize voters. The 2018 election was described by media outlets as the most Islamophobic election ever (Aziza 2018), the 2020 election featured a major backlash to the Black Lives Matter movement and an eruption of anti-AAPI content, and the 2022 and 2024 elections featured anti-LGBTQ+ messaging to an extent not seen in decades. The primary subjects of the right-wing establishment's ire shift according to changes in the political, economic, and social context, but the playbook stays the same.

Shifting Attention to Other Groups

It's clear that those who want to maintain the status quo hierarchy in the US can find different boogeymen to hold up as threats to the prevailing order. As discussed in chapter 4, opposition to Black rights has been a prominent strategy in US politics for most of the country's history. Opposition to gay and lesbian rights, and now to transgender rights, has also been a prominent strategy for decades, particularly among social and religious conservatives. The 9/11 attacks, a major exogenous shock to the system, brought pervasive negative political attention to Muslim Americans. Conservative political and media elites activated public fear and resentment of Muslims and tied it to Barack Obama and the Democratic Party. These actors successfully shifted the norm environment and made anti-Muslim messaging an effective arrow in the conservative quiver. These groups are illustrative of the current social norm environment, but there are several other groups that could have been the focus of the case study chapters in this book.

Another example of an exogenous shock being a catalyst for social norm transformation is the recent COVID-19 pandemic. In March 2020, soon after the first reported case of COVID-19 in the US, Trump referred to the coronavirus as the "Chinese virus" in a tweet (Trump 2020). Many other influential leaders, including Republican elected officials (Slisco 2020), White House staff (Nakamura 2020), and Fox News hosts (Chiu 2020), followed suit with their own anti-Asian and anti-Chinese rhetoric. As the pandemic worsened, the country saw a major increase in documented incidents of anti-Asian racism and violence (Stop AAPI Hate 2022), with much of the heightened anti-Asian sentiment being directly attributable to COVID-19-related anti-Asian rhetoric from Trump and others.

Indeed, heightened anti-Asian and xenophobic attitudes is specifically tied to the pandemic. Using survey data collected in March 2020, Reny and Barreto (2022) found that concerns about the COVID-19 virus were associated with low levels of favorability toward Chinese Americans and Asian Americans and with behaviors such as avoiding Chinese restaurants and "staying away from foreigners." Concern about the virus was also associated with support for a set of xenophobic policies such as reducing visas for people from Asia and mandatory quarantines for Asian travelers. Importantly, the authors found that concern about the virus was not associated with attitudes toward other minority groups like Black and Latino people. During this period, a major societal event—the COVID-19 pandemic—combined with clear signals from influential leaders who blamed China and Asian Americans for spreading the virus made the Asian American community a more urgent threat in the minds of many US residents. In turn, overt anti-Asian sentiment and behavior seemed to become more socially acceptable.

Latinos and immigrants also face significant prejudice in the current political environment. On July 1, 2015, Kathryn Steinle was shot and killed in San Francisco, allegedly by an undocumented immigrant named Juan Francisco Lopez-Sanchez. This became a flashpoint in the ongoing GOP presidential primary for multiple reasons. Immigration was already becoming a major topic in the primary election, largely due to Donald Trump and his anti-immigrant rhetoric. The killing of a young woman by an undocumented immigrant only added fuel to the already vitriolic anti-immigrant environment. Additionally, the incident occurred in San

Francisco, a liberal hotbed and sanctuary city that had refused to comply with federal Immigration and Citizenship Enforcement agents. Trump made this event a major talking point in his speeches and interviews over the coming weeks particularly during the highly televised Family Leadership Summit a few weeks after the incident. Over that same time period, Trump's poll numbers almost doubled from 11.1% on June 29 (two days before the shooting) to 20.4% on July 19 (the day after the summit).[3] This is just one of many examples of campaign rhetoric that explicitly expressed hostility and appeared to be met with enthusiasm from voters.

This anecdote is illustrative of the scholarship. Perez (2016) found that negative and threatening media coverage of Latinos has led white Americans to, implicitly and explicitly, associate the group with illegality, and illegality has developed as a justification for out-group hostility (Sidanius and Pratto 2001). Consequently, hostility toward Latinos is highest when the group is paired with salient stereotypes of foreignness and illegality. Recent work has demonstrated that immigration has had a fundamental impact on American politics by influencing white attitudes and altering partisan attachments (Abrajano and Hajnal 2015). Increases in the immigrant population have activated racial and cultural threat (Hopkins 2010; Newman 2013; Enos 2017) and increased support for anti-immigrant policies (Abrajano and Hajnal 2015). Massey (2014) demonstrated that threatening framing of Latinos by political and media elites moved white people to support restrictive immigration policies. The 2006 immigrant rights marches, while emboldening liberals, also "pushed conservatives in Congress further to the right" (Zepeda-Millan 2017, 193), increasing support for restrictive immigration policy. Importantly, Reny et al. (2020) found that anti-Latino campaign appeals, particularly when Latinos were framed as immigrants, effectively primed racial attitudes without being rejected by voters. My own work, which can be found in the appendix, shows that Republicans are supportive of candidates who overtly signal anti-Mexican and anti-immigrant sentiments in experimental settings.

As long as grievance politics is a dominant strategy for one of the major American political parties, the focus of antiminority politics can shift with changing political, economic, and social circumstances. Indeed, the GOP has made a living by constructing an "other" to appeal to the antiminority sentiments of key constituents within their base. The development of the norm environment and the level of threat felt by the public will determine which group(s) is the current boogeyman and what strategies elites use to activate negative out-group sentiments. If people feel threatened by a group without a constructed norm of equality, then we should expect overt political prejudice to follow. Moreover, even if a norm of equality has been established, that norm can become destabilized if influential actors use their platforms to consistently and forcefully communicate opposition to equality. In sum, the case studies presented in this book do not encompass the full universe of antiminority prejudice in US politics. The findings suggest that different boogeymen will inevitably be constructed to match the social, economic, and political conditions of the time. If groups are not protected by developed and engrained egalitarian norms, they are not safe from the nefarious effects of white grievance politics.

How Will Democrats Respond?

The implications of the theory and findings of this book are largely negative for the well-being of minority groups in the US and for the health of American democracy. However, the findings also point to a growing resistance to prejudice in politics and they provide evidence that prejudicial rhetoric can be neutralized. Each case study presented in chapters 4–6 indicated that norms have developed differently in the Republican and Democratic Parties. The GOP has decidedly become a party that overtly appeals to the prejudicial sentiments of much of its voting base. Each case study showed that the rhetoric of many Republican candidates is overtly antiminority, as are the policies being introduced and passed by GOP-controlled legislative bodies throughout the country. While the GOP is stoking the flames of bigotry and hate for electoral benefit, Democrats are slowly but surely moving in the other direction.

The findings in this book show that Democrats tend to reject antiminority messaging in experimental settings. Democrats have also become more supportive of equal rights in principle, and they've even grown more supportive of equal rights in *practice* since Trump rose to political prominence. For example, chapter 4 showed that Democrats are now more supportive of governmental efforts to improve the economic positions of Black people and that a majority of Democrats now support affirmative action programs. This is especially important because it makes it more likely that equal rights will be enshrined into law.

Democratic elites are also actively taking steps to protect minority rights through rhetoric and legislation. In fact, during Joe Biden's time in office, Democrats and political institutions under Democratic leadership took specific steps to curb the mainstreaming of white supremacy. The Federal Bureau of Investigation and the Department of Homeland Security (2021) identified "racially or ethnically motivated violent extremists," including individuals and organizations who participated in the insurrection, as primary drivers of domestic terrorism and outlined specific action steps being taken to address the problem. One month later, the White House (2021) issued *National Strategy for Confronting Domestic Terrorism*, a report that highlighted the threat of racism and bigotry and laid out a long-term vision to address these societal poisons. Congressional committees led by Democrats, including the January 6 Select Committee, have also taken steps to highlight and address white supremacy.

Egalitarian norms within the Democratic Party are contributing to its at least partial abandonment of the long-held temptation to be silent in the face of prejudice. Indeed, findings in chapter 7 show that a Democratic strategy of condemning antiminority prejudice can be effective in the short term for neutralizing the electoral benefits of antiminority campaign appeals. Further research can test these effects to show replicability, determine the range of condemnations that are effective, and determine the specific election scenarios in which these condemnations will work best. It is also clear that the Democratic Party has not been strong enough in its resistance of grievance politics, and at times leverages antiminority sentiments for its own political gain (see Stephens-Dougan 2020). How forcefully Democrats, progressive activists, the media, and other influential actors resist the normalization of prejudice in coming years will be a key factor to watch.

Democrats will also have to contend with the somewhat fickle attitudes of their base. For example, a recent Democracy Fund report found that 62% of Democrats in the 2024 VOTER Survey said that racial equality is a very important issue, down from 71% who said the same in 2020 (Sides et al. 2024). Similarly, 41% of Democrats in 2024 viewed police reform as a very important issue, down from 53% in 2020. The report also found that Democrats are now less likely to perceive discrimination against Black, Hispanic, and Asian American people, and less likely to support open immigration policies than they were in 2020. After a period in which Democrats had increasingly positive views of racial, ethnic, and religious minority groups, and were increasingly supportive of immigration and governmental efforts to combat racial inequality; attitudes slightly moderated during Biden's presidency. Indeed, the authors of the report argue that there is now a "thermostatic" dynamic to attitudes about minority groups. Though prior work has shown attitudes about race to be quite stable (see Tesler 2015; Atkinson et al. 2021), attitudes may now respond to the policies and rhetoric of the current president. If that is the case, it presents an additional challenge to the solidification of egalitarian norms within the Democratic Party.

Given the plethora of evidence that norms shift over time, and the evidence presented here that racial attitudes may shift in response to presidential administrations, an area ripe for future research is the lasting power or stickiness of egalitarian/inegalitarian norms. The case studies presented in this book show that norms guiding political rhetoric about Black people are actively destabilizing within the GOP; a norm of equality for Muslims may be slowly developing in the Democratic Party; and overt opposition to transgender rights may be contributing to the erosion of egalitarian norms for gay and lesbian people. In chapter 4, I argued that the internalization of norms over time make norms difficult to change and in chapter 6, I presented evidence that internalization happens faster for young people. However, it is still unclear at what point norms are internalized, how that internalization varies across a large population, and how sticky norms are once internalized. Answering these questions can bolster our understanding of norm transformation for subject groups and within target audiences.

Concluding Remarks

On November 5, 2020, two days after the presidential election, Oath Keepers founder Stewart Rhodes sent this message to a group he called "leadership intel sharing secured": "We aren't getting through this without a civil war. Too late for that. Prepare your mind, body, spirit" (Bump 2022a). This was followed by two months of tactical trainings, armament, and violent skirmishes, culminating in the storming of the US Capitol building alongside the Proud Boys and hundreds of other right-wing extremists. While the failed insurrection on January 6, 2021, has mostly been discussed as a last-gasp effort to keep Trump in office, many scholars and public intellectuals viewed it as an attempt to maintain white power (Hayes 2021; Serwer 2021). Hakeem Jefferson, a professor at Stanford University, wrote this two days later: "This is, like so much of American politics, about race, racism, and white Americans' stubborn commitment to white dominance, no matter the cost or the consequence" (Jefferson 2021).

The deep resentments felt by members of the Oath Keepers and Proud Boys and allied supporters of the structure of white supremacy—resentments stoked and enflamed throughout Trump's presidency—were central to the insurrection. White supremacists' anxiety skyrocketed over one of their own vacating the highest political office in the country. Their resentment toward those they blamed for his ouster erupted in a violent attempt to block the peaceful transfer of power. The storming of the Capitol building was a consequence of the normalization and legitimization of dangerous antiminority ideas during the Trump era. Trump pardoning almost all of the insurrectionists furthered entrenched the incident as a legitimate political act in the eyes of much of the public.

The threat to multiracial democracy does not just come from those who participated in the attempted insurrection. It is engrained in the white supremacist ideology of much of the public and in the actions of prominent members of the GOP. A group of eleven GOP senators had previously issued a joint statement demanding the results be overturned and an electoral commission be appointed to investigate election fraud despite there being no evidence of it (Office of Senator Ted Cruz 2021). Mere hours after the insurrection, a majority of Republicans in the US House of Representatives voted to overturn the results of the 2020 presidential election. The reaction from Republican officials should not be surprising. Republicans at the national, state, and local levels have worked hard to pass laws making it more difficult for Black people and other people of color to vote, while blocking legislation to increase voter accessibility. Indeed, they are explicit that some people's votes should matter more than other people's votes.

All of this is made possible by the normalization of prejudice. A June 2022 Monmouth University poll found that a majority (61%) of Republicans viewed the January 6 insurrection as "a legitimate protest" (Monmouth University Polling Institute 2022). This is at least partially because, despite the claim having been repeatedly discredited (Fandos 2017), a similar majority (60%) of Republicans believe unauthorized immigrants vote in elections (Corbett-Davies et al. 2016). About two-thirds of Republicans also believe discrimination against white people has become as big a problem as discrimination against Black people and other minorities (Public Religion Research Institute 2022). The widespread belief among Republican voters in threats to white dominance from people of color and the tendency of GOP officials to demonize minority groups for electoral gain illustrate the lasting power of prejudice in politics and the growing obstacles to building a true multiracial democracy.

The transformation of the Republican Party into one steeped in overt antiminority prejudice and inegalitarian norms has come into sharper focus in 2024. In his successful bid to recapture the presidency, Trump doubled down on his incendiary rhetoric. Philbrick and Bentahar (2023) wrote in *The New York Times* that "Trump's language has become darker, harsher, and more threatening during his third run for the White House." He has frequently advocated violence and referred to the 2024 election as "our final battle." Racist conspiracy theories have remained at the heart of his rhetoric as he portrays Biden's handling of immigration as a "conspiracy to overthrow the United States of America" (Barrow and Colvin 2024). Those within his party who have power to stop him have mostly either stepped aside or enthusiastically supported his efforts. After Trump was found guilty on thirty-four felony charges, most Republican elites lined up to defend him. Even one-time opponents like Nikki Haley and Ron DeSantis and former critics like Mitch McConnell, have fallen in line behind him. Mainstream media continues to give him a platform while conservative media remains unwaveringly loyal to him. Meanwhile, the Supreme Court has delayed other legal cases against him.

Trump's second term in office holds dire consequences for the state of democracy, the normalization of prejudice, and the treatment of minority groups. Trump now has an ironclad grip on the GOP. His defectors have been sidelined and the party has united behind him. Republicans in Congress and in the judiciary have shown almost no willingness to restrain his prejudicial and authoritarian actions. He has also filled his administration with loyalists who are working hard to enact his agenda. As long as Trump is the leader of the Republican Party, inegalitarian norms within the party will only grow stronger. As Ezra Klein recently said on his podcast, "Donald Trump is not a uniquely dangerous person. A few years ago he was a comic figure in American life. . . . Donald Trump is dangerous now because he has taken over the Republican Party."[4] It will take difficult, intentional work from the masses and from influential elites to transform the political environment to one where naked prejudice and violence are not the norm, and in which another Trump-like figure cannot replace Trump as the next leader of the GOP.

Acknowledgments

In 2015, when Donald Trump descended his golden escalator and launched his presidential campaign with a speech branding Mexican immigrants as criminals and rapists, it seemed more like a *Saturday Night Live* sketch or the recreation of an old *Simpsons* episode. However, as Trump escalated his rhetoric against minority communities, his poll numbers rose in tandem. I wanted to understand this phenomenon. Why did such discriminatory rhetoric resonate with so many people? And how could he express his antiminority vitriol so openly without facing widespread public condemnation? These questions marked the beginning of my journey to write this book.

There are so many people who helped me along the way. I am especially grateful to Michael Tesler, without whom this book would not have been possible. Michael was incredibly generous with his time, spending hours talking through ideas with me and reading and editing chapter drafts. I am grateful for the many hours spent in his office, on Zoom, and at Panda Express talking politics, basketball, dogs, pop culture, dating, and so many other topics. His support has meant everything to me. This book is also very much built upon his own work and his influence can be found on almost every page.

In addition to Michael, I am fortunate to have a large support system of people who helped nurture my ideas and gave me the guidance needed to turn them into a published book. Louis DeSipio was infinitely patient with me, listening to my ideas and guiding me in turning them into feasible research questions. I thank Davin Phoenix for giving me hands-on lessons on how to conduct sound research. His comments, and his own work, have greatly influenced the theory and empirics of this book and his thoughtful approach to scholarship has been an inspiration. Claire Kim pushed me to think more deeply and to never confine myself to conventional wisdom while always providing generous encouragement. Bernie Grofman kept me honest, ensured that I truly knew the literature, and reminded me to "think happy thoughts."

Many others have helped me along the way and I am eternally grateful to them. Sara Wallace Goodman was generous in her guidance and mentorship and helped me believe that I belong in academia. Russ Dalton was an invaluable resource for academic knowledge as well as insights into college football recruiting. I would also like to thank Mary McThomas, Graeme Boushey, Matthew Beckmann, Jeffrey Kopstein, Ines Levin, Rein Taagepera, Ann Hironaka, and Evan Schofer for providing advice, guidance, and helpful comments on my work. Thank you also to Hahrie Han for showing me the valuable impact research can have on society and for always providing support and guidance. I am also grateful to Antoine Banks, Andrew Flores, Ashley Jardina, Tom Pepinsky, and Nick Valentino for taking the time to provide helpful feedback on my work. Thank you also to Tom Mowle for his incredible feedback and editing.

I am also grateful to the friends I have made during my academic journey. Hannah June Kim has been the best work partner I could ask for, and without her this book would not have been possible. In-person and virtual writing hours with Hannah and Stacey Liou kept me disciplined, and our Cocktail Fridays helped me get through each week. They have been an invaluable support system throughout the development of this book. Chris Stout has been an incredible mentor and friend to me and his own books have been invaluable resources. This book greatly benefited from Sono Shah's guidance in data analysis and in creating sexy graphs. I am also appreciative of him talking through various aspects of the manuscript with me when I was feeling stuck. I am grateful to Drew Engelhardt for his insightful comments on chapters of this book and his helpful advice on literature and empirical analysis. Many others contributed to the completion of this book in significant ways including Hannah Alarian, Misty Knight-Finley, Trevor Allen, Rob Nyenhuis, Tyler Reny, CJ Lee, Josh Malnight, Shubha Prasad, Archie Delshad, Francisco Jasso, John Emery, Stephen Wandro, Jenny Garcia, Tom Le, Neil Chaturvedi, and Sara Sadhwani. I would also like to thank Peter Miller for his advice and for letting me borrow his name for several of the fictional candidates presented in my survey experiments.

I am forever indebted to the PRIEC community, which helped teach me what it means to be a good colleague and made me feel part of the larger academic community. Specifically, I would like to thank Matt Barreto, Shaun Bowler, Loren Collingwood, Lorrie Frasure-Yokley, Jane Junn, Nazita Lajevardi, Jenn Merolla, Ben Newman, and Karthik Ramakrishnan for their feedback on early versions of my book and for their consistent support. I am especially appreciative of Nazita for her enthusiasm for this project. This manuscript greatly benefited from her guidance and many of the ideas presented in the book were inspired by her own incredible scholarship. I also appreciate the feedback of everyone in attendance at the spring 2019 PRIEC at UC Riverside for their helpful comments on an early version of the manuscript.

I want to thank my department and the administration at Wellesley College for providing me with the time and resources to complete this manuscript. I am particularly grateful to Tom Burke, Paul MacDonald, and Ann Velenchik. Thank you also to my incredible colleagues who have welcomed me to New England and supported me along this journey: Jenn Chudy, Eni Mustafaraj, Chipo Dendere, Danilo Contreras, Igor Logvinenko, Hélène Bilis, Adam Van Arsdale, Dave Olson, Robert Goree, and everyone who I have shared a pint with at beer nights. Thank you also to the incredible Wellesley research assistants who contributed to this manuscript: Hannah Whellan, Anna Lieb, Avery Lumeng, and Anna Nesbitt.

Completion of this book would not have been possible without generous financial support from the Center for the Study of Democracy. I am particularly grateful to Shani Brasier for helping me navigate resource opportunities, and offering encouragement, support, and countless sandwiches.

I would also like to thank Sciences Po-Aix, and especially Taos Boudine, for providing me space to work on this manuscript during my sabbatical. I presented versions of this manuscript at the 2018 and 2019 meetings of the American Political Science Association, the 2019 Western Political Science Association conference, the April 2020 meeting of Brown University's Taubman Center, and as part of Hakeem Jefferson's Identity Politics Workshop at Stanford in January 2020. I am appreciative of the opportunity to present and to the chairs, discussants, and audience members who provided valuable feedback.

Working with Sara Doskow and the rest of the University of Chicago Press team has been a delight. This manuscript is much stronger for their feedback and edits. I am so grateful also to the anonymous reviewers whose comments immeasurably strengthened the final product.

I would also like to acknowledge my friends outside of academia, especially Charles Denson and Arianna Koudounas, without whom I likely would never have made it to grad school and definitely would not have completed this book. Thank you also to Charles for our discussions about norms, prejudice, and politics on our long hikes during the pandemic. Those discussions greatly benefited the resulting manuscript. Thank you to Paul Fowler for listening to me rant about book writing and academia during our late-night ping-pong sessions. Though I did not take him up on it, I appreciated Brendan White's offer to write a foreword for this book.

My family, particularly Nayan, Lindee, Aavi, Saachi, and Mallika, encouraged and supported me, while also providing much-needed escapes from the writing process when I got bogged down. I am grateful for the love and support I have received from all of the Aroras, Mehrotras, Tuckers, and Sutton-Smiths. Finally, and most importantly, I would like to thank my parents for allowing me the freedom to follow my passion and for providing me unconditional love and support throughout the journey; and my wife, partner, and best friend, Robin, for literally everything.

Appendix

Results from Fictional Democratic Primary Elections

In the October 2018 Lucid survey, respondents who identified as Democrats were randomly assigned to one of three primary election scenarios. See below for the wording for each election scenario and results.

Pro-Black Primary Election Scenario

Henry Matthews and Tucker Banks, the two candidates in the Democratic primary election, have similar views on most important policy issues. Both have promised to protect and expand the Affordable Care Act, protect a woman's right to choose, and increase funding for public education. Both candidates are supportive of reforms to the criminal justice system, but candidate Matthews has made it a central campaign promise saying that "we as a nation must end systemic racism in the criminal justice system."

If you lived in this district, which candidate would you vote for?

Pro-Latinx Primary Election Scenario

Tanner Johnson and Luke Davis are the frontrunners in the Democratic primary. Both candidates have worked to expand early childhood education and have promised to enact fairer labor and housing policies to protect the working and middle class. Williams and Davis have both voiced support for immigration reform, and Johnson has made it a central campaign promise "to protect vulnerable Latino communities."

If you lived in this district, which candidate would you vote for?

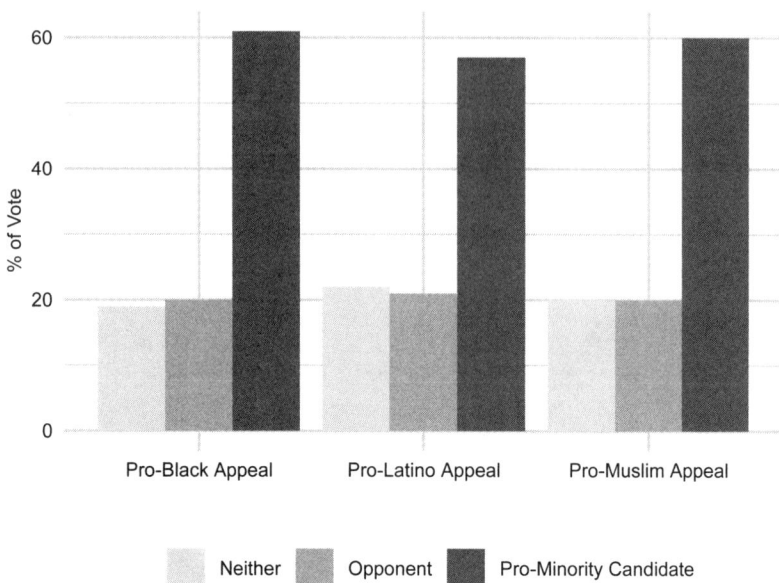

FIGURE A.1. Results from fictional Democratic primary elections pitting pro-minority (pro-Black, pro-Muslim, and pro-Latino) candidates against nonracialized opponents. Data from the October 2018 Lucid survey.

Pro-Muslim Primary Election Scenario

Connor Williams and Luke Davis are the frontrunners in the Democratic primary. Both candidates have worked to expand early childhood education and have promised to enact fairer labor and housing policies to protect the working and middle class. Williams and Davis have both voiced support for protecting the community from hate crimes, and Williams has made it a central campaign promise to "protect Muslim American communities from hate crimes."

If you lived in this district, which candidate would you vote for?

Robustness Checks for Differential Norms

Favorability measures from the July 2018 Lucid survey found that the mean favorability score for Muslim people was .58, compared to .74, .73, and .77 for Black, Hispanic, and white people, respectively. The measure was coded on a 0 to 1 scale. The same measure in the October 2018 Lucid survey found almost identical scores of .59, .74, .73, and .77 for Muslim, Black, Hispanic, and white people, respectively. The January 2019 Lucid survey included favorability measures of undocumented immigrants as well. Mean favorability scores for the various groups were .37 for undocumented immigrants, .58 for Muslim people, .73 for Black people, .72 for Hispanic people, and .78 for white people. The May 2019 Lucid survey found mean scores of .45 for undocumented immigrants, .56 for Muslim people, .72 for Black people, .69 for Hispanic people, and .72 for white people. Across all four surveys, Muslims are rated substantially lower than all other groups except for undocumented immigrants. In the two surveys in which undocumented immigrants were included, favorability scores were the lowest, even lower than favorability of Muslims. These differences are statistically significant according to two-sample *t*-tests.

Another measure, included in a July 2018 Lucid survey, is a question that asks about candidate acceptability: "If your party nominated a generally well-qualified person for president from the following groups, would you vote for that person?" Again, we see a substantial difference between the way Republicans view Muslims versus other groups. Only 37% of Republican respondents say they would probably or definitely vote for a Muslim candidate, compared to 75% and 67%, respectively, for a Black or Hispanic candidate.

TABLE A.1 **Summary statistics of the national samples compared to the US population**

	MTurk 2017	Lucid July 2018	Lucid Oct. 2018	Lucid Jan. 2019	Lucid May 2019	Lucid-Mar. 2023	Lucid June 2023	US pop.
Age	36.9	45.0	46.5	45.8	43.3	45.4	45.8	37.9
Four-year degree	39.2%	39.2%	36.3%	48.8%	35.7%	37.2%	36.0%	30.3%
Female	48.8%	50.5%	53.0%	51.2%	51.8%	50.1%	52.3%	50.8%
White	65.1%	63.8%	64.0%	63.2%	62.2%	62.8%	61.8%	60.7%
Black	8.0%	11.6%	11.3%	11.4%	13.4%	12.1%	12.6%	13.4%
Hispanic	14.5%	17.5%	17.7%	17.8%	17.2%	17.7%	17.8%	18.1%
Asian American and Pacific Islander	8.0%	5.5%	5.7%	5.0%	5.3%	4.8%	5.9%	6.0%

TABLE A.2 **Summary statistics of the YouGov 2020 sample compared to the US white population**

	YouGov 2020	US pop.
Age	45.0	44.0
Four-year degree	41.1%	33.7%
Female	54.4%	50.4%

TABLE A.3 **Confirmatory factor analyses of responses to the social norms index from 2020 YouGov, March 2023 Lucid, and June 2023 Lucid**

Variable	Factor 1
2020 YouGov	
PFA results	1.9917
Vignette 1: Miguel, "greasy food"	0.5853
Vignette 2: Antoine, "playing the race card"	0.7499
Vignette 3: Black student, "laziness"	0.7298
Vignette 4: Muslim family, "terrorism"	0.7444
March 2023 Lucid	
PFA results	2.6627
Vignette 1: Miguel, "greasy food"	0.8165
Vignette 2: Antoine, "playing the race card"	0.7820
Vignette 3: Black student, "laziness"	0.8561
Vignette 4: Muslim family, "terrorism"	0.8073
June 2023 Lucid	
PFA results	2.5935
Vignette 1: Miguel, "greasy food"	0.8105
Vignette 2: Antoine, "playing the race card"	0.7551
Vignette 3: Black student, "laziness"	0.8635
Vignette 4: Muslim family, "terrorism"	0.7879

Source: Data come from the 2020 YouGov sample, the March 2023 Lucid sample, and the June 2023 Lucid sample.

OLS regression analysis of the social norms index (SNI) on support for anti-Black candidates (full model from table 4.2)

	Model: Anti-Black candidate, Mar. 2023 Lucid	Model 2: Primary election, Oct. 2018 Lucid	Model 3: General election, Oct. 2018 Lucid
SNI	.78*** (.04)	.35** (.11)	.16** (.05)
Party ID	.04 (.03)		.18*** (.03)
Female	−.02 (.02)	.05 (.06)	−.1*** (.03)
College degree	−.01 (.01)	0 (0)	0 (0)
Age	−.003*** (.0005)	−.01 (.01)	0 (0)
Racial resentment	.32*** (.04)	.45*** (.15)	.39*** (.06)
Intercept	.11*	.06	.01
R^2	.51	.09	.2
N	744	236	869

Notes: *** $p < .001$, ** $p < .01$, * $p < .05$. Model 1 data from March 2023 Lucid survey. Model 2 and 3 data from October 2018 Lucid survey. The dependent variable in each model is stated intention to vote for an anti-Black political candidate in a US Senate race (model 1), US House Republican primary (model 2), and a US House general election (model 3). Response options for the dependent variable in each model range from 0 to 1. All three models control for gender, education, age, and racial resentment. Model 2 drops partisan identification because the model only includes Republican respondents.

TABLE A.5 **Regression results for figure 5.7**

	Model 1: Anti-Black candidate, Mar. 2023 Lucid	Model 2: Anti-Muslim candidate, Mar. 2023 Lucid
Party ID	.04 (.03)	.04 (.03)
Female	−.02 (.02)	−.03 (.02)
College degree	−.01 (.01)	.01 (.01)
Age	−.003*** (.0005)	−.001 (.01)
Racial resentment	.32*** (.04)	.28*** (.04)
Intercept	.11*	.32
R^2	.51	.26
N	744	754

Notes: * $p < .05$; ** $p < .01$; *** $p < .001$. Data from the March 2023 Lucid survey.

TABLE A.6 **Regression results for figure 5.8**

	Model 1: Anti-Black candidate, Oct. 2018 Lucid	Model 2: Anti-Muslim candidate, Oct. 2018 Lucid
SNI	.35*** (.11)	.39*** (.12)
Female	.05 (.06)	−.09 (.06)
College degree	.00 (0)	.00 (0)
Age	−.01 (.01)	.00 (0)
Racial resentment	.45*** (.15)	.28 (.16)
Intercept	.06	.08
R^2	.09	.09
N	236	240

Notes: * $p < .05$; ** $p < .01$; *** $p < .001$. Data from the October 2018 Lucid survey.

TABLE A.7 **Regression results for figure 6.7**

	Model 1: Control	Model 2: Antitransgender (T1)	Model 3: Antigay (T2)
SNI	.19*** (.03)	.41*** (.03)	.27*** (.04)
Party ID	.03 (.03)	.06* (.02)	−.001 (.03)
Female	−.07*** (.02)	.004 (.02)	−.04* (.02)
College degree	−.04* (.02)	.03 (.02)	.03 (.02)
Age	.001* (.0005)	0 (.0005)	.002** (.0005)
Racial resentment	.06 (.04)	.18*** (.04)	.28*** (.04)
Intercept	.47	.31	.39
R^2	.09	.25	.19
N	748	743	749

Notes: * $p < .05$; ** $p < .01$; *** $p < .001$. Data from the June 2023 Lucid survey.

TABLE A.8 **Regression results for figure 7.2**

	Model 1: Control	Model 2: Islamophobic ad (T1)	Model 3: Condemnation (T2)
SNI	.31*** (.07)	.47*** (.07)	.50*** (.07)
Party ID	.32*** (.04)	.28*** (.04)	.17*** (.04)
Female	−.03 (.03)	.001 (.03)	−.06 (.03)
College degree	−.04 (.03)	−.04 (.03)	−.04 (.03)
Age	−.003** (.001)	−.001 (.001)	−.001 (.0001)
Racial resentment	.43*** (.07)	.36*** (.08)	.28*** (.09)
Intercept	.28	.16	.13
R^2	.40	.42	.35
N	342	327	340

Notes: * $p < .05$; ** $p < .01$; *** $p < .001$. Data from the October 2018 Lucid survey.

TABLE A.9 **Regression results for figure 7.4**

	Model 1: Control	Model 2: Public hanging (T1)	Model 3: Condemnation (T2)
SNI	.22*** (.05)	.44*** (.05)	.50*** (.05)
Party ID	.20*** (.04)	.23*** (.03)	.18*** (.04)
Female	−.03 (.03)	−.03 (.03)	−.01 (.03)
College degree	−.05 (.03)	.0002 (.02)	−.07* (.03)
Age	−.001 (.0008)	−.002** (.0007)	−.002** (.0001)
Racial resentment	.31*** (.06)	.25*** (.05)	.20*** (.06)
Intercept	.22	.19	.11
R^2	.24	.35	.32
N	498	502	488

Notes: * $p < .05$; ** $p < .01$; *** $p < .001$. Data from the May 2019 Lucid survey.

TABLE A.10 **Regression results for figure 7.7**

	Model 1: Control	Model 2: Public hanging (T1)	Model 3: Condemnation (T2)
SNI	.27*** (.04)	.42*** (.03)	.45*** (.04)
Party ID	−.01 (.03)	.06* (.03)	.07* (.03)
Female	−.04* (.02)	.004 (.02)	−.03 (.02)
College degree	−.03 (.02)	−.03 (.02)	−.03 (.02)
Age	−.002*** (.0005)	−.001 (.0005)	−.001 (.0005)
Racial resentment	.28*** (.04)	.19*** (.04)	.20*** (.04)
Intercept	.39	.31	.26
R^2	.19	.25	.27
N	749	743	754

Notes: * $p < .05$; ** $p < .01$; *** $p < .001$. Data from the March 2023 Lucid survey.

Notes

Chapter 1

1. See Killough et al. (2019) for the full story. The one representative who voted against the measure did so because it did not go far enough in condemning his comments.

2. A long line of scholarship shows a principle-implementation gap as it relates to racial equality: Many Americans support racial equality as an ideal but continue to reject interventions designed to bring about this ideal (Sears and Kinder 1971; Kinder and Sanders 1996). Thus, I refer to a norm of racial equality *in principle* throughout the book to differentiate from a norm of equality *in practice* which is yet to be developed.

3. I use the term destabilize throughout the book to refer to situations where the pervading norm, whether egalitarian or inegalitarian, is being put under stress. In these situations, the current norm may destabilize and begin a transition to a new norm. For example, the civil rights movement helped destabilize the pervading norm of racial inequality and ushered in a new norm of racial equality in principle.

Chapter 2

1. Stuart Stevens is a longtime Republican strategist.

2. See Killough et al. (2019) for the full story.

3. Though Boebert's career survived her explicit Islamophobia, it may have been harmed by a series of personal scandals including a viral video showing her vaping and groping her date while attending a play. Boebert decided to leave the Third Congressional District in Colorado where she won reelection in 2022, to run in the Fourth Congressional District in 2024. This decision appears to be because she was being handily out-fundraised by her Democrat opponent in the Third District, Adam Frisch, who she only narrowly defeated by 546 votes in 2022. By comparison, the Fourth District is much more friendly to Republicans. Donald Trump

carried the district in 2020 by 20 percentage points compared to 8 points in the Third District. On June 26, Boebert won the GOP primary for the Fourth District.

4. See appendix for information about the analytical tests and results.

Chapter 3

1. Henry Fernandez works for Fernandez Advisors, a consulting group that helped coordinate the surveys in Virginia conducted by Latino Decisions and the African American Research Collaborative.

2. These questions come from Plant and Devine's (1998) external motivation to respond without prejudice scale.

3. Though social norm adherence and racial attitudes tend to be measured using evaluations of statements, there is precedence for using a series of vignettes. For example, the racial sympathy index (Chudy 2021) also consists of responses to a series of vignettes. One benefit of this construction is that we can gauge respondents' evaluations of the social acceptability of specific instances of prejudice rather than abstract notions of prejudice. Therefore, we can evaluate respondent's perceptions of how others would react to real actions.

4. Respondents who had taken previous surveys were filtered out to ensure that each sample had a unique set of respondents. Respondents were also filtered out of surveys if they did not accurately answer attention-check questions.

5. Cronbach's alpha ranges from 0 to 1, with 1 indicating that a scale explains 100% of the common variance between the items included in the scale.

6. Most of these measures were included in all three Lucid surveys conducted in 2018 and 2019 that make up the pooled Lucid survey data. However, the self-monitoring scale, the racial sympathy scale, and the measure of political correctness were only included in one of the surveys.

7. One reason for this high correlation could be the similar format of the questions. The racial sympathy measure also includes a set of vignettes with five response options.

8. The reference categories for the variables in fig. 3.2 are as follows: Democrats and Independents; women and nonbinary respondents; Black, Asian American, and respondents who identified as "other" when asked about racial identity; respondents who do not have a college degree; and respondents less than fifty years old. The variables "White" and "Latino" are omitted from the YouGov model because the sample only includes white respondents.

Chapter 4

1. See table 3.1A in Schuman et al. (1997).

2. Data from time series Gallup polls that can be accessed at https://news.gal lup.com/poll/1687/race-relations.aspx.

3. There were also respondents in each survey who said they have no opinion.

4. Data from time series Gallup polls that can be accessed at https://news.gal
lup.com/poll/4729/presidency.aspx.

5. See time series at https://news.gallup.com/poll/1687/race-relations.aspx.

6. See the full platform here: https://democrats.org/where-we-stand/party-plat
form/healing-the-soul-of-america/.

7. See appendix table A.1 for a comparison of sample demographics to national
demographics.

8. Results from the other experimental groups are discussed in chap. 5.

9. See appendix table A.1 for a comparison of sample demographics to national
demographics. More information about Lucid can be found in chap. 3.

10. Results from the other experimental group are discussed in chap. 5.

11. Results from the other experimental group are discussed in chap. 5.

12. See appendix table A.1 for a comparison of sample demographics to national demographics. More information about Lucid can be found in chap. 3.

13. The other half of Republican respondents were shown a similar scenario
that included an anti-Muslim campaign appeal instead of an anti-Black appeal.
The results of this test are presented in chap. 5. Respondents who identified as
Democrats were shown a matchup between two Democratic candidates who used
pro-minority campaign appeals. These results can be found in the app. Independents and respondents who supported other political parties were asked to choose
between the Republican and Democratic Parties, and then sorted into the corresponding election scenarios.

14. The questions used to create the SNI were not included in the 2017 MTurk
survey, so the experimental results from that survey are not included in this section.

15. This analysis was conducted on the October 2018 Lucid survey and not the
July 2018 Lucid survey because the SNI was only included in the October survey.

16. Respondents who said they would not vote for either candidate were
grouped with those who said they would vote for the opposing candidate because
they were similar in that, in this election, they would not vote for the candidate
who used the anti-Black campaign appeal.

17. Running tally kept at https://crtforward.law.ucla.edu/.

18. Running tally kept at https://www.chronicle.com/article/here-are-the-states
-where-lawmakers-are-seeking-to-ban-colleges-dei-efforts.

Chapter 5

1. See analysis in chap. 5 of Sides et al. (2018).

2. Analysis comes from the GDELT Project at https://api.gdeltproject.org/api/v2
/summary/summary?d=iatv (Data Source: Internet Archive, Television News Archive; Human Summary: Search for "sharia" or "sharia law" within Fox News, filtering
for publications between January 1, 2010, and December 31, 2017, at 23:59:59 UTC).

3. See data table: https://www.adl.org/sites/default/files/pdfs/2022-05/FBI%20 Hate%20Crime%20Statistics%20Comparison%202000-2020.pdf.

4. Running tally kept at https://www.aclu.org/issues/national-security/nationwide -anti-mosque-activity.

5. Analysis comes from the GDELT Project at https://api.gdeltproject.org/api/v2 /summary/summary?d=iatv (Data Source: Internet Archive, Television News Archive; Human Summary: Search for "sharia" or "sharia law" within Fox News, filtering for publications between January 1, 2010, and December 31, 2017, at 23:59:59 UTC).

6. Among Democrats, 68% said they would and only 9% said they would not. Among Independents, 39% said yes and 26% said no.

7. See appendix table A.1 for a comparison of sample demographics to national demographics.

8. The results from these experiments subset by partisan groups are presented in figure 5.4.

9. See appendix table A.1 for a comparison of sample demographics to national demographics.

10. See appendix table A.2 for a comparison of sample demographics to national demographics.

11. Feeling thermometer measures of Muslims was first included in the ANES in 2004 so I have restricted my analysis to that starting point.

12. See appendix for more detailed results.

13. See chap. 3 for more detailed information about the two surveys. See appendix table A.1 for a comparison of sample demographics to national demographics.

14. The questions used to construct the SNI were not included in the July 2018 Lucid survey.

15. Respondents who said they would not vote for either candidate were grouped with those who said they would vote for the candidate who did not make the racial appeal because they were similar in that, in this election, they would not vote for the candidate who used the anti-Black or Islamophobic appeal. See appendix table A.6 for full model results.

Chapter 6

1. Kelsy Burke is an associate professor of sociology at the University of Nebraska, Lincoln.

2. See chap. 2 for a more detailed discussion of the influence of Fox News.

3. Running tally kept at https://www.aclu.org/legislative-attacks-on-lgbtq-rights.

4. June 5, 2009, is the earliest data available in GDELT. My search terms included "transgender," "trans," and "tranny."

5. These terms were, however, mentioned a lot prior to 2015.

6. A total of 1,837 respondents were dropped from the survey for failing at

least one attention check. Respondents who had taken previous surveys I have conducted on Lucid were disqualified. See chap. 3 for a more detailed description of the sample and see appendix table A.1 for a comparison of sample demographics to national demographics.

7. For Democratic respondents, this may be because they have inferred the party identification of the candidate even though it was not specified. Independents may simply be unmoved by the candidate. More than 40% of Independents (a plurality) in all three experimental conditions said they were neither likely nor unlikely to vote for the candidate.

8. There were also Buddhist, Hindu, Jewish, and Muslim respondents, but the sample size was too small to draw conclusions. Respondents who reported being Protestant specified that they were non-evangelical Protestants.

9. See appendix table A.7 for full model results.

10. See HRC (2022b) for a description of the survey and survey results.

11. See the full blueprint here:·https://static.project2025.org/2025_MandateFor Leadership_FULL.pdf.

Chapter 7

1. James is a pseudonym. His real name is not included to protect his identity.

2. See appendix table A.1 for a comparison of sample demographics to national demographics.

3. See appendix table A.8 for full regression results.

4. See appendix table A.1 for a comparison of sample demographics to national demographics.

5. See appendix table A.9 for full regression results. Each model controlled for partisan identity, gender, education, age, and racial resentment.

6. See appendix table A.1 for a comparison of sample demographics to national demographics.

7. See appendix table A.1 for a comparison of sample demographics to national demographics.

8. See appendix table A.10 for full regression results. Each model controlled for partisan identity, gender, education, age, and racial resentment.

9. See Stout (2020) for a more detailed discussion of the effectiveness of a racialized political approach for the Democratic Party.

Chapter 8

1. Dangerous Speech Project, "Home," June 18, https://dangerousspeech.org/.

2. See chap. 3 for more detailed information about the public opinion polls.

3. See pollster at the *Huffington Post* for smore information on the polling data: https://elections.huffingtonpost.com/pollster/2016-national-gop-primary.

4. The podcast and transcript from the show on June 4, 2024, can be found here: https://www.nytimes.com/2024/06/04/opinion/ezra-klein-podcast-sam-rosenfeld -daniel-schlozman.html.

References

Abbas, Tahir, Inés Bolaños Somoano, Joana Cook, Isabelle Frens, Graig R. Klein, and Richard McNeil-Willson. 2022. "The Buffalo Attack: An Analysis of the Manifesto." *International Centre for Counter-terrorism*, May 18. https://www.icct.nl/publication/buffalo-attack-analysis-manifesto.

Abdelkader, Engy. 2016. *When Islamophobia Turns Violent: The 2016 U.S. Presidential Elections.* The Bridge Initiative, Georgetown University.

Abdo, Geneive. 2005. "Islam in America: Separate but Unequal." *Washington Quarterly* 28 (4): 5–17.

Abrajano, Marisa, and Zoltan L. Hajnal. 2015. *White Backlash: Immigration, Race, and American Politics.* Princeton University Press.

AdImpact. 2024. "2023-2024 Cycle in Review." https://go.adimpact.com/hubfs/Reports/Political%202024/AdImpact_Cycle%20in%20Review_2023-2024.pdf.

Alemany, Jacqueline, and Marianna Sotomayor. 2021. "House Republicans Express Concern over Party Infighting, but Not the Islamophobic Rhetoric That Set It Off." *Washington Post*, December 3. https://www.washingtonpost.com/politics/boebert-mace-islamophobia/2021/12/02/092f8eae-52b8-11ec-8769-2f4ecdf7a2ad_story.html.

Alfaro, Mariana, Marianna Sotomayor, and Felicia Sonmez. 2021. "More than 40 House Democrats Call for Boebert to Be Stripped of Committee Assignments over Anti-Muslim Attacks." *Washington Post*, December 2. https://www.washingtonpost.com/politics/2021/12/02/more-than-40-house-democrats-call-boebert-be-stripped-committee-assignments-over-anti-muslim-attacks/.

Allport, Gordon W. 1954. *The Nature of Prejudice.* Basic Books.

Alsultany, Evelyn. 2022. "Representing Muslims, One Crisis at a Time." *American Quarterly* 74 (3): 544–51.

America's Voice. 2021. *G.O.P. Ad Wars in 2020: Divisive, Anti-immigrant, and Racist.* http://americasvoice.org/wp-content/uploads/2021/01/FINAL-GOP-Ad-Wars-in-2020-Divisive-Anti-immigrant-and-Racist-1.pdf.

American Civil Liberties Union. 2023. "Mapping Attacks on LGBTQ Rights in U.S. State Legislatures." September 15. https://www.aclu.org/legislative-attacks -on-lgbtq-rights.

Anderson, Joanna E., and David Dunning. 2014. "Behavioral Norms: Variants and Their Identification." *Social and Personality Psychology Compass* 8:721–38. https://doi.org/10.1111/spc3.12146.

Anoll, Allison P. 2022. *The Obligation Mosaic: Race and Social Norms in US Political Participation.* University of Chicago Press.

Anti-Defamation League. 2021. "White Supremacists Applaud Tucker Carlson's Promotion of Replacement Theory." Blog, April 22. https://www.adl.org /resources/blog/white-supremacists-applaud-tucker-carlsons-promotion-re placement-theory.

Arango, Tim, Nicholas Bogel-Burroughs, and Katie Benner. 2019. "Minutes Before El Paso Killing, Hate-Filled Manifesto Appears Online." *New York Times*, August 3. https://www.nytimes.com/2019/08/03/us/patrick-crusius-el-paso-shooter -manifesto.html.

Armed Conflict Location and Event Data Project. 2022. "From the Capitol Riot to the Midterms: Shifts in American Far-Right Mobilization Between 2021 and 2022." December 6. https://acleddata.com/2022/12/06/from-the-capitol -riot-to-the-midterms-shifts-in-american-far-right-mobilization-between-2021 -and-2022/.

Arora, Maneesh. 2021. "Rep. Boebert Labels Rep. Omar a Jihadist. Why Don't GOP Leaders Condemn the Slur?" *Washington Post*, December 6. https://www .washingtonpost.com/politics/2021/12/06/boebert-omar-jihad-racism/.

Arora, Maneesh, Davin L. Phoenix, and Archie Delshad. 2019. "Framing Police and Protesters: Assessing Volume and Framing of News Coverage Post-Ferguson, and Corresponding Impacts on Legislative Activity." *Politics, Groups, and Identities* 7 (1): 151–64.

Arora, Maneesh, and Christopher T. Stout. 2019. "Letters for Black Lives: Co-ethnic Mobilization and Support for the Black Lives Matter Movement." *Political Research Quarterly* 72 (2): 389–402.

Astudillo, Carla. 2022. "Election Results: How Texas Voted in the November 2022 Midterms." *Texas Tribune*, November 30. https://apps.texastribune.org /features/2022/texas-2022-election-results/.

Atkinson, Mary Layton, K. Elizabeth Coggins, James A. Stimson, and Frank R. Baumgartner. 2021. *The Dynamics of Public Opinion.* Cambridge University Press.

Axios. 2020. "The Real-Life Changes Won by the Protests." June 12. https://www .axios.com/2020/06/12/black-lives-matter-protest-police-reform.

Aziza, Sarah. 2018. "The 2018 Midterm Cycle Could Be the Most Islamophobic U.S. Election Ever." *The Intercept*, October 22. https://theintercept.com/2018 /10/22/2018-midterms-muslim-candidates-islamophobia/.

Balmer, Randall. 2021. *Bad Faith: Race and the Rise of the Religious Right.* William B. Eerdmans Publishing.

Banks, Antoine J., and Heather M. Hicks. 2019. "The Effectiveness of a Racialized Counterstrategy." *American Journal of Political Science* 63 (2): 305–22.

Barrón-López, Laura, and John Bresnahan. 2019. "Steve King Under Fire After Embrace of White Supremacy." *Politico*, January 11. https://www.politico.com /story/2019/01/10/steve-king-white-supremacy-congress-1077665.

Barrow, Bill, and Jill Colvin. 2024. "Trump Escalates His Immigration Rhetoric with Baseless Claim About Biden Trying to Overthrow the US." Associated Press, March 2. https://apnews.com/article/trump-immigration-biden-gop-voters -border-migrants-1fc6624188f540f495e1087bee64318e.

Batterham, D. 2001. "Modern Racism, Reconciliation and Attributions for Disadvantage: A Role for Empathy and False Beliefs?" Paper presented at 2nd Victorian Postgraduates in Psychology Conference, Swinburne University of Technology, Melbourne.

Bell, D. C., and M. L. Cox. 2015. "Social Norms: Do We Love Norms Too Much?" *Journal of Family Theory & Review*, 7:28–46.

Bennett, Lisa. 1998. *The Perpetuation of Prejudice in Reporting on Gays and Lesbians: Time and Newsweek: The First Fifty Years*. Vol. 21. Joan Shorenstein Center on the Press, Politics, and Public Policy, John F. Kennedy School of Government, Harvard University.

Berinsky, Adam J. 2009. *In Time of War: Understanding American Public Opinion from World War II to Iraq*. University of Chicago Press.

Berrill, Kevin T. 1990. "Anti-gay Violence and Victimization in the United States: An Overview." *Journal of Interpersonal Violence* 5 (3): 274–94.

Bicchieri, Cristina. 2006. *The Grammar of Society: The Nature and Dynamics of Social Norms*. Cambridge University Press.

Bicchieri, Cristina. 2016. *Norms in the Wild: How to Diagnose, Measure, and Change Social Norms*. Oxford University Press.

Blanchard, Fletcher A., Christian S. Crandall, John C. Brigham, and Leigh Ann Vaughn. 1994. "Condemning and Condoning Racism: A Social Context Approach to Interracial Settings." *Journal of Applied Psychology* 79 (6).

Blinder, Scott, Robert Ford, and Elisabeth Ivarsflaten. 2013. "The Better Angels of Our Nature: How the Antiprejudice Norm Affects Policy and Party Preferences in Great Britain and Germany." *American Journal of Political Science* 57 (4): 841–57.

Blueprint. 2024. "Why America Chose Trump: Inflation, Immigration, and the Democratic Brand." https://blueprint2024.com/polling/why-trump-reasons-11-8/.

Blumer, Herbert. 1958. "Race Prejudice as a Sense of Group Position." *Pacific Sociological Review* 1 (1): 3–7.

Bobo, Lawrence, and Vincent L. Hutchings. 1996. "Perceptions of Racial Group Competition: Extending Blumer's Theory of Group Position to a Multiracial Social Context." *American Sociological Review* 61 (6): 951–72.

Bond, Bradley J., and Benjamin L. Compton. 2015. "Gay On-Screen: The Relationship Between Exposure to Gay Characters on Television and Heterosexual

Audiences' Endorsement of Gay Equality." *Journal of Broadcasting & Electronic Media* 59 (4): 717–32.

Bonilla, Tabitha, Alexandra Filindra, and Nazita Lajevardi. 2022. "How Source Cues Shape Evaluations of Group-Based Derogatory Political Messages." *Journal of Politics* 84 (4): 1979–96.

Branigin, Anne. 2022. "A 'Rainbow Wave' of Candidates Made History. What's Next for Them?" *Washington Post*, November 11. https://www.washingtonpost.com/nation/2022/11/11/lgbtq-midterms-2022-candidates/.

Brenan, Megan. 2024. "Same-Sex Relations, Marriage Still Supported by Most in U.S." *Gallup*, June 24. https://news.gallup.com/poll/646202/sex-relations-marriage-supported.aspx.

Broockman, David, and Joshua Kalla. 2016. "Durably Reducing Transphobia: A Field Experiment on Door-to-Door Canvassing." *Science* 352 (6282): 220–24.

Broockman, David E., and Daniel M. Butler. 2017. "The Causal Effects of Elite Position-Taking on Voter Attitudes: Field Experiments with Elite Communication." *American Journal of Political Science* 61 (1): 208–21.

Broockman, David, and Joshua Kalla. 2022. "The Manifold Effects of Partisan Media on Viewers' Beliefs and Attitudes: A Field Experiment with Fox News Viewers." OSF Preprints.

Broockman, David, and Joshua Kalla. 2023. "Selective Exposure and Echo Chambers in Partisan Television Consumption: Evidence from Linked Viewership, Administrative, and Survey Data." OSF Preprints, April 14.

Brown, Jacob R., and Ryan D. Enos. 2021. "The Measurement of Partisan Sorting for 180 Million Voters." *Nature Human Behaviour* 5 (8): 998–1008.

Brown, Jacob R., Enrico Cantoni, Ryan D. Enos, Vincent Pons, and Emilie Sartre. 2022. *The Increase in Partisan Segregation in the United States*. Working paper.

Brummett, Barry. 1994. *Rhetoric in Popular Culture*. Sage.

Buchanan, Larry, Quoctrung Bui, and Jugal K. Patel. 2020. "Black Lives Matter May Be the Largest Movement in U.S. History." *New York Times*, July 3. https://www.nytimes.com/interactive/2020/07/03/us/george-floyd-protests-crowd-size.html.

Buhrmester, Michael, Tracy Kwang, and Samuel D. Gosling. 2011. "Amazon's Mechanical Turk: A New Source of Inexpensive, yet High-Quality, Data?" *Perspectives on Psychological Science* 6 (1): 3–5.

Bump, Philip. 2022a. "Timeline: How Two Extremist Groups Planned for Jan. 6." *Washington Post*, March 15. https://www.washingtonpost.com/politics/2022/03/15/timeline-how-two-extremist-groups-planned-jan-6/.

Bump, Philip. 2022b. "The Unique, Damaging Role Fox News Plays in American Media." *Washington Post*, April 4. https://www.washingtonpost.com/politics/2022/04/04/unique-damaging-role-fox-news-plays-american-media/.

Bump, Philip. 2022c. "Nearly Half of Republicans Agree with 'Great Replacement Theory.'" *Washington Post*, May 9. https://www.washingtonpost.com/politics/2022/05/09/nearly-half-republicans-agree-with-great-replacement-theory/.

Calfano, Brian Robert, Nazita Lajevardi, and Melissa R. Michelson. 2019. "Trumped

Up Challenges: Limitations, Opportunities, and the Future of Political Research on Muslim Americans." *Politics, Groups, and Identities* 7 (2): 477–87.

Campbell, Angus. 1960. *The American Voter.* John Wiley & Sons.

Carmines, Edward G., and James A. Stimson. 1989. *Issue Evolution: Race and the Transformation of American Politics.* Princeton University Press.

Chavez, Leo R., Belinda Campos, Karina Corona, Daina Sanchez, and Catherine Belyeu Ruiz. 2019. "Words Hurt: Political Rhetoric, Emotions/Affect, and Psychological Well-Being Among Mexican-Origin Youth." *Social Science & Medicine.*

Chen, Shawna. 2022. "Where LGBTQ Candidates Made History in the Midterm Elections." Axios, November 10. https://www.axios.com/2022/11/09/midterm-election-lgbtq-candidates.

Chiu, Allyson. 2020. "'China Has Blood on Its Hands': Fox News Hosts Join Trump in Blame-Shifting." *Washington Post,* March 19. https://www.washingtonpost.com/nation/2020/03/19/coronavirus-fox-news-china/.

Chomsky, Daniel, and Scott Barclay. 2013. "The Editor, the Publisher, and His Mother: The Representation of Lesbians and Gays in The New York Times." *Journal of Homosexuality* 60 (10): 1389–408.

Christiani, Leah. 2021. "When Are Explicit Racial Appeals Accepted? Examining the Role of Racial Status Threat." *Political Behavior* 2021:1–21.

Chudy, Jennifer. 2021. "Racial Sympathy and Its Political Consequences." *Journal of Politics* 83 (1): 122–36.

Chudy, Jennifer, and Hakeem Jefferson. 2021. "Support for Black Lives Matter Surged Last Year: Did It Last?" *New York Times,* May 22. https://www.nytimes.com/2021/05/22/opinion/blm-movement-protests-support.html.

Cialdini, R. B., and M. R. Trost. 1998. "Social Influence: Social Norms, Conformity and Compliance." In *The Handbook of Social Psychology,* edited by Daniel T. Gilbert, Susan T. Fiske, and Gardner Lindzey, 151–92. McGraw-Hill.

Clifford, Scott, Ryan M. Jewell, and Philip D. Waggoner. 2015. "Are Samples Drawn from Mechanical Turk Valid for Research on Political Ideology?" *Research & Politics* 2 (4).

Confessore, Nicholas. 2022. "How Tucker Carlson Stoked White Fear to Conquer Cable." *New York Times,* May 4. https://www.nytimes.com/2022/04/30/us/tucker-carlson-gop-republican-party.html.

Converse, Philip E. 1964. "The Nature of Belief Systems in Mass Publics." In *Ideology and Discontent,* edited by David E. Apter, 206–61. Free Press.

Coppock, Alexander, and Oliver A. McClellan. 2019. "Validating the Demographic, Political, Psychological, and Experimental Results Obtained from a New Source of Online Survey Respondents." *Research & Politics* 6 (1).

Corbett-Davies, Sam, Tobias Konitzer, and David Rothschild. 2016. "Poll: 60% of Republicans Believe Illegal Immigrants Vote; 43% Believe People Vote Using Dead People's Names." *Washington Post,* October 24. https://www.washingtonpost.com/news/monkey-cage/wp/2016/10/24/poll-60-of-republicans-believe-illegal-immigrants-vote-43-believe-people-vote-using-dead-peoples-names/.

Cory, David Webster. 1951. *The Homosexual in America*. In *The Path to Gay Rights: How Activism and Coming Out Changed Public Opinion*, edited by Jeremiah J. Garretson, 2018. New York University Press.

Council on American–Islamic Relations. 2002. "Poll: Majority of U.S. Muslims Suffered Post 9/11 Bias." August 21. https://www.cair.com/press_releases/poll -majority-of-u-s-muslims-suffered-post-9-11-bias/.

Craig, Maureen A., and Jennifer A. Richeson. 2014. "More Diverse yet Less Tolerant? How the Increasingly Diverse Racial Landscape Affects White Americans' Racial Attitudes." *Personality and Social Psychology Bulletin* 40 (6): 750–61.

Craig, Maureen A., Julian M. Rucker, and Jennifer A. Richeson. 2018. "The Pitfalls and Promise of Increasing Racial Diversity: Threat, Contact, and Race Relations in the 21st Century." *Current Directions in Psychological Science* 27 (3): 188–93.

Cross, William E. 2003. *Shades of Black: Diversity in African-American Identity*. Temple University Press.

Crandall, Christian S., Amy Eshleman, and Laurie O'Brien. 2002. "Social Norms and the Expression and Suppression of Prejudice: The Struggle for Internalization." *Journal of Personality and Social Psychology* 82 (3): 359–78.

Čvorak, Monika, and Nicholas Williams. 2019. "Ilhan Omar: Congresswoman Receives Death Threats After Trump 9/11 Tweet: Video Report." *The Guardian*, April 16, video, 2:24, https://www.theguardian.com/us-news/video/2019/apr/16 /ilhan-omar-congresswoman-receives-death-threats-trump-911-tweet-video.

Dabashi, Hamid. 2017. *Post-Orientalism: Knowledge and Power in a Time of Terror*. Routledge.

Dale, Daniel. 2022. "Fact Check: The GOP's Dishonesty-Filled Barrage of 'Defund the Police' Attack Ads." CNN, October 23. https://www.cnn.com/2022/10/23 /politics/fact-check-defund-the-police-ads-2022-midterms/index.html.

Daniels, Roger. 2004. *Guarding the Golden Door: American Immigration Policy and Immigrants Since 1882*. Hill and Wang.

Daniels, Roger, Sandra C. Taylor, and Harry H. L. Kitano, eds. 1991. *Japanese Americans: From Relocation to Redress*. University of Washington Press.

Davenport, T. C., A. S. Gerber, D. P. Green, C. W. Larimer, C. B. Mann, and C. Panagopoulos. 2010. "The Enduring Effects of Social Pressure: Tracking Campaign Experiments over a Series of Elections." *Political Behavior* 32 (3): 423–30.

Davidson, Joe. 2019. "State of the Nation: Alleged White-Supremacist Killer Finds Inspiration in Trump." *Washington Post*, March 18. https://www.wash ingtonpost.com/politics/2019/03/18/state-nation-alleged-white-supremacist -killer-finds-inspiration-trump/.

Davis, Darren W., and Brian D. Silver. 2004. "Civil Liberties vs. Security: Public Opinion in the Context of the Terrorist Attacks on America." *American Journal of Political Science* (48) 1: 28–46.

Davis, Darren W. 2006. *Negative Liberty: Public Opinion and the Terrorist Attacks on America*. Russell Sage Foundation.

De Jonge, Chad Kiewiet. 2016. "The Roots of Trumpismo: Populism and Push-back." *ABC News*, March 16. http://abcnews.go.com/Politics/roots-trumpismo -populism-pushback-poll/story?id=37602670.

Del Toro, Juan, and Ming-Te Wang. 2023. "Online Racism and Mental Health Among Black American Adolescents in 2020." *Journal of the American Academy of Child & Adolescent Psychiatry* 62 (1): 25–36.

DellaVigna, Stefano, and Ethan Kaplan. 2007. "The Fox News Effect: Media Bias and Voting." *Quarterly Journal of Economics* 122 (3): 1187–234.

DeSante, Christopher D., and Candis Watts Smith. 2019. *Racial Stasis: The Millennial Generation and the Stagnation of Racial Attitudes in American Politics.* University of Chicago Press.

Dixon, Travis L. 2008. "Crime News and Racialized Beliefs: Understanding the Relationship Between Local News Viewing and Perceptions of African Americans and Crime." *Journal of Communication* 58 (1): 106–25.

Dixon, Travis L. 2017. "Good Guys Are Still Always in White? Positive Change and Continued Misrepresentation of Race and Crime on Local Television News." *Communication Research* 44 (6): 775–92.

Doherty, Erin. 2022. "The Number of LGBTQ-Identifying Adults Is Soaring." Axios, February 19. https://www.axios.com/2022/02/17/lgbtq-generation-z-gallup.

Domonoske, Camila. 2017. "State Department Apologizes for Decades of Anti-LGBT Discrimination." NPR, January 9. https://www.npr.org/sections /thetwo-way/2017/01/09/508966318/state-department-apologizes-for-decades -of-anti-lgbt-discrimination.

Drennen, Ari (@AriDrennen). 2023a. "Michael Knowles' Speech." X, March 8, 9:06 a.m. https://x.com/aridrennen/status/1633499328387104768.

Drennen, Ari (@AriDrennen). 2023b. "This Is an Eliminationist Movement." X, February 7, 3:50 p.m. https://x.com/aridrennen/status/1623091839388749824.

Druckman, James N., Matthew S. Levendusky, and Audrey McLain. 2018. "No Need to Watch: How the Effects of Partisan Media Can Spread via Interpersonal Discussions." *American Journal of Political Science* 62 (1): 99–112.

Duncan, Ryan. 2022. "Christians Started the 'Groomer' Lie—Now We Need to End It." *Sojourners*, April 20. https://sojo.net/articles/christians-started-groomer -lie-now-we-need-end-it.

Dunivin, Zackary Okun, Harry Yaojun Yan, Jelani Ince, and Fabio Rojas. 2022. "Black Lives Matter Protests Shift Public Discourse." *Proceedings of the National Academy of Sciences* 119 (10).

Edgell, Penny, Joseph Gerteis, and Douglas Hartmann. 2006. "Atheists as Other: Moral Boundaries and Cultural Membership in American Society." *American Sociological Review* 71 (2): 211–34.

Edsall, Thomas Byrne, and Mary D. Edsall. 1992. *Chain Reaction: The Impact of Race, Rights, and Taxes on American Politics.* W. W. Norton & Company.

Edsall, Thomas B., and Brian Faler. 2002. "Lott Remarks on Thurmond Echoed 1980 Words." *Washington Post*, December 11. https://www.washingtonpost.com

/archive/politics/2002/12/11/lott-remarks-on-thurmond-echoed-1980-words
/c613ae1c-e17d-41c1-836a-4dd0741ec7c8/.

Edwards, Griffin Sims, and Stephen Rushin. 2018. "The Effect of President Trump's
Election on Hate Crimes." *SSRN Electronic Journal*, January. http://dx.doi.org
/10.2139/ssrn.3102652.

Engelhardt, Andrew M. 2021. "Racial Attitudes Through a Partisan Lens." *British
Journal of Political Science* 51 (3): 1062–79.

Engelhardt, Andrew M. 2023. "Observational Equivalence in Explaining Attitude
Change: Have White Racial Attitudes Genuinely Changed?" *American Journal
of Political Science* 67 (2): 411–25.

Enos, Ryan D. 2017. *The Space Between Us: Social Geography and Politics*. Cambridge University Press.

Erb, Hans-Peter, Gerd Bohner, Knut Schmilzle, and Susanne Rank. 1998. "Beyond
Conflict and Discrepancy: Cognitive Bias in Minority and Majority Influence."
Personality and Social Psychology Bulletin 24 (6): 620–33.

Esposito, John L. 1999. *The Islamic Threat: Myth or Reality?* Oxford: Oxford University Press.

Eugenios, Jillian. 2022. "How 1970s Christian Crusader Anita Bryant Helped
Spawn Florida's LGBTQ Culture War." *NBC News*, April 14. https://www.nbc
news.com/nbc-out/out-news/1970s-christian-crusader-anita-bryant-helped-spawn
-floridas-lgbtq-cult-rcna24215.

Evans, Erin. 2019. "If It's Racist, Call It Racist: Associated Press Stylebook Changes
Guidelines for Journalists." *NBC News*, March 29. https://www.nbcnews.com
/news/nbcblk/if-it-s-racist-call-it-racist-associated-press-stylebook-n989056.

Factbase. 2020. "Tweet from @realDonaldTrump, December 26, 11:23 p.m."
Image. https://media-cdn.factba.se/realdonaldtrump-twitter/1342974373632876
545.jpg.

Fandos, Nicholas. 2017. "Trump Won't Back Down from His Voting Fraud Lie.
Here Are the Facts." *New York Times*, January 24. https://www.nytimes.com
/2017/01/24/us/politics/unauthorized-immigrant-voting-trump-lie.html.

Federal Bureau of Investigation and Department of Homeland Security. 2021.
"Strategic Intelligence Assessment and Data on Domestic Terrorism." May
2021. https://www.fbi.gov/file-repository/fbi-dhs-domestic-terrorism-strategic-re
port.pdf/view.

Feinberg, Ayal, Regina Branton, and Valerie Martinez-Ebers. 2022. "The Trump
Effect: How 2016 Campaign Rallies Explain Spikes in Hate." *PS: Political Science & Politics* 55 (2): 257–65.

Fiske, Susan T. 1998. "Stereotyping, Prejudice, and Discrimination." In *The Handbook of Social Psychology*. Vol. 2, edited by Daniel T. Gilbert, Susan T. Fiske,
and Gardner Lindzey, 357-411. 4th ed. McGraw-Hill.

Forestal, Jennifer. 2019. "Beyond Gatekeeping: Propaganda, Democracy, and the
Organization of Digital Publics." *Journal of Politics*.

Futrell, Robert, and Pete Simi. 2004. "Free Spaces, Collective Identity, and the Persistence of U.S. White Power Activism." *Social Problems* 51 (1): 16–42.

Gabriel, Trip. 2019. "Before Trump, Steve King Set the Agenda for the Wall and Anti-immigrant Politics." *New York Times*, January 10. https://www.nytimes.com/2019/01/10/us/politics/steve-king-trump-immigration-wall.html.

Gardiner, Dustin, and Mark Olalde. 2019. "These Copycat Bills on Sharia Law and Terrorism Have No Effect. Why Do States Keep Passing Them?" *Arizona Republic, USA Today*, and the Center for Public Integrity, July 17. https://www.usatoday.com/in-depth/news/investigations/2019/07/17/islam-sharia-law-how-far-right-group-gets-model-bills-passed/1636199001/.

Garretson, Jeremiah J. 2018. *The Path to Gay Rights: How Activism and Coming Out Changed Public Opinion.* NYU Press.

Gass, Nick. 2015. "The 15 Most Offensive Things That Have Come Out of Trump's Mouth." *Politico*, December 8. https://www.politico.eu/article/15-most-offensive-things-trump-campaign-feminism-migration-racism/.

Gerber, Alan S., Donald P. Green, and Christopher W. Larimer. 2008. "Social Pressure and Voter Turnout: Evidence from a Large-Scale Field Experiment." *American Political Science Review* 102 (1): 33–48.

Germar, Markus, and Andreas Mojzisch. 2019. "Learning of Social Norms Can Lead to a Persistent Perceptual Bias: A Diffusion Model Approach." *Journal of Experimental Social Psychology.*

Gilens, Martin. 1999. *Why Americans Hate Welfare: Race, Media, and the Politics of Antipoverty Policy.* University of Chicago Press.

Gilliam, Franklin D. Jr., and Shanto Iyengar. 2000. "Prime Suspects: The Influence of Local Television News on the Viewing Public." *American Journal of Political Science.*

Gilliam, Franklin D. Jr., Nicholas A. Valentino, and Matthew N. Beckmann. 2002. "Where You Live and What You Watch: The Impact of Racial Proximity and Local Television News on Attitudes About Race and Crime." *Political Research Quarterly* 55 (4): 755–80.

Gillion, Daniel Q. 2013. *The Political Power of Protest: Minority Activism and Shifts in Public Policy.* Cambridge University Press.

Glaun, Dan. 2021. "A Timeline of Domestic Extremism in the U.S., from Charlottesville to January 6." *PBS Frontline*, April 21. https://www.pbs.org/wgbh/frontline/article/timeline-us-domestic-extremism-charlottesville-january-6/.

Goffman, Erving. 1956. *The Presentation of Self in Everyday Life.* Doubleday Anchor Books.

Goffman, Erving. 1967. *International Ritual: Essays on Face-to-Face Behavior.* Double Day Anchor Books.

Goldmacher, Shane. 2024. "Trump and Republicans Bet Big on Anti-Trans Ads Across the Country." *New York Times*, October 8. https://www.nytimes.com/2024/10/08/us/politics/trump-republican-transgender-ads.html.

Goode, Chris, Rhonda H. Balzarini, and Heather J. Smith. 2014. "Positive Peer Pressure: Priming Member Prototypicality Can Decrease Undergraduate Drinking." *Journal of Applied Social Psychology* 44 (8): 567–78.

Gottfried, Jeffrey, Galen Stocking, and Elizabth Grieco. 2018. "Partisans Remain Sharply Divided in Their Attitudes About the News Media." Pew Research Center, September 25. https://www.journalism.org/2018/09/25/partisans -remain-sharply-divided-in-their-attitudes-about-the-news-media/.

Graham, David A., Adrienne Green, Cullen Murphy, and Parker Richards. 2019. "An Oral History of Trump's Bigotry." *The Atlantic*, June. https://www.theatlan tic.com/magazine/archive/2019/06/trump-racism-comments/588067/.

Green, Donald P., Bradley Palmquist, and Eric Schickler. 2002. *Partisan Hearts and Minds: Political Parties and the Social Identities of Voters.* Yale University Press.

Green, Joshua. 2011. "The Heroic Story of How Congress First Confronted AIDS." *The Atlantic*, June 8. https://www.theatlantic.com/politics/archive/2011/06/the -heroic-story-of-how-congress-first-confronted-aids/240131/.

Hackett, Ashley. 2021. "Why National Republicans Love Talking About 'Defund the Police.'" *MinnPost*, September 9. https://www.minnpost.com/national/2021/09 /why-national-republicans-love-talking-about-defund-the-police/.

Haney López, Ian. 2014. *Dog Whistle Politics: How Coded Racial Appeals Have Reinvented Racism and Wrecked the Middle Class.* Oxford University Press.

Hansler, Jennifer. 2017. "Bipartisan Condemnation for 'Unite the Right' Rally." CNN, August 13. https://www.cnn.com/2017/08/12/politics/parties-condemn-white-na tionalist-rally/index.html.

Harriot, Michael. 2022. "War on Wokeness: The Year the Right Rallied Around a Made-Up Menace." *The Guardian*, December 21. https://www.theguardian .com/us-news/2022/dec/20/anti-woke-race-america-history.

Hatewatch. 2017. "Live-Blog: ACT for America's 'March Against Sharia' Rallies." Southern Poverty Law Center, June 10. https://www.splcenter.org/hate watch/2017/06/10/live-blog-act-americas-march-against-sharia-rallies.

Hatewatch. 2020. "Trump Tweets, 'When the Looting Starts, the Shooting Starts,' Extremists Will Respond." Southern Poverty Law Center, May 29. https:// www.splcenter.org/hatewatch/2020/05/29/trump-tweets-when-looting-starts -shooting-starts-extremists-will-respond.

Hayes, Chris. 2021. "Ta-Nehisi Coates." Produced by MSNBC. *Why Is This Happening?*, episode 144, January 17. Podcast, YouTube, 1:01:18. https://www.you tube.com/watch?v=O0p_vJVAiDg.

Hemmer, Nicole. 2016. *Messengers of the Right: Conservative Media and the Transformation of American Politics.* University of Pennsylvania Press.   .

Henry, Patrick J., and David O. Sears. 2009. "The Crystallization of Contemporary Racial Prejudice Across the Lifespan." *Political Psychology* 30 (4): 569–90.

Hensch, Mark. 2015. "Romney Slams Trump on Muslim Ban." *The Hill*, December 8. https://thehill.com/blogs/blog-briefing-room/news/262472-romney-trump -fired-before-aiming-at-muslims/.

Hobbs, William, and Nazita Lajevardi. 2019. "Effects of Divisive Political Campaigns on the Day-to-Day Segregation of Arab and Muslim Americans." *American Political Science Review* 113 (1): 270–76.

Hoewe, Jennifer, Kathryn Cramer Brownell, and Eric C. Wiemer. 2020. "The Role and Impact of Fox News." *The Forum* 18 (3): 367–88.

Hollinsworth, David. 1992. *Race and Racism in Australia*. Social Science Press.

Hopkins, Daniel J. 2010. *Politicized Places: Explaining Where and When Immigrants Provoke Local Opposition*. Princeton University Press.

Huber, Gregory A., and John S. Lapinski. 2006. "The 'Race Card' Revisited: Assessing Racial Priming in Policy Contests." *American Journal of Political Science* 50 (2): 421–40.

Huddy, Leonie, Stanley Feldman, Charles Taber, and Gallya Lahav. 2005. "Threat, Anxiety, and Support of Antiterrorism Policies." *American Journal of Political Science* 49 (3): 593–608.

Huff, Connor, and Dustin Tingley. 2015. "'Who Are These People?' Evaluating the Demographic Characteristics and Political Preferences of MTurk Survey Respondents." *Research & Politics* 2 (3).

Human Rights Campaign (HRC). 2022a. "Breaking: In Final Weeks of Election, Extremist Candidates, Anti-LGBTQ+ Orgs Funnel Tens of Millions of Dollars in Ads Attacking Trans Youth, Targeting Black and Spanish-Speaking Voters." October 28. https://www.hrc.org/press-releases/breaking-in-final-weeks -of-election-extremist-candidates-anti-lgbtq-orgs-funnel-tens-of-millions-of -dollars-in-ads-attacking-trans-youth-targeting-black-and-spanish-speaking -voters.

Human Rights Campaign (HRC). 2022b. "New Post-Election Poll: Equality Voters Stopped the Red Wave, Rejecting Extremism and Anti-LGBTQ+ Attacks." November 17. https://www.hrc.org/press-releases/new-post-election-poll-equality -voters-stopped-the-red-wave-rejecting-extremism-and-anti-lgbtq-attacks.

Hurwitz, Jon, and Mark Peffley. 2005. "Playing the Race Card in the Post-Willie Horton Era: The Impact of Racialized Code Words on Support for Punitive Crime Policy." *Public Opinion Quarterly* 69 (1): 99–112.

Hutchings, Vincent L., Hanes Walton, and Andrea Benjamin. 2010. "The Impact of Explicit Racial Cues on Gender Differences in Support for Confederate Symbols and Partisanship." *Journal of Politics* 72 (4): 1175–88.

Iftikhar, Arsalan. 2020. "Christchurch Anniversary: The Islamophobic 'Great Replacement' Theory." The Bridge Initiative, March 14. https://bridge.george town.edu/research/christchurch-anniversary-the-islamophobic-great-replace ment-theory/.

Iyengar, Shanto, and Donald R. Kinder. 1987. *News That Matters: Television and American Opinion*. University of Chicago Press.

Iyengar, Shanto, Gaurav Sood, and Yphtach Lelkes. 2012. "Affect, Not Ideology: A Social Identity Perspective on Polarization." *Public Opinion Quarterly* 76 (3): 405–31.

Jachimowicz, Maia, and Ramah McKay. 2003. "'Special Registration' Program."
    Migration Policy Institute, April 1. https://www.migrationpolicy.org/article/spe
    cial-registration-program.

Jardina, Ashley. 2019. *White Identity Politics*. Cambridge University Press.

Jardina, Ashley, and Trent Ollerenshaw. 2022. "The Polls—Trends: The Polarization
    of White Racial Attitudes and Support for Racial Equality in the US." *Public
    Opinion Quarterly* 86 (S1): 576–87.

Jardina, Ashley, and Spencer Piston. 2019. "Racial Prejudice, Racial Identity, and
    Attitudes in Political Decision Making." In *Oxford Research Encyclopedia of
    Politics*.

Jardina, Ashley, and Spencer Piston. 2022. "The Effects of Dehumanizing Attitudes
    About Black People on Whites' Voting Decisions." *British Journal of Political
    Science* 52 (3): 1076–98.

Jardina, Ashley, and LaFleur Stephens-Dougan. "The Electoral Consequences of
    Anti-Muslim Prejudice." *Electoral Studies* 72 (2021): 102364.

Jefferson, Hakeem. 2021. "Storming the U.S. Capitol Was About Maintaining
    White Power in America." *FiveThirtyEight*, January 8. https://fivethirtyeight
    .com/features/storming-the-u-s-capitol-was-about-maintaining-white-power
    -in-america/.

Johnson, Benny (@bennyjohnson). 2023. "The Colorado Springs Shooter Identi-
    fied as Non Binary." X, March 27, 4:16 p.m. https://x.com/bennyjohnson/status
    /1640477904839614466.

Johnson, Jenna. 2015a. "Donald Trump: Syrian Refugees Might Be a Terrorist
    Army in Disguise." *Washington Post*, September 30. https://www.washington
    post.com/news/post-politics/wp/2015/09/30/donald-trump-syrian-refugees-might
    -be-a-terrorist-army-in-disguise/.

Johnson, Jenna. 2015b. "Trump Calls for 'Total and Complete Shutdown of Mus-
    lims Entering the United States.'" *Washington Post*, December 7. https://www
    .washingtonpost.com/news/post-politics/wp/2015/12/07/donald-trump-calls
    -for-total-and-complete-shutdown-of-muslims-entering-the-united-states/.

Johnson, Jenna, and Abigail Hauslohner. 2017. "'I Think Islam Hates Us': A Time-
    line of Trump's Comments About Islam and Muslims." *Washington Post*,
    May 20. https://www.washingtonpost.com/news/post-politics/wp/2017/05/20/i-think
    -islam-hates-us-a-timeline-of-trumps-comments-about-islam-and-muslims/.

Johnson, Ted. 2023. "Fox News Dominated February Cable News Viewership, but
    All Networks Were Down vs. 2022." *Deadline*, February 28. https://deadline
    .com/2023/02/fox-news-ratings-february-cnn-msnbc-1235274986/.

Jones, Robert P., and Daniel Cox. 2011. *Most Support Congressional Hearings on Al-
    leged Extremism in U.S. Muslim Communities*. Public Religion Research Institute.
    https://www.prri.org/research/majority-say-congressional-hearings-on-alleged
    -extremism-in-american-muslim-community-%E2%80%98good-idea%E2%8
    0%99/.

Jones, Sam, and Roudabeh Kishi. 2022. "Fact Sheet: Anti-LGBT+ Mobilization in the United States." Armed Conflict Location and Event Data Project, November 23. https://acleddata.com/2022/11/23/update-fact-sheet-anti-lgbt-mobilization-in-the-united-states/.

Joyella, Mark. 2023. "With 3.5 Million Viewers, Tucker Carlson Has the Week's Highest-Rated Cable News Show." *Forbes*, February 14. https://www.forbes.com/sites/markjoyella/2023/02/14/with-35-million-viewers-tucker-carlson-has-the-weeks-highest-rated-cable-news-show.

Kaczynski, Andrew. 2014. "GOP Congressman: Spy on U.S. Mosques to Stop ISIS Recruitment." *Buzzfeed News*, September 12. https://www.buzzfeednews.com/article/andrewkaczynski/gop-congressman-spy-on-us-mosques-to-stop-isis-recruitment.

Kaczynski, Andrew. 2021. "Another Video Shows Lauren Boebert Suggesting Ilhan Omar Was Terrorist." CNN, November 30. https://edition.cnn.com/2021/11/30/politics/lauren-boebert-ilhan-omar-video-comments/index.html.

Kalin, Michael, and Nazita Lajevardi. 2017. "Breathing While Muslim in the Age of Trump." Political Violence at a Glance.

Kalkan, Kerem Ozan, Geoffrey C. Layman, and Eric M. Uslaner. 2009. "'Bands of Others?' Attitudes Toward Muslims in Contemporary American Society." *Journal of Politics* 71:847–62.

Kalkstein, David A., Cayce J. Hook, Bridgette M. Hard, and Gregory M. Walton. 2022. "Social Norms Govern What Behaviors Come to Mind—And What Do Not." *Journal of Personality and Social Psychology*.

Kam, Cindy D., and Donald R. Kinder. 2007. "Terror and Ethnocentrism: Foundations of American Support for the War on Terrorism." *Journal of Politics* 69 (2): 320–38.

Kellstedt, Paul M. 2000. "Media Framing and the Dynamics of Racial Policy Preferences." *American Journal of Political Science* 44 (2): 245–60.

Kernahan, Cyndi, and Tricia Davis. 2007. "Changing Perspective: How Learning About Racism Influences Student Awareness and Emotion." *Teaching of Psychology* 34 (1): 49–52.

Kernahan, Cyndi, and Tricia Davis. 2009. "What Are the Long-Term Effects of Learning About Racism?" *Teaching of Psychology* 37 (1): 41–45.

Killough, Ashley, Lauren Fox, and Elizabeth Landers. 2019. "House Votes to Reject White Supremacy After Steve King's Comments." CNN, January 15. https://www.cnn.com/2019/01/15/politics/steve-king-pressure-to-resign/index.html.

Kim, Eunji, and Cindy Kam. 2023. "Othering in Everyday Life: Anti-Chinese Bias in the COVID-19 Pandemic." *Public Opinion Quarterly* 87 (3): 733–48.

Kinder, Donald R., and Lynn M. Sanders. 1996. *Divided by Color: Racial Politics and Democratic Ideals*. University of Chicago Press.

Kinder, Donald R., and Cindy D. Kam. 2010. *Us Against Them: Ethnocentric Foundations of American Opinion*. University of Chicago Press.

Kleefeld, Eric, and Courtney Hagle. 2023. "Right-Wing Media Ramped Up Anti-trans Vitriol Following Nashville Shooting." Media Matters for America, March 31. https://www.mediamatters.org/fox-news/right-wing-media-ramped-anti-trans-vitriol-following-nashville-shooting.

Knefel, John. 2022. "Right-Wing Media Is Targeting Boston Children's Hospital for Providing Care to Trans Youth." Media Matters for America, August 19. https://www.mediamatters.org/tucker-carlson/right-wing-media-targeting-boston-childrens-hospital-providing-care-trans-youth.

Knight Foundation. 2018. "Indicators of News Media Trust." September 11. https://knightfoundation.org/reports/indicators-of-news-media-trust/.

Kuhnhenn, Jim, and Lisa Lerer. 2015. "For Obama and Clinton, Twisty Paths to 'Yes' on Gay Marriage." Associated Press, June 27. https://apnews.com/united-states-government-general-news-63f51fcd69bb4ce18ed6b7306d1b3c89.

Kuklinski, James H., and Norman L. Hurley. 1994. "On Hearing and Interpreting Political Messages: A Cautionary Tale of Citizen Cue-Taking." *Journal of Politics* 56 (3): 729–51.

Lajevardi, Nazita. 2020. *Outsiders at Home: The Politics of American Islamophobia.* Cambridge University Press.

Lajevardi, Nazita, and Marisa Abrajano. 2019. "How Negative Sentiment Toward Muslim Americans Predicts Support for Trump in the 2016 Presidential Election." *Journal of Politics* 81 (1): 296–302.

Lajevardi, Nazita, and Kassra A. R. Oskooii. 2018. "Old-Fashioned Racism, Contemporary Islamophobia, and the Isolation of Muslim Americans in the Age of Trump." *Journal of Race, Ethnicity and Politics* 3 (1): 112–52.

Latino Decisions. 2017. "Virginia Election Eve Poll Results." Blog, November 8. https://latinodecisions.com/blog/virginia-election-eve-poll-results/.

Lee, Taeku. 2002. *Mobilizing Public Opinion: Black Insurgency and Racial Attitudes in the Civil Rights Era*. University of Chicago Press.

Legros, Sophie, and Beniamino Cislaghi. 2020. "Mapping the Social-Norms Literature: An Overview of Reviews." *Perspectives on Psychological Science* 15 (1): 62–80.

Leonhardt, David, and Ian Prasad Philbrick. 2022. "Culture War, Redux. How Did L.G.B.T. Rights Again Become the Subject of a Culture War?" *New York Times*, April 8. https://www.nytimes.com/2022/04/08/briefing/culture-war-lgbt-rights-us-politics.html.

Levendusky, Matthew. 2009. *The Partisan Sort: How Liberals Became Democrats and Conservatives Became Republicans*. University of Chicago Press.

Levendusky, Matthew. 2013. "Partisan Media Exposure and Attitudes Toward the Opposition." *Political Communication* 30 (4): 565–81.

Levy, Sheri R., Steven J. Stroessner, and Carol S. Dweck. 1998. "Stereotype Formation and Endorsement: The Role of Implicit Theories." *Journal of Personality and Social Psychology* 74 (6).

LGBTQ+ Victory Fund. 2022. "Out on the Trail 2022 Report." https://victoryfund.org/out-on-the-trail-2022/.

LGBTQ+ Victory Fund. 2023. "When We Run: The Motivations, Experiences and Challenges of LGBTQ+ Candidates in the United States." September 7. https://victoryinstitute.org/resource/when-we-run-the-motivations-experiences-and-challenges-of-lgbtq-candidates-in-the-united-states/.

LGBTQ+ Victory Fund. 2024. "Out on the Trail 2024 Report." https://victoryfund.org/out-on-the-trail-2024/.

Lichtblau, Eric. 2016. "Hate Crimes Against Muslims Most Since Post–9/11 Era." *New York Times*, September 17. https://www.nytimes.com/2016/09/18/us/politics/hate-crimes-american-muslims-rise.html.

Lillis, Mike. 2016. "Trump's 'Law-and-Order' Gamble." *The Hill*, July 14. http://thehill.com/homenews/campaign/287635-trumpslaw-and-order-gamble.

Lind, Dara. 2018. "The Conspiracy Theory That Led to the Pittsburgh Synagogue Shooting, Explained." *Vox*, October 29. https://www.vox.com/2018/10/29/18037580/pittsburgh-shooter-anti-semitism-racist-jewish-caravan.

Lotz, Amanda D. 2007. *The Television Will Be Revolutionized*. NYU Press.

Mackie, Gerry, Francesca Moneti, Holly Shakya, and Elaine Denny. 2015. "What Are Social Norms? How Are They Measured?" University of California at San Diego-UNICEF Working Paper.

Mansfield, Erin, and Candy Woodall. 2022. "Republican Politicians All over the Country Have Repeated the Great Replacement Theory." *USA Today*, May 29. https://www.usatoday.com/story/news/politics/2022/05/29/republicans-great-replacement-theory/9798199002.

Marshall, Thomas R. 1987. "The Supreme Court as an Opinion Leader: Court Decisions and the Mass Public." *American Politics Research* 15 (1): 147–68.

Martin, Gregory J., and Ali Yurukoglu. 2017. "Bias in Cable News: Persuasion and Polarization." *American Economic Review* 107 (9): 2565–99.

Mason, Lilliana. 2018. *Uncivil Agreement: How Politics Became Our Identity*. Chicago University Press.

Massey, Douglas S. 2014. *Categorically Unequal: The American Stratification System*. Russell Sage Foundation.

Massey, Douglas S., and Nancy A. Denton. 1993. *American Apartheid: Segregation and the Making of the Underclass*. Harvard University Press.

Mazumder, Soumyajit. 2018. "The Persistent Effect of US Civil Rights Protests on Political Attitudes." *American Journal of Political Science* 62 (4): 922–35.

McAlister, Melani. 2005. *Epic Encounters: Culture, Media, and U.S. Interests in the Middle East Since 1945*. Vol. 6. University of California Press.

McCarthy, Justin. 2021. "Mixed Views Among Americans on Transgender Issues." *Gallup*, May 26. https://news.gallup.com/poll/350174/mixed-views-among-americans-transgender-issues.aspx.

McElwee, Sean. 2018. "The Rising Racial Liberalism of Democratic Voters." *New York Times*, May 23. https://www.nytimes.com/2018/05/23/opinion/democrats-race.html.

McIlwain, Charlton D., and Stephen M. Caliendo. 2011. *Race Appeal: How Candidates Invoke Race in US Political Campaigns.* Temple University Press.

Media Matters for America. 2023. "Daily Wire Host Says 'There Can't Be a Genocide' of Trans People: 'Transgender People Is Not a Real Ontological Category.' " February 28. https://www.mediamatters.org/daily-wire/daily-wire-host-says-there-cant-be-genocide-trans-people-transgender-people-not-real.

Mendelberg, Tali. 1997. "Executing Hortons: Racial Crime in the 1988 Presidential Campaign." *Public Opinion Quarterly* 61 (1): 134–57.

Mendelberg, Tali. 2001. *The Race Card: Campaign Strategy, Implicit Messages, and the Norm of Equality.* Princeton University Press.

Mendelberg, Tali. 2018. "From the Folk Theory to Symbolic Politics: Toward a More Realistic Understanding of Voter Behavior." *Critical Review* 30 (1–2): 107–18.

Michelson, Melissa R., and Brian F. Harrison. 2020. *Transforming Prejudice: Identity, Fear, and Transgender Rights.* Oxford University Press.

Miller, Cassie. 2022. "SPLC Poll Finds Substantial Support for 'Great Replacement' Theory and Other Hard-Right Ideas." Southern Poverty Law Center, June 1. https://www.splcenter.org/news/2022/06/01/poll-finds-support-great-replacement-hard-right-ideas.

Monmouth University Polling Institute. 2020. "Protestors' Anger Justified Even If Actions May Not Be." June 2. https://www.monmouth.edu/polling-institute/reports/monmouthpoll_us_060220/.

Monmouth University Polling Institute. 2022. "National: Faith in American System Drops." July 7. https://www.monmouth.edu/polling-institute/documents/monmouthpoll_us_070722.pdf/.

Moreau, Julie. 2022. "These Recently Elected Trans Lawmakers Say Anti-LGBTQ Bills Inspired Them to Run." *NBC News*, November 30. https://www.nbcnews.com/nbc-out/out-politics-and-policy/recently-elected-trans-lawmakers-say-anti-lgbtq-bills-inspired-run-rcna59188.

Morris, Michael W., Ying-yi Hong, Chi-yue Chiu, and Zhi Liu. 2015. "Normology: Integrating Insights About Social Norms to Understand Cultural Dynamics." *Organizational Behavior and Human Decision Processes* 129:1–13.

MSNBC. 2015. "Rep. Steve King on Islamophobia." December 9. Video, 6:05, https://www.msnbc.com/all-in/watch/rep.-steve-king-on-islamophobia-583276099760.

Mueller, Zachary. 2022. "Republicans Embrace Dangerous White Nationalist 'Replacement' and 'Invasion' Conspiracies as a Midterm Strategy." *America's Voice* (blog). https://americasvoice.org/blog/replacementinvasionreport/.

Mullinix, Kevin J., Thomas J. Leeper, James N. Druckman, and Jeremy Freese. 2015. "The Generalizability of Survey Experiments." *Journal of Experimental Political Science* 2 (2): 109–38.

Munger, Kevin, and Joseph Phillips. 2022. "Right-Wing YouTube: A Supply and Demand Perspective." *International Journal of Press/Politics* 27 (1): 186–219.

Murib, Zein. 2024. "New Findings from the 2022 U.S. Transgender Survey." *Good Authority*, February 27. https://goodauthority.org/news/new-findings-2022-us-transgender-survey/.

Muslim Advocates. 2018. "Running on Hate: 2018 Pre-election Report." https://muslimadvocates.org/advocacy/addressing-anti-muslim-political-rhetoric/.

Muslim Advocates. 2022. "New Report Documents Nationwide Spread and Failure of Anti-Muslim 2018 & 2017 Campaigns." October 22. https://muslimadvocates.org/2018/10/new-report-documents-nationwide-spread-and-failure-of-anti-muslim-2018-2017-campaigns/.

Nacos, Brigitte Lebens, and Oscar Torres-Reyna. 2007. *Fueling Our Fears: Stereotyping, Media Coverage, and Public Opinion of Muslim Americans*. Rowman & Littlefield.

Nagourney, Adam, and Jeremy W. Peters. 2023. "How a Campaign Against Transgender Rights Mobilized Conservatives," *New York Times*, April 16. https://www.nytimes.com/2023/04/16/us/politics/transgender-conservative-campaign.html.

Nakamura, David. 2020. "With 'Kung Flu,' Trump Sparks Backlash over Racist Language — and a Rallying Cry for Supporters," *Washington Post*, June 24. https://www.washingtonpost.com/politics/with-kung-flu-trump-sparks-backlash-over-racist-language--and-a-rallying-cry-for-supporters/2020/06/24/485d151e-b620-11ea-aca5-ebb63d27e1ff_story.html.

National Conference of State Legislatures. 2022. "Law Enforcement Legislation: Significant Trends 2022." August 22. https://www.ncsl.org/civil-and-criminal-justice/law-enforcement-legislation-significant-trends-2022.

NBC News, and *Wall Street Journal*. 2020. "Full July Results." July. https://www.documentcloud.org/documents/6998891-July-Full-Results.html.

Neiwert, David. 2017. "When White Nationalists Chant Their Weird Slogans, What Do They Mean?" Southern Poverty Law Center, October 10. https://www.splcenter.org/hatewatch/2017/10/10/when-white-nationalists-chant-their-weird-slogans-what-do-they-mean.

Newman, Benjamin J. 2013. "Acculturating Contexts and Anglo Opposition to Immigration in the United States." *American Journal of Political Science* 57 (2): 374–90.

Newman, Benjamin, Jennifer L. Merolla, Sono Shah, Danielle Casarez Lemi, Loren Collingwood, and S. Karthick Ramakrishnan. 2021. "The Trump Effect: An Experimental Investigation of the Emboldening Effect of Racially Inflammatory Elite Communication." *British Journal of Political Science* 51 (3): 1138–59.

Newport, Frank. 2015. "Six in 10 Americans Would Say 'Yes' to Muslim President." *Gallup*, September 22. https://news.gallup.com/opinion/polling-matters/185813/six-americans-say-yes-muslim-president.aspx.

New York Times. 2016. "Transcript of the Main Republican Presidential Debate." January 28. https://www.nytimes.com/2016/01/29/us/politics/republican -presidential-debate-transcript.html.

New York Times. 2020. "Do You Think the United States Is a Racist Country?" https://www.nytimes.com/interactive/2020/us/politics/racism-in-america-20 -questions.html.

Ngai, Mae M. 2004. *Impossible Subjects: Illegal Aliens and the Making of Modern America.* Princeton University Press.

Nirappil, Fenit. 2023. "The Right Exploits Nashville Shooting to Escalate Anti-trans Rhetoric." *Washington Post,* March 30. https://www.washingtonpost.com /health/2023/03/30/nashville-shooting-transgender-shooter/.

Nolan, Brendan J., Sav Zwickl, Peter Locke, Jeffrey D. Zajac, and Ada S. Cheung. 2023. "Early Access to Testosterone Therapy in Transgender and Gender-Diverse Adults Seeking Masculinization: A Randomized Clinical Trial." *JAMA Network Open* 6 (9): e2331919. https://doi.org/10.1001/jamanetworkopen.2023.31919.

NYC LGBT Historic Sites Project. 2021. "Stonewall Inn." https://www.nyclgbtsites .org/site/stonewall-inn-christopher-park/.

O'Brien, Connor. 2019. "Kaine: Trump's Rhetoric 'Emboldens' White Nationalists." *Politico,* March 17. https://www.politico.com/story/2019/03/17/kaine-trump -white-nationalists-klobuchar-1224199.

Office of Senator Ted Cruz. 2021. "Joint Statement from Senators Cruz, Johnson, Lankford, Daines, Kennedy, Blackburn, Braun, Senators-Elect Lummis, Marshall, Hagerty, Tuberville." January 2. https://www.cruz.senate.gov/newsroom /press-releases/joint-statement-from-senators-cruz-johnson-lankford-daines -kennedy-blackburn-braun-senators-elect-lummis-marshall-hagerty-tuberville.

Otten, Tori. 2023. "The Tennessee House Just Passed a Bill Completely Gutting Marriage Equality." *New Republic,* March 7. https://newrepublic.com/post /171025/tennessee-house-bill-gutting-marriage-equality.

Owens, John E. 2021. "The Trump Party: Republican in Name Only." *Political Insight* 12 (2): 32–35. https://doi.org/10.1177/20419058211022938.

Padgett, Donald. 2023. "Pro-Trump Candidate Calls for Executing Parents of LGBTQ+ Kids." *The Advocate,* May 31. https://www.advocate.com/news/2022 /6/14/pro-trump-sc-candidate-mark-burns-calls-executing-allies-lgbtq-kids.

Paluck, Elizabeth Levy, and Donald P. Green. 2009. "Prejudice Reduction: What Works? A Review and Assessment of Research and Practice." *Annual Review of Psychology* 60: 339–67.

Panagopoulos, Costas. 2006. "The Polls-Trends Arab and Muslim Americans and Islam in the Aftermath of 9/11." *Public Opinion Quarterly* 70 (4): 608–24.

Park, Bernadette, and Charles M. Judd. 2005. "Rethinking the Link Between Categorization and Prejudice Within the Social Cognition Perspective." *Personality and Social Psychology Review* 9 (2): 108–30.

Parker, Christopher S., and Matt A. Barreto. 2013. *Change They Can't Believe In: The Tea Party and Reactionary Politics in America.* Princeton University Press.

Patel, Faiza, and Rachel Levinson-Waldman. 2017. "The Islamophobic Adminis-tration." Brennan Center, April 19. https://www.brennancenter.org/our-work /research-reports/islamophobic-administration.

Paterson, Alex. 2022. "Fox News Attacked LGBTQ People on over 100 Days in the First Half of 2022—Including Nearly 90% of Days During Pride Month." Media Matters for America, July 25. https://www.mediamatters.org/fox-news/fox-news -attacked-lgbtq-people-over-100-days-first-half-2022-including-nearly-90-days.

Pauly, Madison. 2023. "Inside the Secret Working Group That Helped Push Anti-trans Laws Across the Country." *Mother Jones*, March 8. https://www .motherjones.com/politics/2023/03/anti-trans-transgender-health-care-ban -legislation-bill-minors-children-lgbtq/.

PBS Frontline. n.d. "'Employment of Homosexuals and Other Sex Perverts in Government' (1950)." https://www.pbs.org/wgbh/pages/frontline/shows/assault /context/employment.html.

Perez, Efrén O. 2016. *Unspoken Politics: Implicit Attitudes and Political Thinking*. Cambridge University Press.

Petrizzo, Zachary. 2021. "White Nationalists Go Wild for Tucker Carlson's 'Great Replacement' Theory." *Salon*, April 14. https://www.salon.com/2021/04/14 /white-nationalists-go-wild-for-tucker-carlsons-great-replacement-theory/.

Pettigrew, Thomas F., and Linda R. Tropp. 2006. "A Meta-analytic Test of Intergroup Contact Theory." *Journal of Personality and Social Psychology* 90 (5): 751–83.

Pew Research Center. 2017. "Americans Express Increasingly Warm Feelings To-ward Religious Groups." February 15. http://www.pewforum.org/2017/02/15 /americans-express-increasingly-warm-feelings-toward-religious-groups/.

Pew Research Center. 2019. "Attitudes on Same-Sex Marriage." May 14. https:// www.pewresearch.org/religion/fact-sheet/changing-attitudes-on-gay-marriage/.

Philbrick, Ian Prasad, and Lyna Bentahar. 2023. "Donald Trump's 2024 Campaign, in His Own Menacing Words." *New York Times*, December 5. https://www.ny times.com/2023/12/05/us/politics/trump-2024-president-campaign.html.

Phillips, Amber. 2017. "'They're Rapists.' President Trump's Campaign Launch Speech Two Years Later, Annotated." *Washington Post*, June 16, https://www .washingtonpost.com/news/the-fix/wp/2017/06/16/theyre-rapists-presidents -trump-campaign-launch-speech-two-years-later-annotated/.

Pilkington, Ed. 2016. "Ted Cruz Campaign's Anti-Muslim Propagandists Called 'Ter-rifying.'" *The Guardian*, March 25. https://www.theguardian.com/us-news/2016 /mar/25/ted-cruz-anti-muslim-sentiment-dangerous-trump-groups-warn.

Place, Nathan. 2021. "White Nationalist Website Calls Tucker Carlson's 'Replace-ment' Rant 'One of the Best Things Fox News Has Ever Aired.'" *Independent*, April 13. https://www.the-independent.com/news/world/americas/us-politics/tucker -carlson-white-nationalist-vdare-b1830829.html.

Plant, E. Ashby, and Patricia G. Devine. 1998. "Internal and External Motivation to Respond Without Prejudice." *Journal of Personality and Social Psychology* 75 (3).

Politico. 2017. "Full Text: Trump's Comments on White Supremacists, 'Alt-Left' in Charlottesville." August 15. https://www.politico.com/story/2017/08/15/full -text-trump-comments-white-supremacists-alt-left-transcript-241662.

Public Religion Research Institute. 2022. "Challenges in Moving Toward a More Inclusive Democracy: Findings from the 2022 American Values Survey." October 27. https://www.prri.org/research/challenges-in-moving-toward-a-more -inclusive-democracy-findings-from-the-2022-american-values-survey.

Putnam, Lara, Jeremy Pressman, and Erica Chenoweth. 2020. "Black Lives Matter Beyond America's Big Cities." *Washington Post*, July 8. https://www.washington post.com/politics/2020/07/08/black-lives-matter-beyond-americas-big-cities/.

Reed, Erin. 2023a. "Anti-trans Legislative Risk Assessment Map: New Adult Map." *Erin in the Morning*, September 6. https://www.erininthemorning.com/p /anti-trans-legislative-risk-assessment.

Reed, Erin (@ErinInTheMorn). 2023b. "Charlie Kirk." X, February 7, 5:55 p.m. https://x.com/erininthemorn/status/1626747081275715585.

Reny, Tyler T., and Matt A. Barreto. 2022. "Xenophobia in the Time of Pandemic: Othering, Anti-Asian Attitudes, and COVID-19." *Politics, Groups, and Identities* 10 (2): 209–32.

Reny, Tyler, Ali Valenzuela, and Loren Collingwood. 2020. "No, You're Playing the Race Card: Anti-Black and Anti-Latino Appeals in the Post-Obama Era." *Political Psychology* 41 (2): 283–302.

Republican Party of Texas. 2022. *Report of the Permanent 2022 Platform & Resolutions Committee.* https://texasgop.org/wp-content/uploads/2022/06/6-Perma nent-Platform-Committee-FINAL-REPORT-6-16-2022.pdf.

Rivera, Christopher. 2014. "The Brown Threat: Post-9/11 Conflations of Latina/os and Middle Eastern Muslims in the US American Imagination." *Latino Studies* 12 (1): 44–64.

Rizzo, Salvador. 2018. "Indicted Congressman Falsely Ties Opponent to Terrorism." *Washington Post*, October 1. https://www.washingtonpost.com/politics /2018/10/01/indicted-congressman-falsely-ties-opponent-terrorism/.

Rodden, J. A. 2019. *Why Cities Lose: The Deep Roots of the Urban-Rural Political Divide.* Basic Books.

Rosenberg, Eli, and Kayla Epstein. 2019. "President Trump Targets Rep. Ilhan Omar with a Video of Twin Towers Burning." *Washington Post*, April 13. https://www.washingtonpost.com/politics/2019/04/13/president-trump-targets -rep-ilhan-omar-with-video-twin-towers-burning/.

Rothman, Lily. 2017. "50 Years Ago This Week: How to Win a War in One Week." *Time*, June 12. https://time.com/4798084/1967-dayan-six-day-war/.

Rummler, Orion. 2022. "Republicans in Midterm Races Are Embracing Anti-trans Rhetoric Like Never Before." *The 19th*, November 3. https://19thnews .org/2022/11/election-transgender-rhetoric-gop-campaign-ads/.

Said, Edward. 1979. *Orientalism: Western Representations of the Orient.* Pantheon.

Saleem, Muniba, Grace S. Yang, and Srividya Ramasubramanian. 2016. "Reliance on Direct and Mediated Contact and Public Policies Supporting Outgroup Harm." *Journal of Communication* 66 (4): 604–24.

Sargent, Greg. 2023. "GOP States Take an Ugly New Turn in the Culture Wars with 'Forced Outing.'" *Washington Post*, August 24. https://www.washingtonpost .com/opinions/2023/08/24/forced-outing-lgbtq-rights-pen-america-transgender/.

Schaffner, Brian F. 2020. *The Acceptance and Expression of Prejudice During the Trump Era*. Cambridge University Press.

Schickler, Eric. 2016. *Racial Realignment: The Transformation of American Liberalism, 1932–1965*. Princeton University Press.

Schneider, Gregory S. 2017. "Did Gillespie Ads Turn Off African American Voters in Virginia?" *Washington Post*, November 11. https://www.washingtonpost .com/local/virginia-politics/did-gillespie-ads-turn-off-african-american-voters -in-virginia/2017/11/16/64a6f74c-caed-11e7-b0cf-7689a9f2d84e_story.html.

Schuman, Howard, Charlotte Steeh, and Lawrence Bobo. 1985. *Racial Trends in America: Trends and Interpretations*. Harvard University Press.

Schuman, Howard, Charlotte Steeh, Lawrence Bobo, and Maria Krysan. 1997. *Racial Attitudes in America: Trends and Interpretations*. Harvard University Press.

Sears, David O., and Donald R. Kinder. 1971. *Racial Tension and Voting in Los Angeles*. Vol. 156. Institute of Government and Public Affairs, University of California.

Sears, David O., Colette Van Laar, Mary Carrillo, and Rick Kosterman. 1997. "Is It Really Racism? The Origins of White Americans' Opposition to Race-Targeted Policies." *Public Opinion Quarterly* 61 (1): 16–53.

Sechrist, Gretchen B., and Charles Stangor. 2001. "Perceived Consensus Influences Intergroup Behavior and Stereotype Accessibility." *Journal of Personality and Social Psychology* 80 (4).

Serwer, Adam. 2021. "The Capitol Riot Was an Attack on Multiracial Democracy." *The Atlantic*, January 7. https://www.theatlantic.com/ideas/archive/2021/01/multi racial-democracy-55-years-old-will-it-survive/617585/.

Shaheen, Jack. 2001. *Reel Bad Arabs: How Hollywood Vilifies a People*. Olive Branch Press.

Shanmugasundaram, Swathi. 2018. "Anti-Sharia Law Bills in the United States." Southern Poverty Law Center, February 5. https://www.splcenter.org/hatewatch /2018/02/05/anti-sharia-law-bills-united-states.

Sherkat, Darren E. 2019. "Public Opinion and Religion: Gay Rights in the United States." In *Oxford Research Encyclopedia of Politics*.

Sidanius, Jim, and Felicia Pratto. 2001. *Social Dominance: An Intergroup Theory of Social Hierarchy and Oppression*. Cambridge University Press.

Sides, John, and Kimberly Gross. 2013. "Stereotypes of Muslims and Support for the War on Terror." *Journal of Politics* 75 (3): 583–98.

Sides, John, Michael Tesler, and Lynn Vavreck. 2018. *Identity Crisis: The 2016 Presidential Campaign and the Battle for the Meaning of America*. Princeton University Press.

Sides, John, Chris Tausanovitch, and Lynn Vavreck. 2022. *The Bitter End: The 2020 Presidential Campaign and the Challenge to American Democracy*. Princeton University Press.

Sides, John, Michael Tesler, and Robert Griffin. 2024. *Pushed and Pulled: How Attitudes About Race and Immigration are Settling and Shifting After Trump*. Democracy Fund Voter Study Group.

Simonov, Andrey, Szymon Sacher, Jean-Pierre Dubé, and Shirsho Biswas. 2022. "Frontiers: The Persuasive Effect of Fox News: Noncompliance with Social Distancing During the COVID-19 Pandemic." *Marketing Science* 41 (2): 230–42.

Simonovits, Gabor, Jennifer McCoy, and Levente Littvay. 2022. "Democratic Hypocrisy and Out-Group Threat: Explaining Citizen Support for Democratic Erosion." *Journal of Politics* 84 (3): 1806–11.

Slisco, Aila. 2020. "GOP Senator Defends 'Chinese Virus' Name, Says It's Not Racist Because China Is Where 'These Viruses Emanate From.' " *Newsweek*, March 18. https://www.newsweek.com/gop-senator-defends-chinese-virus-namesays-its -not-racist-because-china-where-these-viruses-1493145.

Smietana, Bob. 2015. "One in Three Americans Worry About Sharia Law Being Applied in America." Lifeway Research, February 11. https://research.lifeway .com/2015/02/11/1-in-3-americans-worry-about-sharia-law-being-applied-in -america/.

Sniderman, Paul M., and Louk Hagendoorn. 2007. *When Ways of Life Collide: Multiculturalism and Its Discontents in the Netherlands*. Princeton University Press.

Snyder, Mark. 1974. "Self-Monitoring of Expressive Behavior." *Journal of Personality and Social Psychology* 30 (4).

Southern Poverty Law Center (SPLC). 2005. "A Dozen Major Groups Help Drive the Religious Right's Anti-gay Crusade." April 28. https://www.splcen ter.org/fighting-hate/intelligence-report/2005/dozen-major-groups-help-drive -religious-right%E2%80%99s-anti-gay-crusade.

Southern Poverty Law Center (SPLC). 2016. "The Trump Effect: The Impact of the Presidential Campaign on Our Nation's Schools." April 13. https://www.splcenter .org/20160413/trump-effect-impact-presidential-campaign-our-nations-schools.

Southern Poverty Law Center (SPLC). 2023. "Anti-Muslim." https://www.splcen ter.org/fighting-hate/extremist-files/ideology/anti-muslim.

Southern Poverty Law Center (SPLC). n.d. "ACT for America." https://www .splcenter.org/fighting-hate/extremist-files/group/act-america.

Sprunt, Barbara. 2020. "Iowa Rep. Steve King, Known for Racist Comments, Loses Reelection Bid." NPR, June 3. https://www.npr.org/2020/06/03/865823546/iowa -rep-steve-king-ousted-in-gop-primary-ap-projects.

Stangor, Charles, Gretchen B. Sechrist, and John T. Jost. 2001. "Changing Racial Beliefs by Providing Consensus Information." *Personality and Social Psychology Bulletin* 27 (4): 486–96.

Steiner, Linda, Fred Fejes, and Kevin Petrich. 1993. "Invisibility, Homophobia and Heterosexism: Lesbians, Gays and the Media." *Critical Studies in Mass Communication* 10 (4): 395–422.

Stephens-Dougan, LaFleur. 2020. *Race to the Bottom: How Racial Appeals Work in American Politics*. University of Chicago Press.

Stop AAPI Hate. 2022. "National Report (Through December 31, 2021)" March. https://stopaapihate.org/2022/03/04/national-report-through-december-31-2021/.

Stout, Christopher J. 2015. *Bringing Race Back In: Black Politicians, Deracialization, and Voting Behavior in the Age of Obama*. University of Virginia Press.

Stout, Christopher T. 2020. *The Case for Identity Politics: Polarization, Demographic Change, and the Growing Significance of Racial Appeals*. University of Virginia Press.

Suarez, Miranda. 2022. "Billboards and 'Hate Mail' with Anti-LGBTQ+ Messages Target Texas Candidates." KUT Public Media, October 28. https://www.kut.org/politics/2022-10-28/billboards-and-hate-mail-with-anti-lgbtq-messages-target-texas-candidates.

Sunstein, Cass R. 2001. *Republic.com*. Princeton University Press.

Suro, Roberto. 1991. "The 1991 Election: Louisiana; Bush Denounces Duke as Racist and Charlatan." *New York Times*, November 7. https://www.nytimes.com/1991/11/07/us/the-1991-election-louisiana-bush-denounces-duke-as-racist-and-charlatan.html.

Tajfel, Henri. 1982. *Social Identity and Intergroup Relations*. Cambridge University Press.

Tajfel, Henri, and John C. Turner. 1979. "An Integrative Theory of Intergroup Conflict." In *The Social Psychology of Intergroup Relations*, edited by William G. Austin and Stephen Worchel, 33–47. Monterey, CA: Brooks/Cole.

Tampa Bay Times. 2015. "Religious Groups React to Supreme Court Ruling on Same-Sex Marriage." June 26. https://www.tampabay.com/news/courts/religious-groups-react-to-supreme-court-ruling-on-same-sex-marriage/2235233/.

Tankard, Margaret E., and Elizabeth Levy Paluck. 2016. "Norm Perception as a Vehicle for Social Change." *Social Issues and Policy Review* 10:181–211.

Tankard, Margaret E., and Elizabeth Levy Paluck. 2017. "The Effect of a Supreme Court Decision Regarding Gay Marriage on Social Norms and Personal Attitudes." *Psychological Science* 28 (9): 1334–44.

Tazamal, Mobashra. 2019. "Fox News: A Megaphone for Anti-Muslim Hatred." The Bridge Initiative, March 18. https://bridge.georgetown.edu/research/fox-news-megaphone-for-anti-muslim-hatred/.

Telhami, Shibley, and Stella Rouse. 2022. "American Public Attitudes on Race, Ethnicity, and Religion." University of Maryland. https://criticalissues.umd

.edu/sites/criticalissues.umd.edu/files/American%20Attitudes%20on%20Race
%2CEthnicity%2CReligion.pdf.

Terkildsen, Nayda. 1993. "When White Voters Evaluate Black Candidates: The Processing Implications of Candidate Skin Color, Prejudice, and Self-Monitoring."
American Journal of Political Science.

Tesler, Michael. 2013. "The Return of Old-Fashioned Racism to White Americans'
Partisan Preferences in the Early Obama Era." *Journal of Politics* 75 (1): 110–23.

Tesler, Michael. 2015. "Priming Predispositions and Changing Policy Positions: An
Account of When Mass Opinion is Primed or Changed." *American Journal of
Political Science* 59 (4): 806–24.

Tesler, Michael. 2016. *Post-racial or Most-Racial? Race and Politics in the Obama
Era.* University of Chicago Press.

Tesler, Michael. 2018. "Democrats and Republicans Used to Agree About the
N-Word. Now They Don't." *Washington Post*, August 30. https://www.washington
post.com/news/monkey-cage/wp/2018/08/30/democrats-and-republicans-didnt
-use-to-disagree-about-the-n-word-now-they-do/.

Tesler, Michael. 2022. "President Obama and the Emergence of Islamophobia in
Mass Partisan Preferences." *Political Research Quarterly* 75 (2): 394–408.

Tesler, Michael, and David O. Sears. 2010. *Obama's Race: The 2008 Election and the
Dream of a Post-Racial America.* University of Chicago Press.

Tokeshi, Matthew, and Tali Mendelberg. 2015. "Countering Implicit Appeals:
Which Strategies Work?" *Political Communication* 32 (4): 648–72.

Trevor Project. 2023. "2023 U.S. National Survey on the Mental Health of LGBTQ
Young People." https://www.thetrevorproject.org/survey-2023/.

Trounstine, J. 2018. *Segregation by Design: Local Politics and Inequality in American Cities.* Cambridge University Press.

Trump, Donald J. 2015. "Trump Statement on Preventing Muslim Immigration Online by Gerhard Peters and John T. Woolley." The American Presidency Project.
https://www.presidency.ucsb.edu/node/314221.

Trump, Donald J. (@realDonaldTrump). 2020. "The United States Will Be Powerfully Supporting Those Industries." X, March 16, 4:51 p.m. https://x.com
/realDonaldTrump/status/1239685852093169664.

Ulfelder, Jay. 2023a. "Pushing Back Against Anti-LGBTQ Legislation." *Counting
Crowds* (blog), Crowd Counting Consortium, March 15. https://countingcrowds
.org/2023/03/15/pushing-back-against-anti-lgbtq-legislation/.

Ulfelder, Jay. 2023b. "2023 Trans Day of Visibility." *Counting Crowds* (blog),
Crowd Counting Consortium, April 2. https://countingcrowds.org/2023/04/02
/2023-trans-day-of-visibility/.

Vaitla, Bapu, Alice Taylor, Julia Van Horn, and Ben Cislaghi. 2017. *Social Norms
and Girls' Well-Being: Integrating Theory, Practice, and Research.* Washington,
DC: Data2X.

Valentino, Nicholas A. 1999. "Crime News and the Priming of Racial Attitudes
During Evaluations of the President." *Public Opinion Quarterly* 63 (3): 293.

Valentino, Nicholas A., Vincent L. Hutchings, and Ismail K. White. 2002. "Cues That Matter: How Political Ads Prime Racial Attitudes During Campaigns." *American Political Science Review* 96 (1): 75–90.

Valentino, Nicholas A., Fabian G. Neuner, and L. Matthew Vandenbroek. 2018a. "The Changing Norms of Racial Political Rhetoric and the End of Racial Priming." *Journal of Politics* 80 (3).

Valentino, Nicholas A., James Newburg, and Fabian G. Neuner. 2018b. "From Dog Whistles to Bullhorns: Racial Rhetoric in U.S. Presidential Campaigns, 1984–2016." Paper presented at the 2018 American Political Science Association Conference, September.

Valentino, Nicholas A., and David O. Sears. 2005. "Old Times There Are Not Forgotten: Race and Partisan Realignment in the Contemporary South." *American Journal of Political Science* 49 (3): 672–88.

Valentino, Nicholas A., and Kirill Zhirkov. 2018. "Blue Is Black and Red Is White? Affective Polarization and the Racialized Schemas of US Party Coalitions." Paper presented at the 2018 Midwest Political Science Association Conference, Chicago, March.

Van Dijk, Teun A. 2015. *Racism and the Press*. Routledge.

Vargas, Edward D., Kimberly R. Huyser, Vickie D. Ybarra, Justin Hollis, and Gabriel R. Sanchez. 2018. "The Influence of the Great Recession on Racial Attitudes Among Non-Hispanic Whites in the United States." *Journal of Economics, Race, and Policy* 1:196–203.

Virtanen, Simo V., and Leonie Huddy. 1998. "Old-Fashioned Racism and New Forms of Racial Prejudice." *Journal of Politics* 60 (2): 311–32.

Weil, Julie Zauzmer, and Fenit Nirappil. 2020. "D.C. Toughens Officer Hiring and Discipline, as Wave of Police Reform Sweeps the U.S." *Washington Post*, June 9. https://www.washingtonpost.com/local/dc-politics/dc-council-police-reform/2020/06/09/c77ae6b0-aa49-11ea-a9d9-a81c1a491c52_story.html.

White House. 2001. "'Islam Is Peace' Says President." September 17. https://georgewbush-whitehouse.archives.gov/news/releases/2001/09/20010917-11.html.

White House. 2002. "Backgrounder: The President's Quotes on Islam." https://georgewbush-whitehouse.archives.gov/infocus/ramadan/islam.html.

White House. 2021. "National Strategy for Confronting Domestic Terrorism." June. https://www.whitehouse.gov/wp-content/uploads/2021/06/National-Strategy-for-Countering-Domestic-Terrorism.pdf.

White House. 2025. "Ending Radical and Wasteful Government DEI Programs and Preferenncing." January. https://www.whitehouse.gov/presidential-actions/2025/01/ending-radical-and-wasteful-government-dei-programs-and-preferencing/.

White, Ismail K. 2007. "When Race Matters and When It Doesn't: Racial Group Differences in Response to Racial Cues." *American Political Science Review* 101 (2): 339–54.

White, Ismail K., and Chryl N. Laird. 2020. *Steadfast Democrats: How Social Forces Shape Black Political Behavior*. Princeton University Press.

Wilcox, Clyde. 2020. "Anti-LGBT and Religious Right Movements in the United States." In *Oxford Research Encyclopedia of Politics*.

Wilkins, Clara L., and Cheryl R. Kaiser. 2014. "Racial Progress as Threat to the Status Hierarchy: Implications for Perceptions of Anti-white Bias." *Psychological Science* 25 (2): 439–46.

Winter, Nicholas J. G. 2008. *Dangerous Frames: How Ideas About Race and Gender Shape Public Opinion*. University of Chicago Press.

Wong, Scott. 2022. "GOP Leaders Denounce Greene, Gosar for Speaking at White Nationalist Event." *NBC News*, February 28. https://www.nbcnews.com/poli tics/congress/gop-leaders-denounce-greene-gosar-speaking-white-nationalist -event-rcna18050.

Wright, David. 2016. "Bernie Sanders Blasts Trump Birther Statement: 'This Is Pathetic.'" CNN, September 16. http://www.cnn.com/2016/09/16/politics /bernie-sanders-donald-trump-birthers/.

Woodly, Deva R. 2021. *Reckoning: Black Lives Matter and the Democratic Necessity of Social Movements*. Oxford University Press.

Yadon, Nicole, and Spencer Piston. 2019. "Examining Whites' Anti-Black Attitudes After Obama's Presidency." *Politics, Groups, and Identities* 7 (4): 794–814.

YouGov. 2020. "Is Systemic Racism Something That Should Be Addressed by the 2020 Presidential Campaigns?" August 31. https://today.yougov.com/topics /politics/survey-results/daily/2020/08/31/ed8ec/3.

YouGov. 2022. "Daily Survey: Don't Say Gay Bill." April 2022. https://docs.cdn .yougov.com/a0gojsm4ca/tabs_Dont_Say_Gay_Bill_20220405%20(2).pdf.

Zaller, John. 1992. *The Nature and Origins of Mass Opinion*. Cambridge University Press.

Zepeda-Millan, Chris. 2017. *Latino Mass Mobilization: Immigration, Racialization, and Activism*. Cambridge University Press.

Zhang, Peng, Yanhe Deng, Xue Yu, Xin Zhao, and Xiangping Liu. 2016. "Social Anxiety, Stress Type, and Conformity Among Adolescents." *Frontiers in Psychology* 7 (May). https://doi.org/10.3389/fpsyg.2016.00760.

Zoledziowski, Anya. 2023. "'Under His Wings': Leaked Emails Reveal an Anti-trans 'Holy War.'" *Vice News*, March 21. https://www.vice.com/en/article/7kxpky /leaked-emails-reveal-an-anti-trans-holy-war.

Index

Page numbers in italics refer to figures and tables.

Run for Something, 66
Ryan, Paul, 176

same-sex adoption rights, 124
same-sex marriage: increase in support for, 20, 123–24, 133; Massachusetts as first state to legalize, 124; Respect for Marriage Act, 119; *United States v. Windsor*, 124
Sanders, Bernie: condemnation of racism in Trump's election campaigns, 164; condemnation of Unite the Right rally, 64
Schilling, Terry, 118
Scott, Tim, criticism of Steve King, 176
Sears, David O., 22, 89
self-monitoring scale (SM): measure of use of self-awareness to guide behavior in social situations, 41; moderately correlated with social norms index (SNI), 49, 204n6
September 11, 2001, terrorist attacks: anti-Muslim rhetoric by conservative political leaders and media, 6, 23, 93; leveraging of public fear and anger through government measures against Muslim rights, 6, 23, 93; manipulation of by political actors to restrict minority rights, 25–26, 183; public view of Muslims as threat and increase in hate crimes against, 22–23, 25, 92–93, 95–96, 115; shift in norm environment, 93, 182; USA PATRIOT Act and opening of Guantanamo Bay prison, 25, 93
Shaheen, Jack, 92
Sharia law: Fox News obsession with, 94, 97, 205n2; myth of spread, 93–94
Sides, John, 95
SNI. *See* social norms index
social desirability bias, 44
social identity theory, ethnocentric or in-group bias, 53
social norm adherence: difficulty measuring, 180–81; limitations of measures, 39–41; measurement methods, 204n3. *See also* social norms; social norms index
social norms: definitions of, 17; expression of social approval or disapproval of behaviors, 18; influence on wide variety of beliefs and behaviors, 17–18, 38, 97; supported by desire of people to control impressions of others, 17–18; support

for what behavioral responses are warranted or acceptable in a given situation, 18, 41–42
social norms, development and transformation: competition among factors influencing norm transformation, 27–28; development from signals of influential actors to public, 19–20, 23; development through media influence, 20–22; development through political institutions such as Supreme Court rulings and US Congress, 20; development through social movements, 22, 23; transformation from exogenous shocks, 19, 22–23, 184; transformation from social movements and organized social action, 19. *See also* Black Americans, norm of racial equality; LGBTQ+ community, historical development of social norms; Muslim Americans, social norms for
social norms index (SNI): construction of, 41–44; designed to avoid social desirability bias, 44; designed to determine normative expectations of appropriateness, 44; four vignettes, 42, *43*; measure of normative beliefs about what others think they should do, 42
social norms index (SNI), and antiminority political messaging, 112–13, *113*, 115; differing levels of support for candidates based on use of explicit anti-Black, anti-Muslim, or anti-LGBTQ+ messages, 53; individual-level measure of norm adherence for acceptance or rejection of antiminority political messages, 5, 43; marginal effects on support for anti-Black and anti-Muslim candidates, 112–13, *113*, 115, *200*, 206n15; marginal effects on support for anti-Black and anti-Muslim candidates and their opponents across two fictional Republican primary elections, 113–14, *114*, 115, *200*; OLS regression analysis of social norms index (SNI) on support for anti-Black candidates, 80–82, *81*; strong predictor of support for candidates who use explicit antiminority appeals, 53, 71, 80–82, *81*, 91; test of effect of norm adherence on evaluation of candidates who issue antiminority political messages, 52–53, 58